Human Systems Are Different

Human Systems are Different

by

Geoffrey Vickers

Harper & Row, Publishers
London

Cambridge
Hagerstown
Philadelphia
New York

San Francisco
Mexico City
Sao Paulo
Sydney

© Jeanne Vickers 1983
All rights reserved

Harper & Row Ltd
28 Tavistock Street
London WC2E 7PN

No part of this book may be used or reproduced in any manner whatsoever without written permission except in the case of brief quotations embodied in critical articles and reviews.

British Library Cataloguing in Publication Data

Vickers, Geoffrey
  Human systems are different
  1. Social evolution
  2. Social systems
  I. Title
  303.4′4   GN360

ISBN 0 06 318262 9

Typeset by Alan Sutton Publishing Ltd, Gloucester
Printed and bound by Butler & Tanner Ltd, Frome and London

SIR GEOFFREY VICKERS: AN AFFECTIONATE PORTRAIT

I met Sir Geoffrey Vickers in the early 1970s during one of his trips to the United States. In 1977 I joined the small, regular stream of people who visited him in Goring-on-Thames to seek his counsel. My purposes, however, were somewhat out of the ordinary. I had heard of his recent removal from his house to quarters in a retirement home, and I wanted to know what was to become of his papers for I had recognized him as a splendid subject for biography, if not by me certainly by someone else; might he consider autobiography? The suggestion took Geoffrey completely by surprise. He remarked that, since he was neither a film star nor a politician, there would be no audience for such a volume. Further conversation revealed his exquisitely refined sense of what ought, and ought not, to be placed in the public domain – a variation on the theme of the tacit and the explicit which appears in his writings. And then, as though to lay my question permanently to rest, he confessed cheerfully to having discarded a great many papers when he moved. I winced.

But the idea of biography did not dispose of itself so easily. Geoffrey and I began a correspondence about biographical forms and his life, about identity and self-knowledge. In March 1979 he unexpectedly started to write what we referred to as 'The Life and Times of G.V.', but a few months later he reported that his effort was 'stillborn', and lay where he had abandoned it, in mid-sentence. Later he wrote, with more certainty: 'No, there will be no autobiography and, I hope, no biography.' What follows, then, is a biased portrait, drawn largely from unpublished materials. It is written with respect for privacy, warmth, and admiration for a man of many parts: soldier, lawyer, administrator, public servant, poet, friend, humanist, sage.

'The year I was born – 1894 – was the best year in a decade in which one year was not as good as another', Geoffrey reflected as he looked back across a distance of eight decades. 'For those born even a few years earlier would probably have to interrupt a new career in order to fight a war, whilst those born even a few years later would finish their education in schools devoid of teachers and preoccupied with death; and if they went on to a university, they would find the junior common room monopolized by colonels and naval commanders discussing the Somme and Gallipoli while they finished their education. Above all, they would miss the privilege of having grown up in England in the "pre-war world", a precious though incommunicable experience.'

Geoffrey was the youngest child of Jessie Lomas and Charles Henry Vickers of Nottingham. Charles ran the successful, if not exactly prosperous, lace manufacturing business that had been founded by his grandfather and passed down to him by his father. In 1882 Charles married Jessie, a beautiful woman of independent convictions who had declined seven offers of marriage from others before succumbing to his persuasions. In 1883 she gave birth to a daughter, Margery. She was solemnly advised, however, against further adventures in motherhood, a warning she chose to ignore in deference to what Geoffrey called 'her own inner assurances'. The next child, a son, died at birth; but in 1890 Jessie bore William Burnell and, four years later, the future author of *Human Systems Are Different*.

After seventy-five years of encounters with men, Geoffrey wrote simply, 'My father was the best and most lovable man I ever knew; and he seemed to combine the two superlatives without the slightest effort. His enthusiasms were boundless, his gaiety endemic and his energies limitless. He bathed his children in his own excitement and delights, pleased when they shared and responded but showing no disappointment when they did not.' Shadows fell upon Geoffrey's memories of his mother, of some sorrow beyond his reach, but they did not cast doubt upon his affection. 'My mother was both vulnerable and tough. . . . Over part of my childhood there floats an image of a mother who needed a kind of forethought that I did not know how to give – a mother who could not be taken for granted so completely as my father. But the dominant image is of one who was both gay and fey. . . . When she died, I felt that the uniqueness which characterizes every human being had been raised in her to an unusual level, because it was so very much of her making, rather than of life's shaping.'

For most of Geoffrey's childhood the family lived in a small, semi-detached house on Vickers Street, named in honour of William, the original lace-maker, who had once been Mayor of Nottingham. The love of nature, of learning, and of language that accompanied Geoffrey throughout his life was given to him early. Poetry was among the delights that filled time and mind in that gadget-free home. One favourite family pastime began with each player writing a question and a noun on separate slips of paper which were then shuffled. 'Each then drew at random a question and a noun and wrote a poem, answering the question and bringing in the noun. Spontaneity was essential; fifteen minutes was the longest period of gestation allowed.' Jessie and Charles created an atmosphere that encouraged curiosity, original thought, confidence, and a sense of humour. They did so more by generous example than by design. Perhaps their creation succeeded because it was spontaneous, unencumbered by fancy theories of child rearing. 'The home my parents made was a place of unalloyed happiness', Geoffrey wrote. 'The only stresses of time came from the external world of school or the internal world of awakening conflict and confusion. Home was a place of accepted ways and standards which were unquestioned then and which survive question now; a place of mutual acceptance and total security.'

One childhood memory above all imprinted itself in Geoffrey's mind, gathering meaning as he reviewed it at various moments in life: it centred on a piece of furniture. On the day the family moved to Vickers Street, when Geoffrey was about three, he watched two moving men haul a huge Victorian double wardrobe into the new house. The spectacle of humans carrying an article that he had believed to be fixed in place astonished him. Years later he wrote: 'It seems to me in retrospect that, as I watched that wardrobe edge through the door, I caught my first glimpse of the fact that human order and disorder are largely made by men, consciously or blindly, compulsively or deliberately, with understanding or with grotesque misunderstanding of the delicate medium in which they work and of the endless repercussions of everything they do.'

Another memory: 'I only once remember being bored even for a moment. I must have been about six at the time. I wonder what went wrong.'

Geoffrey got off to a bad start at school. 'My first day school introduced me to the anguish reserved for nonconformists who long to conform and for the awkward who long to excel in dexterity.' When Jessie asked the teacher why her son was so miserable, the latter replied, 'If the children are cutting out rabbits in newspaper and one of them cuts off his rabbit's ears, he just starts again. But if Geoffrey cuts of his rabbit's ears, he throws the scissors across the room and bursts into tears.' Eventually he adjusted, made friends, and enjoyed two more day schools and a boarding school, called Bramcote, in Scarborough. His next educational phase proved less satisfying. 'From 1908 to 1912 I tried with meagre success to fit in to the public school system as expressed at Oundle.' Characteristically, he disposed of what must have been a most disagreeable experience in a single sentence. It was not his custom to dwell on personal disaster.

Early in 1913 Geoffrey spent a few months in Germany, at least part of the time in the company of his father who had himself been at school there. 'When I first visited the Continent, no frontier asked to see my passport, and a golden sovereign (there were no one pound notes) was exchangeable at a fixed rate for any currency from Antwerp to Athens. My standards of stability were set in a world which still looked and felt far more stable than it was or has ever been since that glorious sunset.' He went up to Merton College, Oxford, in October 1913 to read Greek and Latin, or 'Greats', but the outbreak of war in August 1914 interrupted his studies. 'At Oundle and Oxford I had been in what was then called the Officers' Training Corps, so I was deemed fit, without further screening, to command in battle men of whom many were much older than I. I was given a commission in our local territorial battalion, the 7th (Robin Hood) Battalion of the Sherwood Foresters, without even a medical examination. I was with them before the end of 1914 and in France in February of the next year.' Geoffrey did not call into question the war or his participation in it. As he observes in this book, 'Before 1914, war, though mildly deplored in Britain, was still regarded as an alternative and sometimes necessary instrument of foreign policy.'

Geoffrey took part in the heavy fighting in Flanders, in the neighbourhood of Ypres, during the spring of 1915. (The Germans introduced poison gas into the conflict during the Battle of Ypres.) Autumn found him at the Battle of Loos, in a strategic situation which duplicated almost exactly a crab-apple war in his childhood – but with grenades as weapons and quite different results. Sir Arthur Conan Doyle described the incident in his history of *The British Campaign in France and Flanders, 1915*, as follows: 'In the early morning of the 14th [October], Captain Checkland, with a company of the 5th Sherwood Foresters, pushed an advance up to the place where their comrades of the 7th Battalion had been, and found Captain Vickars [*sic!*] of that regiment who, with a bravery which deserves to be classical, defended almost single-handed a barrier, while he ordered a second one to be built behind him, cutting him off from all succour. He was desperately wounded, but was brought back by his comrades.' Thus did Geoffrey spend his 21st birthday, October 13th, and the first day of his 22nd year. He was awarded the Victoria Cross for his courage. He repaired from his wounds in a convalescent home in Bournemouth. Healed, he returned to battle, saw a great deal more action, and received the Croix de Guerre in 1918. Meanwhile, his brother Burnell had died, 'killed by a shell in his battery in some untenable position in the Ypres salient', in 1916.

After his discharge Geoffrey resumed his studies at Oxford and earned a Master of Arts degree. He proceeded to read law, and was admitted to the profession as a solicitor in 1923. 'I was educated almost wholly in the humanities, that is to say in the study of human experience. The subjective domain was assumed to be paramount in importance for human subjects such as we. Mathematics and logic were honoured though perhaps not adequately stressed. They were important intellectual tools in the ordering of experience. But the Word was paramount.'

Geoffrey acquired a family during his student days. In 1918 he married Helen Tregoning Newton. Their first child, Pamela, was born in 1921, and the second, Douglas Burnell, in 1922. Geoffrey also wrote a number of poems during the early 1920s. Some, his 'jingles', were humorous:

> For those upon house-hunting bent
> How fearful is the map of Kent!
> How could I brook inglorious ease
> At SMARDEN, SNAVE or OLD WIVES LEES;
> Or have men cast it in my teeth:
> 'He lives at SMEETH! He *lives* at SMEETH!'

written at Charing Cross Station in 1924. But there was in him as well a battlefield which he explored in verse. One sonnet, called 'Blindness', and composed in 1922, ends,

> God! I would give all man can know or guess
> to pass the veil of man's self-consciousness.

Around 1925 his poetic voice became still for almost thirty years while he wrote stories, essays, and fables.

It was also during the 1920s that Geoffrey became a sailor. In recreation, as in his other pursuits, he aimed for excellence: he sailed competitively and came in second in the Fastnet Race shortly before the Second World War. His daughter, Pamela, recalls another of her father's 'mad exploits' was to pioneer 'balloon pole jumping' in 1928 – a sort of hybridization of pole-vaulting and ballooning.

Youthful marriages do not always wear well, and Geoffrey's grew 'blindly muddled'. The union was dissolved in 1934. In 1935 Geoffrey wed Ethel Ellen Tweed, a match that brought him three decades of happiness. Their son, Hugh, was born in 1939.

Meanwhile, as 'an analyst and architect of legal relations', Geoffrey quickly earned the respect of his peers. His friend and sometime colleague, Donald Hall, recalls that 'when he arrived at Slaughter and May as a new partner in 1926, I was still only an articled clerk. In that prestigious firm there were then only four partners; he was 33, had won the Victoria Cross on his 21st birthday, and was already reputed to be an almost dangerously brilliant lawyer.' Geoffrey described his career in the law in these words: 'I lived as a lawyer in the ethical and the aesthetic dimensions. I did virtually no contentious work. My chief activity was to design structures of legal relation and therewith human relations, to give effect to the wishes of anyone who engaged me to do so, provided that both the ends proposed and the means available seemed to me to be both legal and proper. Since in private practice a lawyer's clients are only those who are able to pay for his help and whom he is happy to work with, life (given success) is almost improperly easy. There was plenty of work and plenty of money.'

Slaughter and May had clients with foreign investments, and Geoffrey travelled frequently. He recorded his sensations during one such trip, a five-day flight to India during the first year of commercial airline service between Britain and India (1930), in an autobiographical story. Except for naming his protagonist 'Ambrose', Geoffrey did not bother to disguise himself. 'Ambrose reached for the black bag in the rack above his head', the story reads. 'This bag contained about four pounds in weight of paper covered with information about a jute mill in Bengal. For three months Ambrose had concentrated his whole being upon the disentangling of its obscure and sordid affairs. And, because loyalties are generated by rendering and not receiving services, the continued existence of this jute mill, which did not belong to him and which he had never seen, had become to Ambrose more important than his own.' Suspended in time, 'Ambrose' loses his need for the black bag; he speculates about the shards of alien cultures observed during frequent stops for refuelling; and he makes acquaintance with the thoughts of Buddha, finding them at once compelling and perplexing. One might analyse the story at some length because it contains as seedlings many ideas which Geoffrey brought to maturity later. But its biographical interest lies chiefly in the implication that success in the practice of law did not quite fulfil – though its author would have been hard pressed at the time to identify the source of his dissatisfaction.

Geoffrey's most important and time-consuming legal work during the interwar years involved arranging 'the extension of a fabulous volume of German debt', a task which took him back and forth between London and Berlin. 'It was the beginning of the Nazis;' Donald Hall remembers; 'we discussed them when he came to stay with us, and when I naively remarked that their worst trait seemed their awful tactlessness, he said severely and forever memorably, "My dear Donald, tactlessness implies an absolute inability to understand other human beings; it is one of the most terrifying sins against the spirit." ' But Geoffrey did not recognize the threat of Nazi Germany until Britain had yielded to Hitler's demands for the cession of the Sudetenland in September 1938. The terms of the Munich agreement struck Geoffrey instantly and with brute force. 'How *could* I have been so blind?', he asked – and would continue to ask for the rest of his life.

The fact of his failure to anticipate Nazi intentions, rather than the events themselves, precipitated a profound and permanent change in Geoffrey's view of the world and his place in it. 'It seems all to have begun in 1938 at Munich, which left me intensely, permanently politically conscious, absorbed in the historical process of cultural growth, change and conflict, whether between and within nations or large institutions', he wrote in one letter. In another he said, 'Suddenly in 1938 . . . I became politically conscious, not just of the approaching war but of an unworthy state of affairs at home. I started a "movement" in the City which went off like a bomb.' The movement, The Association for Service and Reconstruction, had as its 'manifesto' a statement written by Geoffrey and Hugh Quennell, issued October 21st 1938 – evidence that no time had been wasted since Munich. The statement opened with these words:

> We believe that this country is in danger from without and from within.
>
> The danger from without lies in the policies of those nations whose governments accept war as an instrument of policy and approve it as a stimulus to virility.
>
> The danger from within lies in the confusion both in our moral and in our material resources; in the sluggishness of our over-burdened government; in our acceptance of fear as a dictator of policy; and in our smugness. . . .

> The national effort needed will evidently require citizens to accept both sacrifices and opportunities – on the one hand, a reduction in the standard of living of the wealthier classes and perhaps temporarily of all; a tolerance of far reaching regulation of life; a weakening in the power of vested interests – on the other, a more vital social relationship; a sense of responsibility, springing from the realization that all work is public as well as private; greater opportunities for service.

A bomb indeed. Geoffrey, as Chairman, addressed the first meeting of Association members in December, greeting them as follows: 'I have developed on the one hand a sense of the most uncontrollable dissatisfaction with the conditions of things as they are, and on the other hand a conviction that as an ordinary man I have, in common with other ordinary men, a power and hence a duty to do something to make that condition other than it is. I can tell you that nothing but that would have got me here.'

The Association created a sensation but, said Geoffrey, 'I didn't know what to do with it and it was a relief when the outbreak of war scattered the leaders, including me, to a variety of wartime jobs. But the impetus remained and had some part in deciding me to leave the City (and soon the law). . . .'

Geoffrey also belonged to a group called the Moot, which had grown out of an ecumenical conference held at Oxford in 1937 on 'Church, Community, and State.' The Moot's membership included Reinhold Niebuhr, T. S. Eliot, Kark Mannheim, J. H. Oldham (the group's guiding spirit), Michael Polanyi, and Adolph Löwe. The last three became Geoffrey's valued friends, particularly Löwe. Through the Moot, Geoffrey became involved in the founding of the *Christian News-Letter* in 1939. Edited by Oldham, it was intended as a means of communication among people who wanted to keep a spirit of internationalism alive. Geoffrey contributed a number of articles.

The inevitable war arrived. Geoffrey reinlisted as an infantry lieutenant in 1940, spent six weeks in Scotland 'learning to blow things up', and fully expected to be parachuted into battle. Instead he found himself a 'bogus' colonel assigned to an intelligence mission in South America, appraising the potential for fifth columnists. While he 'shipped out to safety', his wife Ellen stayed back in England – which they had vowed not to abandon – during the Battle of Britain, watching for enemy parachutists and tending baby Hugh. Geoffrey completed his work and returned with the bombing still in progress. 'I was *never* so glad to get home!' He passed the remainder of the war, from 1941 to 1945, as Deputy Director-General of the Ministry of Economic Warfare in charge of economic intelligence – a position that had previously been held by Hugh Gaitskell – and member of the Joint Intelligence Committee of the Chief of Staff. Mr. M. Y. Watson, who served with Geoffrey in the Ministry, wrote: 'There was soon no doubt in any of us that we had a chief of unusual intellectual powers, with a keen nose for muddled thinking and the second-rate. There were some who found they were left behind by the speed and mode of his thought. One of my friends, emerging visibly shaken from an interview with Geoffrey, said, "Next time I am summoned by that man I shall take my legal adviser with me". But no one understood better than he how to draw the best out of his staff and for those who passed the tests of this rather stern man (stern because he expected of others the same high standards he set himself) there were rich rewards. No one was more generous with deserved praise. I think all Geoffrey's staff respected him deeply; many, especially those who got to know him away from his always uncluttered desk, loved him also.' It was for this work – what Sir Anthony Eden referred to in his letter of thanks as 'providing our armed services with all the intelligence required to enable them to penetrate the chinks of our enemy's armour' – that Geoffrey received his knighthood, in 1946.

After the war Geoffrey went into 'that most basic and English occupation, coal'. A client who had agreed to become chairman of the new National Coal Board asked him to be legal adviser and to help organize the board. The offer presented him with an opportunity to practise the principles of public service in peacetime that had been fundamental to the Association for Service and Reconstruction. 'I was . . . sure that the public sector was bound to become so important that large public monopolies of this kind had to be made to work.' In 1948 he ceased functioning as the board's lawyer and became board member in charge of manpower, training, education, health, and welfare, until 1955. A gargantuan task in any situation, made more difficult by the fact of nationalization and the need to create confidence and new organizational forms.

Of the individuals he met during his years with the Coal Board, Geoffrey spoke with particular respect and affection for Arthur Horner, an official of the National Union of Mineworkers and a Communist. Pamela heard that 'my father once asked Arthur Horner why, when he was addressing the board, he always looked at him. "Because you seem to be the only one who is listening," came the reply.'

Geoffrey also served on a number of public and professional bodies, notably the London Passenger Transport Board (1941–1946), the Council of the Law Society (1944–1948), and the Medical Research Council (1952–1960). He was appointed to two Royal Commissions, on the Press (1947–1949) and the later Committee of Enquiry into the Cost of the National Health Service (1956). He was Chairman of the Research Committee of the Mental Health Research Fund for sixteen years, from 1951 to 1967. Professor J. M. Tanner, Secretary of that committee for most of this period, spoke at Geoffrey's memorial in 1982 and offered these insights into the quality of Geoffrey's presence as a leader: 'The Research Committee had about twenty members and they were deliberately drawn from many different fields of science and medicine.... It sounds like the recipe for a nightmare, but Geoffrey ran this extraordinary menagerie for fifteen years with never a resignation, never a caucus, scarcely even a sigh of despondency.

'It was the most extraordinary committee I have ever served on.... The decisions, when they came, were perfectly hard-edged and operational. But nobody on that committee ever felt his views had been slighted by the Chairman, and after an attendance or two each member picked up the same scent and he didn't slight his colleagues' views either, whatever his discipline. Such was the effect of Geoffrey Vickers' example: for Geoffrey was no preacher; it was simply that other people recognized an integrity which went beyond the intellectual, and found it a model they wished to imitate.'

During the post-war years Geoffrey began to write and lecture about the coal industry in particular, and institutions in general, and to think 'about how large organizations of people hang together'. His discovery of cybernetics and information theory provided further stimulation by suggesting an organizational framework for understanding human affairs. However, Geoffrey responded to systems theory 'in a way which was to diverge increasingly from that of everyone else I know'. When he retired from the Coal Board in 1955, he began to write and talk more 'and also to read more and so to realize for the first time that what I was saying was not orthodox. So my utterance became increasingly a protest against what seemed to me the three errors built into contemporary culture, notably unwillingness (1) to recognize human concern as a causal factor in human behaviour, (2) to regard human understanding as an exercise in constructing complementary pictures of reality each with a different figure and correspondingly different relevant ground, and (3) to accept that social constraints and commitments can and should be enlargements of the person and are indeed necessary to the growth of personality.'

Altogether Geoffrey published approximately a hundred papers and eight books, including the classic *The Art of Judgment* (1965), *Value Systems and Social Process* (1968), *Freedom in a Rocking Boat* (1970), *Making Institutions Work* (1974), and this volume. He tackled huge issues – responsibility, love, morality, culture, history, commitment – because he valued their place in human experience and, therefore, in human institutions. Although his writings speak most directly to the concerns of managers, policy makers, and planners, they do not fit snugly into any category, and his following is a more motley group. For he was, above all, a passionate humanist – a most under-represented species.

Thus in retirement Geoffrey became a writer, a 'para-academic', a 'wandering scholar'. Beginning in the early 1960s, when he was invited to be a consultant to conferences at the University of Toronto on 'Man and Industry', he travelled frequently to North America. The United States Department of Health, Education, and Welfare sought his advice in organizing the U.S. National Institute of Mental Health. Geoffrey lectured in such diverse settings as the Institute for International Studies at the University of California, Berkeley, and the Division for Study and Research in Education at the Massachusetts Institute of Technology. (It was at the latter institution that he became deeply suspicious of various efforts to model human experience on the computer, not to mention what seemed to him inflationary claims about the power of the computer as an educational tool for small children. But before expressing his objections he thought he ought to have a better grasp of the technology, so he prevailed upon a graduate student to spend a day with him in a computer laboratory and teach him rudimentary programming. Geoffrey proved to be a splendid, receptive student – at the age of 80! But he was no convert. After this adventure he wrote to a friend at M.I.T.: 'In the beginning was the Word, not the equation.')

Geoffrey's success in his new 'career' and in the New World surprised him; he observed from time to time that, in this new role, he was better known on the American side of the Atlantic than on his own. The infirmities of age caught up with him in the late 1970s, and his trans-oceanic travels came to an end. He continued to write and to lecture in England where his reputation was on the increase. He died in March 1982, at the age of 87, still filled with wonder.

There are many pieces of Geoffrey that slip outside the chronological order. Any picture of him must include his 'back room boys' – his metaphor for his mental activity which seemed to him a dialogue between his 'back room' and his 'front parlour'. The back room produced exciting thoughts; the front parlour played the critic, sometimes resubmitting material for improvement. Thus it would sometimes happen that Geoffrey might not respond to some provocative question in a conversation, only to appear the next day with a memorandum dictated during the night 'by the Back Room Boys'.

Geoffrey was a superb listener. He was an embarrassingly faithful correspondent. He had a particularly fine rapport with young people, both small children and young adults, whose ideas he entertained with utmost seriousness. He had a delicious, often mischievous wit, usually at his own expense. He felt at home with insects and birds and all manner of creatures, and especially with the vegetable world. Though humans often puzzled him, he felt comfortable in history. For him historical time began with the geological strata beneath his long legs as he strode across his beloved chalk downs – his awareness of layers beneath the surface soil no doubt enhanced by visits to the coal pits; and the Enlightenment happened the day before yesterday. He belonged to this process, as an Englishman and a 'lapsed Victorian'.

At the age of 84 Geoffrey wrote: 'I once said to someone that I felt like a very minor prophet who arose and said, "The Lord gave me a most important message for you; but I couldn't quite hear what he said". I have now almost abandoned hope of discovering what the message was. On the other hand, people keep on coming and talking and asking me to utter; and I still occasionally do. Some message must be getting out. . . .' Through his writings he recalled the real meanings of words devalued by usage: love, knowledge, responsibility, morality, appreciation; he offered tools for understanding and action in a world which, he reckoned, sorely required attention. By example, he set a standard of integrity. As Antony said of Brutus, 'His life was gentle, and the elements so mixed in him that Nature might stand up and say to all the world: "This was a man!".'

S. B. Sutton
Boston, Massachusetts, USA
April 1983

CONTENTS

Foreword		xix
Part I	**Systems Thinking**	
Chapter 1	The Relevance of Systemic Thinking	1
Chapter 2	The Characteristics of Open Systems	12
Chapter 3	Regulation, Organic and Technological	20
Chapter 4	The Emergence of Ecological Systems	27
Chapter 5	The Emergence of Human Systems	33
Chapter 6	The Peculiarities of Human Systems	41
	Communication	
	Culture	
	Government	
	War	
Chapter 7	Appreciation and Action	54
	Concern	
	Ethic	
	Reason	
Chapter 8	The Bonding of Human Systems	59
Chapter 9	Four Dimensions of Instability in Human Systems	65
Part II	**Western Systems Since The Enlightenment**	
Chapter 10	Regulating Political Systems: Three Decaying Hopes	69
Chapter 11	The Emergence of the Nation State	76
Chapter 12	The Emergence of the Autonomous Individual	81
Chapter 13	Autonomy, Alienation, and Authenticity	89
Chapter 14	The Declining Force of Membership	98

Part III The Threat to Human Systems

Chapter 15	Six Escalating Instabilities	107
Chapter 16	Unstable Relations with the Natural Milieu	112
Chapter 17	Unstable Relations in the Human Milieu	122
	War	
	Development	
	Inflation and the standard of living	
	Unemployment	
Chapter 18	The Changing Role of the Technologist	141
Chapter 19	Analysts, Modellers, and Governors	152
Chapter 20	Understanding, Deciding, and Policy Making	162
Chapter 21	How Different are Human Systems?	169
Bibliography		178
Index		180

The publishers gratefully acknowledge the editorial assistance of Dr. Margaret Blunden of The Open Systems Group at the Open University.

FOREWORD

This book is an attempt to apply systems thinking to human history to the extent needed to understand the present predicament of Britain in particular, and more generally of the industrial Western countries which share the cultural inheritance of the Enlightenment,[1] a phase of history which I believe to be abruptly ending now.

I claim no academic authority as a historian or as a scientist – certainly not as a 'systems scientist', though I have been influenced and, I think, helped by contact with systems concepts. My active experience has lain in the partly overlapping fields of law, war, and public administration, and the chief focus of my interest has been on the regulation of behaviour in human organizations, especially those involving some formal distribution of power.

This is both a historical and an ethical study. It is historical because all human societies emerge, grow, change and disappear in the dimension of time and are affected to some extent by their own past. It is ethical because all human societies are governed in greater or less degree by standards of self-expectation and mutual expectation, some explicitly formalized in laws or specific agreements, some partly or wholly tacit but none the less powerful. I have found what I understand by systems thinking to be immensely helpful in understanding this historical and ethical process; and I hope that the outcome is sufficient to justify the particular contribution which I wish to make to the growing literature on 'the future'.

In this book I want to stress two factors, neither of which seem to me to have had sufficient attention in the 'futures' literature. The first of these factors is the systemic nature of human history, and also of human experience, which is by no means the same thing.

The esssence of systems thinking, as I understand it, is the concept of form or order, sustained through time by a self-corrective process, that notices deviations from the standards which define order and responds with actions which sustain or restore it. Biology and ecology offer many examples of self-sustaining order, and technology has become adept at applying the principle to the creation and maintenance of mechanical – though not of political – 'orders' devised by man.

To a mind accustomed to systems thinking, time is an ever present dimension, and the preservation of order through time is the basic problem both in understanding the past and in influencing the future. Stability, even more than change, demands to be explained, aspired to and regulated. Form may be preserved through change but change may also disrupt form. In particular, linear change is bound in time to be self-limiting or self-reversing and may even destroy the form which it has defined.

The second and more contentious of the factors which I wish to stress is that the standards by which human order is defined are in part culturally set by the human societies which they organize, and change with time by a process which is not wholly beyond human understanding or control. The development of standards is a dialectic process, in the sense that it breeds its own changes; but it is neither circular nor guaranteed to arrive at any ultimate state of stability. On the contrary, it may easily prove self-destructive.

If seen in this way, the history of human affairs and the history of the standards of judgement which human beings apply to those affairs, evolve partly autonomously and partly interdependently.

In the past, people have often exaggerated the extent of their mental autonomy. In reaction against this, scientific theory has been reluctant to acknowledge the possibility that mental activity can be even partly self-determining. Yet I know no scientific ground for the presumption that the human mind is not free – except of course the convenience of the scientist. The element of self-determination which has emerged in our species with its capacity to represent to itself (however mistakenly) its situation as it is and as it might be, and even as it 'ought to be', is not necessarily an asset. But I shall be much concerned with it.

The idea that linear development cannot continue indefinitely was buried during the age of accelerating 'progress' in material abundance which marked the nineteenth century and our own, at least until the present time. But the idea is now painfully winning its way back into public consciousness. It is resisted mainly because both scientific knowledge and technological expertise seem to be continuing to expand linearly and even exponentially. There is also a widespread belief, as old as Adam Smith (though not to be attributed to him without massive qualification) that, in a world of expanding science and technology, economic and social order will take care of themselves.

Some futurists, such as Alvin Toffler[2] in his recent book *The Third Wave*, seem to see no inconsistency in the concept of an ever more interdependent and crowded human world sustaining its harmony with no 'consensus' at all.

To me, on the contrary, human societies are primarily remarkable as political and social systems, rather than technological ones. Even their economic stability seems to depend increasingly on their political and social stability. And the political and social trends which can be discerned as 'linear' in the last few centuries of Western development appear to point clearly to the limiting factors which they are themselves engendering and to the price which would have to be paid to stabilize them.

The historical imagination is not greatly encouraged in these days; yet it seems to me especially needed if we are to give perspective to contemporary changes. Consider then very briefly one aspect of 'order', political and social order, as it has developed in Britain over the last five centuries. This is not a long time, when judged by the basic scale of one individual human life. Five hundred years are spanned by seven consecutive lifetimes, or by 15–20 generations. Imagine ten individuals, each born in England fifty years later than the next, and each reflecting on his life experience as it neared its end.

My first example, an old man at the end of the fifteenth century, looked back over a life spent under a feudal order which had defined the rights and duties of a highly classified society with little change for four or five centuries. He may have been aware that that order was in the last stages of self-destruction; but he could not have foreseen the new age which was dawning. His junior by fifty years, when reaching the same age in about 1550, had experienced the rise of a highly centralized monarchy, under an excommunicated king, Henry VIII, which had disarmed the nobility, expropriated the monasteries, nationalized the Church and fortified its power by creating a new class of bureaucrats. How could he guess that his junior by only fifty years, when reaching the same age in 1600, would be celebrating the euphoria of Elizabeth's later years, Protestantism established, Spain vanquished and a still class-structured people united in self-confident alliance with a trusted executive monarchy? How could that junior guess that his junior by fifty years would at his age be living in 1650 under the rule of a 'Protector', Cromwell, supported by an army, and would remember the blood spurting from the mutilated body of a king on a scaffold in Whitehall? He would have been comforted if he could have known that his junior fifty years later would be celebrating the 'glorious revolution' of 1689, the only landmark in the calendar of my chosen time span to introduce a period of political stasis long enough not to surprise the next of my series, who could, in 1750, compare the newly evolving institutions of his government with the turbulent times of his youth.

Yet even that complacent age was not to last a century. An ideological ferment begat the American and French Revolutions and accompanied them throughout. It was believed that liberty could be married to equality without either partner being restricted by the union, a proposition that the logical de Tocqueville questioned when it was expounded in America in the 1830s. So, a decade later, did a German political analyst called Karl Marx. But the eighth of my imaginary experiments might have lived long enough to hear the Prince Consort, when opening the Great Exhibition in 1851, declare as a matter of common assurance, that the unity of all mankind was about to be achieved in a Great Commercial Republic. And the ninth, attending Queen Victoria's diamond jubilee celebrations in Spithead in 1897, would probably have found no cause to disbelieve in the conjunction between economic increase and political betterment.

He would have been shaken to know that his junior by fifty years would in 1950 look back on ten years of global war, twenty years of interwar depression and the rise of rival political ideologies claiming far more numerous subjects, perhaps even devotees, than his own. But even that sobered individual, if he had lived to mid-century, would have had substantial ground for hope that his treasured political institutions could deal with the social as well as the economic problems of his day. Political democracy, he was sure, had always been social democracy in embryo.

His junior, my contemporary, would not be so sure.

We can play this game with other variables which yield a more consistent pattern – with geographical exploration, with the multiplication of populations, with the exploitation of resources, with changing public responses to poverty and unemployment, with the multiplication and fragmentation of diffused knowledge – and, of course, with the growth of both science and technology and of their interaction. Some of these developments have reached or passed their climax, as have geographical exploration and the colonization of empty (terrestrial) space. Some, like science and technology, are still in full spate. But even in the political dimension which I have chosen to explore some linear trends are discernible.

There has been a wider devolution of political power, but in two directions which are not easily to be reconciled. On the one hand, the universal franchise has vested in a majority of virtually all the adult members of the population the power to choose a legislature, and indirectly an executive, from whatever alternatives may be available. On the other hand, single-interest pressure groups of several kinds have been created to which governments, however elected, are more responsive – at least between elections – than they are to their electors as such.

Governments are particularly susceptible to opposition from such groups. The power to veto grows faster than the power to impose order; and both powers cause division and polarization as other constraints and commitments weaken.

In the meantime economic and technological development continue, but on what may be divergent lines. Economic growth, buoyant for two decades, then flagging for one, has run into what may be more than a cyclical depression. Technology has taken a new turn; but the age of the computer should not blind us to the immense development of engineering in the field of energy, especially armaments, and to the increasingly complex relation between industry and government in a world where the making of jobs has become as politically important as the making of goods or even money.

Political systems of this uncertainty are not to be modelled on computers, unless they are simplified either by ignoring their more important aspects, which only makes the result misleading, or by controlling their outcome with a completeness, which, if it were possible, would be highly threatening – as it already is in those regimes where it is attempted. None the less they do not wholly escape our understanding. Even a horseback survey as superficial as the one summarized in previous paragraphs may give a sense of change with time, which is better than its absence, however uncomfortable it may be.

This sense of change is intensified if we concentrate attention on the last two hundred years, which is the focus of this book. In this time, marked in its origin by unparalleled hope and confidence, the world's independent states have multiplied as ten multinational empires have dissolved, and the resultant fragments are, for the most part, unstable. The last empty continents have been colonized and apportioned and their multiple populations are constrained by rising barriers against immigration into 'developed' countries and in some cases against emigration. Grotesque disparities of wealth have developed between countries and within them.

In many countries destitution increases. Unemployment and inflation have become endemic and wars multiply.

The environment of each society and of each individual in each society is becoming increasingly a human environment, created by other societies and other individuals. The interdependence of all of them mounts but the means of regulating their mutual relations, even including markets for commodities, products, currencies, skill, and 'labour' is breaking down. Even the relations between the human species and its habitat are becoming problematic, not through failure of technological inventiveness but through the failing responses of the patient earth. The growth of the natural sciences has not resulted in a common or even a convergent world view of world 'order'. On the contrary, such dreams as the epoch has produced have faded and rival ideologies have grown in strength and ferocity to a degree as intense and on a scale far more world-wide than at the height of the religious wars. There is awareness of disorder but it is not mitigated, at least in the West, by any dream of some realistic alternative order, other than the desperate fantasies of the technological imagination.

The twelfth in my series of imaginary experiments, in around the year 2030, may just possibly look around him and backwards and forwards in time with the same confident content as attended the happiest of his predecessors in my series of potted scenarios – but I see no present reason to hope that he will. The minimal changes which he and his fellows would have had to absorb if they are to enjoy a political and social order even as acceptable and as stable as our own today, are daunting. These changes are considered in the last part of this book. They may seem impossible to achieve. They may be impossible. But if they are impossible the cost to him and his generation and their children will be very high. He and they may simply not survive. And if he does survive, we may, I think, assume that his state will reflect in part not only the 'realism' with which we in our time perceive our situation but also the quality of our hopes, our fears, our perceptions and our choices.

This reference to 'realism' leads me from the first of the two factors this book is concerned with – the systemic nature of human history – to the second, the cultural roots of the human standards that determine what is seen as 'real' in any particular era.

Human societies express specific cultures, which speak to their members both in the indicative and in the imperative moods, what is and what ought to be. 'This is true', 'that is admirable', 'that is not acceptable'. Even the scope of what is thinkable and what is possible are culturally defined. History records acts of individuals and societies – heroic resistances, outrageous destructions, strange self-dedications – made in the name of beliefs which are no longer held and of imperatives which are no longer binding but which in their time were potent creative or destructive forces. Even the great innovators who have changed the conceptual, the ethical, or the aesthetic standards of their day were rebels against an existing culture and designers of another. Our knowledge of reality is always indirect, a cultural construct interpreting our experience; and in the more important fields of our experience it is not only an interpreter but a designer. However inconvenient it may be for purposes of organized study, it does not seem to me to be questionable that human systems constantly generate and respond to their own understanding of what is and what might be and what ought to be. Human systems both design and predict their own future history – they are sometimes blind, often obdurate, often misguided, but seldom negligible as agents in the unfolding, sustainment and sometimes destruction of their own and each other's orders.

This means that there are limits to the possible rate at which human history can change without disintegration, since coherent change involves change in the whole set of cultural standards by which a society interprets its situation; and these standards are related to the life experience and hence the life span of individuals. But, of course, life expectancy is getting longer, so that while the rate of change of everything else is increasing, the rate of turnover of human lives, a key element in the rate of experiental adaptation, is actually decreasing. My series of scenarios may challenge the common assumption that the rate of change in human affairs has speeded only in the last two or three generations; but that rate has certainly speeded by comparison with the centuries over which my first experient looked back. Moreover, rates of change vary in importance not merely in terms of their speed but also in terms of the significance of what it is that is changing and its closeness to whatever threshold turns it into a major and immediate threat.

These then are the major themes which I pursue in this book. I have extended its time perspective further into the past than some may feel the need to do and more selectively than may seem acceptable to others. I do so in order to stress two points which are essential to my argument. The first concerns the differences which throughout recorded time have distinguished our species even from those most closely akin to us. Our technological age tends to equate human 'progress' with the development of technology and later of 'science'. I shall seek to show that there are other distinguishing differences not directly related to developing technology, notably the development of government within specific societies and of war between them. Ethologists are more interested in detecting similarities between human and nonhuman behaviour than in exploring the manifest differences. This imbalance needs, I think, to be corrected.

The second point which I wish to emphasise is, that in our attempts to regulate relations within and between human societies, and between them and their physical milieu, technology creates problems as well as solving them. This is a highly ambivalent role and one which is basically destabilising, like all linear developments. The present state of confusion, I shall suggest, may be more radical than that which always accompanies the transition of human societies from one cultural phase to another.

Three further explanatory notes are perhaps required. First, I conceive my approach to be that of the professional, rather than the academic. The professional has a built-in test of relevance; and he seeks knowledge wherever he can find whatever is relevant to the exercise of the skills he professes. The professions with which I identify myself are the professions of management and government. But I am conscious that, though the art of being managed and governed is not yet recognized as a profession, those who profess it (as we all need to do, in some form or another) must seek understanding where they can, regardless of conventional academic boundaries. Academic fragmentation is useful only in so far as agent experients can synthesize the fragments back together so as to make their actions more effective, or at least less lethal and their experience more sensitive, more profound, and more bearable than it would otherwise be. I am also conscious that the more closely the managed and governed claim to participate in their own governance (as they are so conspicuously claiming to do) the more they need to share an understanding of the process involved and of their own power to thwart it or to contribute to it.

Secondly, I am concerned that the word 'system' should not develop a purely technological flavour, as it is in danger of doing. Looking back over the development of study and education in governance (to use the most general term) an activity which burgeoned in Britain only after the Second World War, I am dismayed at the extent to which the word has become linked to the valuable but limited technique of systems modelling, to the exclusion of its wider conceptual meaning. I have found this wider meaning to be liberating and illuminating both during my last years of practical administration and during the more than twenty-five years since then which nature has allowed me for study and reflection. I describe the view with which it has left me in the hope that this will contribute to the equally personal views which others, as I assume, must constantly make and revise in order to place themselves in the changing scene in which they live and work, both as individuals and as role players in the complex business of collective living.

It follows that the book is concerned not with solving problems but with understanding situations. It is motivated by a cogent belief that a deeper commitment to systems thinking will provide a deeper understanding of the rhythms of human history; and by a corresponding fear that this potential liberation of the human understanding may be blocked by the technological culture in which it has been released.

This hope and this fear explain the arrangement and the emphasis of the whole study.

And yet there is a 'problem' inherent in the theme. It does not invite a technological solution, but it is, none the less, important to technologists, as to others – perhaps even more, as the latter half of this book suggests.

It can be firmly stated, and this is my third point.

The ideology deriving from the Enlightenment which has dominated the West for two hundred years, has aspired to realize both liberty and equality, at first for the 'greatest number' and later for each and all. And it has hoped to do so by a self-regulating and self-exciting or self-stimulating process, powered by technology and directed by human 'reason'. In its pursuit of the doubtfully compatible goals of liberty and equality, this ideology has produced much that we should be sorry to forgo; but the contemporary outcome is the reverse of what the nineteenth century expected. An ever more scientific world was never less predictable. An ever more technological world was never less controllable. A world dedicated to majority rule is increasingly run by militant minorities. 'Free' individuals, increasingly dependent on each other, are subject to increasing demands to share the commitments, accept the constraints and accord the trust required by the multiplying systems and subsystems to which they belong and on which they wholly depend. And these distribute their favours and, still more, their responsibilities, with the equality of a battlefield. For good and ill the ideology of the Enlightenment has worked itself out, paid its dividends and revealed its shortcomings.

In what new form can its inherent nobility of aspiration be realized in an overcrowded world, filled with confident, cultural competitors? Has it a future? If so, what and at what cost?

And if not, what?

Goring-on-Thames,
England
July 1981

Footnotes

1. The immense cultural change, euphemistically termed the Enlightenment, had five particularly important aspects: the market economy, utilitarian political philosophy, the narrowing of science as a concept, the explosive interaction of science and technology, and, above all, the concept of the autonomous individual. (G. Vickers, 'The Weakness of Western Culture', *Futures*, December 1977, p. 457). This cultural phase has bred its own reversals – for instance, the age of the individual has led to collectivities on a scale never dreamed of before – and is now in a trough of confusion. (Ibid p. 467).
2. A. Toffler, *The Third Wave*, London, William Collins, 1980.

PART I

Systems Thinking

CHAPTER 1

THE RELEVANCE OF SYSTEMIC THINKING

Systems is an old word. The Greeks were using it more than 2000 years ago to describe 'a whole composed of related parts'. Since then, as might be expected from so broad a term, it has been used in many contexts – in astronomy, meteorology, physics, biology; in politics, law and economics; in medicine and psychiatry; and even in the study of those related ways of thinking, feeling and acting which anthropologists have taught us to refer to as a people's culture.

Of course, the definition begs all the questions which it raises. Can something be regarded as more or less a whole or as a whole for some purposes but not others? Can a whole be also part of another whole or even of several other wholes? And if the answer to all these questions is 'yes', as it clearly is, can a concept so wide and vague be useful?

It has at least proved powerful. Many of the world's greatest wars have been directed either to freeing some part of a political 'whole' so that it might itself become politically 'whole' or to capturing some 'whole' and incorporating it as part of the capturing whole. And at less dramatic levels organization theory has always been beset by the problem of how much autonomy to devolve on an organization's parts. This of itself shows that we conceive of 'wholeness' as divisible, something which can exist more or less. A local authority or a business subsidiary may have a restricted but defined area of autonomy; it may be free to decide and act within certain limits or for some purposes but not others. Local authorities, for example, are required to make some provisions, allowed to make others, and forbidden to make yet others; and the enabling or restricting power may be expressed in the granting or witholding of funds or of legal authority.

These external constraints are not confined to the exercise of power by a superior authority. Facts, no less than decisions, are limiting factors, notably limitations of resources of all kinds – money, men, skill, materials, time and attention. To be autonomous is not to be all powerful. It is merely to be free from the constraint of a superior human will.

Even within this limited freedom a 'whole' is not necessarily 'free' to do anything within its authority and its resources. It has also to be so organized and so inclined that it is able to act as a whole on its surround for that purpose. For it is composed of constituent parts which may or may not be willing and able to combine in joint action, to act 'as a whole'. The more 'autonomy' these parts enjoy, the more extensive will be the power of any of them to block joint action by the 'whole'. The peculiar difficulty of government, whether political or industrial, in Western democracies at the present time is clearly due to the rise to power of organized sectional minorities, each with an effective power to veto the others and thus to curtail the area within which the system which they constitute can in fact act as a whole, despite the fact that it has the authority and the resources to do so.

So clearly there is an important relation and also an important difference between internal relations which enable any society or organization to act as a whole, and the external relations between it and all the other wholes to which it relates hierarchically or otherwise. Internal relations within a whole can either limit or facilitate its powers to act as a whole at its own level for any specific purpose or indeed at all.

It is not surprising that as human populations have multiplied and become more differentiated and more interdependent both internally and externally, their problems of organization have grown greater; and such skill as men have developed in the art of organization has been more than offset by these increasing difficulties. This has been accentuated in the West over the last four hundred and, still more, the last two hundred years by a sharp increase in the consciousness of individual persons and in their expectation and demand for autonomy at the personal level.

Because consciousness is a personal experience and can easily become an isolating one, the problem of wholes and parts has always been most sensitive in the context of human individuals and their relations with each other and with the manifold societies in which they are always associated. The 'individual' has not always and everywhere claimed to be the basic unit, more 'whole' than any of the wholes which he might participate in forming. None the less even in the most traditional societies men have probably been aware, at least intermittently, of their individual as well as their social identity. To this extent our understanding of the social organization of men even at their closest contrasts sharply with our growing biological knowledge of the ways in which organisms develop and control their related parts; and equally with our ethological knowledge about how apes and other social species regulate the communities in which they live. A huge spectrum includes the wolf pack, the herds of herbivores, the familial groupings of the primates, and the almost organic association of bees and termites. But human societies and organizations differ from all of these in ways so distinctive as to make the differences at least as striking as the similarities.

None the less we knew a lot about human systems and their management before what we now call *systems thinking* – or, more narrowly, *systems science* – emerged on the intellectual scene as a way of thought sufficiently characteristic to deserve a name; and even before the social sciences (including psychology) began to order and extend our knowledge of human relations. It began, in the West, more than twenty centuries ago with the study of history and the formulation of political and ethical philosophies; and it grew more intense as the rate of change quickened, both within human societies and in their environment, often through the willed, and more often through the unwilled, acts of men. This brought with it both threats and promises which challenged the human understanding and developed a much sharper awareness of time.

The social sciences did much to clarify familiar concepts, as well as to introduce new ones. The concept of role, for example, is as old as the theatre and has always been used in contexts much wider than the theatrical. But sociology gave it depth and precision and made it an invaluable term of art in describing human relationships. Similarly, it had been known since the great voyages of discovery began (indeed much earlier) that other societies had languages, customs and techniques radically different from those of the West and of each other. But the self-confident West arranged them in an ascending hierarchy of development, leading from savagery, through barbarism to the one and only pinnacle of accomplishment – their own. It was the anthropologist, patiently immersing himself in these alien milieux, who developed the idea of cultures, including his own native culture, as a number of alternative forms of social life, each with a history of its own, and searched for laws which would explain their differences and similarities.

It is to be noted that these insights had their limitations. Most sociologists, I think, accept the fact that the playing of a role is more than the keeping of a set of explicit rules, however complex, and cannot be completely formulated in express terms, because it depends on the manifold contexts in which it may be played. It is significant that one of the most disruptive industrial practices of our day is 'working to rule'. But neither psychologists nor epistemologists have got far in describing the mental processes by which role playing is judged adequate or otherwise, either by role players themselves or by those whom their roles affect. Many people are still loth to recognize that such mental processes must exist and must be partly tacit, and we have as yet nothing very conclusive to say about why they change with time or how far such changes are controllable by human policy. Yet these are matters essential to education, to management, and to government.

Similarly, cultural anthropologists are not agreed on the reasons why human cultures differ so widely or on the common source of those elements which they have in common. And international bodies seeking to establish trans-cultural agreements on human rights encounter the same difficulty. It has, indeed, always haunted the study of human systems. Some historians purport to record only 'what happened' disclaiming, as H. A. L. Fisher does,[1] any ability to discern in history 'a plot, a rhythm, a predetermined pattern' and stressing 'the play of the contingent and the unforeseen'. Yet even they must use some criteria, however tacit, in selecting what to record from the immense flux of event. Others discern a 'rhythm', as Toynbee did in his *Study of History* but fail to account for it. And those who think they see more deeply into the process, as Hegel and Marx did, find it difficult to define the area and importance of human initiative in what they wish to regard as a determined sequence of events.

Marx accepted the ambiguity but did not bother to explain it. How, if history was determined, could its course be altered, even slowed or speeded by revealing its laws to those who were subject to them? Was that not illogical? If so, so much the worse for logic. He knew that his exposition of historical laws would change history, and it did. He was a political activist, seeking theory only to guide action. 'The philosophers have *interpreted* the world in various ways, the point, however, is to *change* it.'

Professor Marvin Harris, by contrast, is equally committed to establishing the laws of history by pure scientific standards. In his great book, *The Rise of Anthropological Theory*,[2] he blames Marx for mixing up scientific theory and political practice. The politicians are sure to debase science for their own purposes. He points to the pseudo-scientific ideologies of the USSR. He knew they would debase science for political ends and they have. He was right too.

But he misses the point which Marx saw and which everyone except the scientist is bound to see – that as agents seeking to manage the world, or even their own lives, men seek knowledge to guide action, not vice versa. Politicians do not make revolutions or devise new constitutions in order to prove a theory. As agents, they have other goals, other criteria. If they choose to impose on their fellows beliefs which are not scientifically true, may not these beliefs alter the course of history? Every revolution of our century confirms that it may.

And if, on the contrary, they allow themselves to be guided by valid new knowledge, may not this also make a difference? Consider the movements towards a more humane penology which accelerated in Europe from the turn of this century, or the change in attitudes towards those once called lunatics who are now regarded as mentally ill and thus assimilated to the realm of the healing and caring professions. Would these changes have happened if changing scientific beliefs about the nature of man had not helped to relax the standards of universal and equal responsibility?

Professor Harris sums up Marx' view of cultural materialism as resting on three major socio-cultural distinctions: (1) the economic base; (2) the legal-political arrangements, that is, the social structure; and (3) social consciousness or ideology. This is a useful classification more than a century later, though some today would prefer to call the first the technological base, remembering that the largest industry in the world today is the armament industry. Professor Harris then defends Marx and Engels against charges of 'oversimplification' for having subsumed the second (legal-political) and third (ideology) segment under the first (economics). But neither Professor Harris nor Marx (though I think for quite different reasons) admits that however powerful the unconscious unfolding of history may be, men as agents talk, listen, think and feel about it in their efforts to understand it, often misconceive it and act as they would not have acted if they had understood their situation better or sometimes even achieve desired ends which would not otherwise have been realized. This phenomenological dimension obtrudes whenever people in active life seek to inform themselves and to influence others by changing the mental model in terms of which they and their fellows perceive and value their situations.

I do not wish in this book to enter the controversy about determinism any further than is needed to explain why in Chapters 5 and 6 I stress so strongly what I believe to be the role of diverse cultures in determining the response of men and societies to (amongst other things) the technological changes around them – responses which allow the second and third segments of the Marxist analysis (legal-political arrangements and ideology) to become semiautonomous forces codetermining the outcomes of history. If this makes human history refractory to the methods of pure science, we must use such methods as are open to us. That will be less unscientific than to ignore the facts to be explained.

This seems to me particularly important at a time when technological evolution has created a new and threatening relationship between and within human societies and between all of them and their planetary milieu, and when science has begun to provide in systems theory a model of the dialectic process more complete than Marx could command, which policy makers need urgently to understand.

Many great minds before and after Marx have pondered on the government of men by men – in other words, on the management of human systems. I do not think that Professor Harris exaggerates when he compares Marx' contribution to that of Darwin's. But Darwin's theories also have been developed and modified in important ways since they were first stated, notably by the impact of ecology, in which man (the 'ethical animal'[3] as a great evolutionary biologist has called him) has a still inadequately charted but obviously alarming role. So I do not apologize for acknowledging that a human culture once established becomes a partly autonomous force in its own future development, even though it be impossible to distinguish its contribution from all the other influences, outside and inside the society concerned, which are operating to change it or to stabilize it.

From those problems of human governance the main stream of science remained aloof, preoccupied with its major task of distinguishing and analysing matter and energy. For more than a century after technology had produced the telegraph, 'science' even declined to admit information as a change agent distinct from energy.

And then, over the last fifty years, came a change. Science contributed two clarifying concepts and technology a powerful tool. The concepts – control and information – are not new, but the making of technological systems has greatly clarified them; and the tool, the digital computer, has opened new scope for their application. It seems exceedingly strange to me that ideas which have been current for millenia should become familiar and even acceptable only after they have been incorporated in a machine; and I have no doubt that this fact tells us something either about the human understanding or more probably about the limitations inherent in

Western technological culture. But fact it is, and highly important in several ways.

The incorporation of control and information in computers is important in its own right, in so far as it enables men to make machines which can not only take over tasks formerly done by men but can often do them both faster and more reliably than men can. A sea-rescue helicopter, for example, can maintain its position and height above turbulent water in turbulent air by automatic controls with a precision beyond anything that could be achieved by a human nervous system, however alert and however well trained.

The incorporation of control and information in computers is further important in its own right in so far as it can supplement what the human brain and central nervous system can do. Everyone knows the computer's facility for storing and retrieving information and for applying to information any sequence of logical operations which can be fully specified. It is still a moot point how far and in what conditions this power enables it to build models of human situations more reliable than those on which the human policy maker has had to rely in peace and war in the aeons before this century. But it is a manifest fact that such models are proliferating and that governments are relying on them increasingly, and indeed find it increasingly hard not to rely on them.

Thirdly, the incorporation of control and information in computers is important because it has greatly clarified the confused distinction between wholes and parts and is capable of clarifying it much further and thereby making possible a taxonomy or 'natural history' of systems, an enormous boon at all levels, including our understanding of the vitally important and neglected study of human history. Its impact on our scientific ideology is emerging only slowly but it has already clarified, though not resolved, at least one bogus 'problem', the 'body-mind' problem. Although it is much too soon to tell how far the programming of computers throws light on the way the brain or any part of it organizes the experience of a human individual, it is not too soon to welcome the fact that science has no longer any scientific ground for banning the distinction which direct experience has always drawn between the mind and the brain. It cannot be less than the distinction between hardware and software.

A computer without a program cannot compute. A program without a computer cannot be run. The two are complementary but disparate. The program needs the computer. But an account of the electronic activities of the computer would throw no light on the nature or purpose of the program. Equally it would be futile to expect an electronics engineer to remedy an error in a program or a programmer to detect and correct a faulty element in the machine.[4]

The fourth impact of technological systems making is more dubious but not less familiar. Everyone knows, or should know by now, that men and their cultures are profoundly influenced by the tools they use. In this sense technology is not and never can be 'neutral'. It shapes its users' minds and habits; it limits as well as enlarges. 'To a man who has only a hammer,' it has been said, 'everything tends to look like a nail.' A comprehensive survey of the computerized models now in use would surely show how closely concentrated they are on situations which lend themselves to such modelling. At a recent conference of systems analysts, supposed to be concerned with urban problems, all but one of the presentations made dealt with problems of urban transportation. Transport is an important element in the working of urban systems, but there are others – crime, housing, unemployment, education, health, the treatment of ethnic and other minorities – all no less likely than traffic jams to reduce such systems to chaos. I do not complain that they were not 'modelled'; but I do regard it as highly sinister that none of them was 'analysed'.

Finally, and most important, systems theory as applied to computers throws no light whatever on the source of the standards by which any particular system is regulated. It makes beautifully clear why learning a role is different from acquiring a conditioned response, but it adds nothing to our understanding of the way regulative standards emerge, grow, change and sometimes perish in the ongoing life of men and societies. Nothing? Let us make one exception. By establishing the reality and importance of such standards it focuses attention on them and attests the reality of some process of mutual self-determination among conscious, communicating members of our kind and thus the reality and importance of some peculiarity which distinguishes human systems.

These are the themes which I pursue in this book. I begin with an analysis of the features which all open systems have in common and proceed to the peculiarities of systems in which human beings play a part. Then I explore the peculiarly threatening features which the contemporary world scene presents, especially to the West, in terms of instability, fearfully magnified by the proudest technological achievements of the past. In conclusion I review the developments which in the West, in the brief two centuries before today presented the technologist as the saviour of the world, and I draw some conclusions about the equally important but different role which awaits him in the future – in the immediate future; for contemporary trends will, I think, close today's cultural phase for the West in less than a generation.

I shall be largely concerned with human systems; that is, with human persons and the societies and organizations in which they are always found. This will include, so far as need be, their biological aspects as organisms without which they would not exist, and their social and cultural aspects without which they would not be human; and it will be at some pains to distinguish the different types and levels of organization, political, economic and social, which unite and divide them and the different mix of factors which determine the stability of each. Among these it includes those global relations which today so greatly dominate their present concerns and so clearly threaten their survival. These are not relationships for which biological evolution has selected them and may be far beyond their power, still more beyond their control. But no study of human systems today can ignore the elements both physical and cultural which have come to create systemic relations between human societies and between each of them and the fragile biosphere on which they all depend.

At all levels of this immense field my object is to show the usefulness of systemic thinking as a means to the better understanding of the human condition at the present time. How far that better understanding may lead to wiser policies and more reliable organizations is a question to be answered in the context of particular situations. It does not offer a blueprint for the design of human societies. I hope it will weaken the contemporary urge to regard such activities as akin to engineering rather than (at most) to gardening. It will probably burden us with a livelier consciousness of all those aspects of the contemporary human condition which we deplore but cannot abate. We and the world in general will, none the less, be the better for a clearer understanding of the processes of which we form part and of our real, however limited, scope for intervening in them. Not least we should be better equipped to bear what we cannot alter.

My particular concern is to emphasize the net of cultural and subcultural systems which so diversify both human experience and the different ways in which this is perceived and interpreted in different human societies. This is an unpopular and neglected viewpoint, especially among scientists, who tend to equate successful understanding with the discovery of general laws. I personally regard this as itself a feature of the culture of science which should not be immune from enquiry. In so far as the subject matter of human experience is historical and conditioned by a variety of cultures which are themselves both agents and outcomes of historical change, this subject matter is resistant to the methods of the natural sciences. But it is not on that account wholly beyond our understanding, especially when this is illuminated by an understanding of systemic interaction.

This concern with history will inevitably involve a deep concern with ecology and the character of ecological systems. I do not share the view common among anthropologists a few decades ago (though perhaps less common today) that human history is no more than human ecology. But I do regard it as hugely important that an awareness of ecological relations has developed over the last fifty years simultaneously with the development of control technology, though technology is still reluctant to accept the limitations of ecology.

The appearance of dustbowls in the American prairies in the 1920s and 1930s was perhaps the first widely recognized popular signal that means-ends technology (that is, technology concerned with finding *means* to ends, rather than evaluating ends) might be self-defeating if it operated without adequate awareness of the complexities of the system in which it was intervening. Through the prewar years, while technologists were developing control devices such as automatic pilots, biologists were becoming more aware of the far more subtle controls on which the stability of the biosphere depends. In the years immediately after the Second World War, when the development of control and communication technology was in full spate both practically and theoretically, the episode of London's 'smog' – a word coined on that occasion – brought home to millions of city dwellers outside as well as within England that human systems were at best petty contrivances compared with the ecological systems on which whole populations depend for their existence. The euphoria of the moon landings contrasted strangely with the sombre warnings of *Limits to Growth*. The technologist, who for generations had built his reputation on his ability to change the world, found himself at a loss in a world increasingly concerned with stability and increasingly aware that stability did not depend wholly or even chiefly on engineers but primarily on the institutions of human governance and culture by which alone technology was directed or misdirected and which technology itself had so profoundly changed in the previous hundred years.

So today everyone – and especially every technologist – has a primary concern to understand so far as may be the ecological system of which mankind is part and in which even the most ambitious technological enterprise is a mere intervention, dependent for its success or failure on its effect on forces far more powerful than its own – forces historical and cultural as well as physical. The scope for the technologist is not thereby reduced. It is vastly increased, especially in its difficulty, because of the much more complex criteria by which it has to be judged. The reader therefore should not be surprised that my approach to human systems leads through a brief survey of the other forms of regulation which impose stability or instability on life on earth, irrespective of the activities of its most disturbing element – man; and not merely man but men in the countless specific cultural forms in which alone they are to be found.

Footnotes

1. H. A. L. Fisher, *A History of Europe*, London, Arnold, 1936.
2. Marvin Harris, *The Rise of Anthropological Theory*, London, Routledge & Kegan Paul, 1969.
3. C. H. Waddington, *The Ethical Animal*, London, W. H. Allen, 1960.
4. Michael Polanyi, in *Personal Knowledge: Towards a Post-critical Philosophy*, London, Routledge & Kegan Paul, 1973, pointed out that even a locomotive cannot be explained simply in terms of physics and chemistry. Human synthesis in human design for a human purpose are necessary to understanding how and why the thing came into existence, as well as how it works. Even an aggregation of all its parts would throw no light on their synthesis and potentialities except to a human mind which could infer the intentions of the fellow human who designed it.

CHAPTER 2
THE CHARACTERISTICS OF OPEN SYSTEMS

The most essential characteristic of an open system is that its *form* is more enduring than the presence of the substances which constitute it at some moment of time. The Greek philosopher who said that we never step twice into the same river was, I think, being wilfully perverse in presenting an important truth. For he surely knew as well as anyone that a river is the name we give to a form; not to the water which happens to constitute it at some moment of time. All the other characteristics of open systems flow from this basic concern with form, rather than substance.

Though form is no new concern to the human mind, it is a relatively new concern of science. For two hundred and fifty years before the beginning of this century, natural science was dominated by the need to distinguish energy from matter, with which at the beginning of that time it was profoundly entangled. Matter appeared to include what were then called corporeals and incorporeals. Solids and liquids were comfortably corporeal. But what of air? And heat? And light? And life? Descartes was reduced to postulating a special kind of matter, *res cogitans*, which thought, as distinct from the more familiar *res extensa*.

Two hundred and fifty years later that job was apparently done. Energy was established as a basic property of the physical world, despite the fact that it lacked what had been supposed to be the essential qualities of that world – it had no weight and it took up no space. Its forms, its transfers and transformations had been charted and its two most essential and paradoxical qualities had been defined. It was indestructible; but it was none the less degradable. Entropy, it seemed, was inescapable and universal. The time was ripe for Einstein with his famous equation to establish a link between matter and energy, a relation in which it seemed that energy was the senior partner.

The study of forms which outlast their substances was the natural complement to this massive work. Of course the substances are conserved.

The water which flows through the river will ultimately find its way back into the atmosphere through evaporation or transpiration in the course of a passage in which it may have been part of many forms, including animal and vegetable forms. The forms, by contrast, are far from indestructible. On the other hand, if they survive, they tend to become more complex. The questions are how they endure long enough to earn a name; and how some of them elaborate their forms with the passage of time.

Some forms are imposed almost wholly by independent factors external to themselves – as the river is largely determined by the contours of its catchment area and the volume and distribution of its supply of water from rain and springs. Some sustain their form largely by internal directives and regulators, such as those which determine the growth and form of an animal and the levels of its internal heat and chemical constituents. Some owe their form to both factors, as where external factors are themselves changed by the behaviour of the form and react upon it to change it, as with men in a market place or on a battlefield. All these questions concerning the ways in which open systems preserve their form even through change are questions of *regulation*, the second focus of interest which naturally arises in the study of form.

An open system seldom preserves its form absolutely unchanged even for a brief period. One major reason for this is that its regulation consists partly in correcting deviations from its 'normal' state and some deviation is usually required to signal the need for a regulatory act. But apart from this, no open system lasts for ever. Its stability can never be taken for granted; it fluctuates and it may at any time escape from even the minimal regulation needed to sustain it and dissolve or change into something else. The animal dies, the skater falls, the business goes into liquidation, the community is absorbed by another or scattered or destroyed by natural forces (like Pompeii) or more frequently by human forces (like Carthage). So the third focus of interest, a counterpart of the second, is *stability*, or rather the whole dimension from maximal stability to dissolution. With this we must associate a concern with *growth*. For growth involves change both within a system and in the relations between it and its surround and these changes are bound to affect stability unless the regulative process takes care of them. The growth of a human organism from a single cell into the immense complexity of its adult form could not be achieved except by a marvel of internal regulation including most refined timing. There is a radical difference between cancerous and organic growth.

Open systems, by definition, do not exist in isolation. They depend on complex exchanges with their surround; exchanges of matter, of energy, of information, and of other communications not conveniently included in the useful but very narrow concept of information. The variety and reliability of these exchanges vary vastly. The giant sloth does not ask much of its surround or offer much to it, by comparison with his human fellow creatures in cabinets and boardrooms.

The progress towards greater interdependence which comes with growth involves limitations as well as enlargements, for it involves both mutual and, far more, complementary constraints and commitments. For example, the rights and duties of parent to child, teacher to taught, even buyer to seller, are not identical with the converse rights and duties of the other members of each pair, except for a few, such as honesty, respect, and compassion, which are regarded by the culture as the rights and duties of all. Moreover, as the individual and the systems to which he belongs become engaged in an increasingly complex net of interdependence, both the constraints and the commitments tend to impose more contradictory imperatives. Organization can mitigate this but not remove it. We must then add to our list of concerns the words *interdependence, limitation* and *organization*.

It is sobering to reflect that even three or four decades ago it was still possible for intelligent people to debate whether a 'whole' could possibly be more than the sum of its 'parts', and if so how. Today it is perfectly apparent, though not yet completely accepted, that every whole must necessarily be both more and less than the sum of its parts. It is less because its parts are constrained by being organized. They can no longer do some things which were open to them in their unorganized state. For example, the constituents of a dead body are free to combine in other forms, once the discipline of the living organism is relaxed. But they are also more than their sum because, when organized, they can do what they could not do alone or as an unorganized aggregate.

Thus the study of systems has validated the concept of organization and established what was regarded as a heresy in the heyday of reductionism. At every new level of organization constraints and enablements emerge which could not have been detected or even predicted from a study of their constituent parts in isolation. Vitalism, the theory that the origin and phenomena of life are due to a vital principle or life force, as distinct from a purely chemical or physical force, was once a dreaded heresy; it is seen today as a name for one of the many steps in organization. Organisms do indeed behave differently from inorganic systems. They do not defy or elude or contradict the laws which govern their constituents but they add other and new regularities which are functions of their new level of organization. And this would remain no less true if we could synthesize them from their inorganic components.

Of what then do systems consist? They consist of relationships. Surely there must be objects, entities which support these relationships? It seems probable to me that the relationships are more basic than the entities related; that we abstract or infer these entities solely from our experience of relationships. To avoid such metaphysical speculations let us agree that there are entities to be related. But they are curiously elusive and relative to the concerns which draw our attention to them.

A commuter train needs a driver. But the commuters who use it daily do not know when one driver gives place to another. The laws of England define relationships and apply to all the individuals who for the time being are subject to them. It may be important to an individual to establish whether he is or is not subject to that body of law; but it makes no difference to the law. The entities which support relations are neither more nor less than the relations demand. If the train were transferred to remote control and ran successfully without a driver, the commuters would not know.

Take a more elaborate example. To an architect a school is a building designed to accommodate and facilitate specified activities. Its siting is irrelevant except for physical features of the actual site. To a planner it is a service to a community and its location is important to its utility and convenience. To an educator it is a community of teachers and students assembled for a number of related purposes. To an individual teacher it is a workplace, a responsibility, an opportunity, and a step in a teaching career. To the local sanitary engineer it is one among many generators of sewage of which he has to dispose. He is not concerned with what else goes on there. But his concern with sewage disposal may make him sensitive to some factor which is irrelevant to most or all of the others – for example, to its height above sea level relative to the contour on which his sewage disposal works is situated. And if this concern were anticipated, it might even have affected the activities of the planner in siting the school, through the medium of the local authority's finance committee, concerned with the cost of providing services. How many kinds of fragmented entity is a school? Of how many wholes is it a part? How far is it itself a whole – or many different wholes?

These are unreal problems, derived from our habit of attaching labels to 'entities' and thus exaggerating their integrity. It is, however, possible and important to draw a distinction between those internal relations which enable any assembly to sustain its 'form' (any of its forms) and those which enable it to act as a whole on its surround. From the viewpoint of parents, teachers, and students the school remains not only a school but *the* familiar school so long as teaching, attendance and activities proceed 'as usual', even though teachers and students change. A host of internal relationships have to be maintained if this is to happen. Teachers must attend and teach; students must attend and keep their disruptive activities below whatever threshold has become acceptable. A host of external relationships must also be maintained between the school as a whole and its surround, the physical support systems (including the drains already mentioned) the arrangements for recruiting trained teachers to replace those who leave or are promoted, the payment of salaries, the maintenance of structures, even the minimal good will of the parents (if they are to be regarded as wholly 'external', as in England they so often are). All these relationships, both internal and external, have limits beyond which they cannot be pushed without escalating instability which may result in irreversible change or even dissolution of the system. Within these limits change can be accommodated sometimes almost unnoticed, sometimes welcomed. Unhappily it is often difficult to predict where these limits lie until they have been passed.

So the relation between wholes and parts begins to become clearer. An organization is a whole in so far as it acts as a whole on its surround. These external relations can be sustained only so long as its internal relations support them. This relation between inner and outer is not a simple dichotomy; for systems may be related hierarchically. The commuter train as such cannot replace an absent driver, but the management of the local sector of the railway system probably can. And to the commuters, external to the local management systems as well as to the train, it will be neither evident nor important which level of the organization furnished the adaptability needed to keep the train running on time.

One further important point remains to be noted. Forms are indeed often related hierarchically and it is this which encourages us to differentiate them as wholes and parts. Cells, each a complex marvel of organization, combine to form organs which together create organisms which support persons, which combine in societies. But relations are not necessarily arranged hierarchically, as the example of the school has shown. Many 'entities' form part of many different systems which are not themselves related in any hierarchic fashion, though events may raise one or other to a status of overriding importance. Few urban activities, for example, can continue for long if the sewage system stops working. Yet whilst it works, it is taken for granted as one of many physical support systems.

In the chapters which follow I will develop some of these ideas further; but I hope this introduction has made the basic ideas as I see them sufficiently clear to be summarized.

1. Systems are nets of *relations* which are sustained through *time*. The processes by which they are sustained are the process of *regulation*. The limits within which they can be sustained are the conditions of their *stability*.

2. Open systems depend on and contribute to their surround and are thus involved in *interdependence* with it as well as being dependent on the interaction of their internal relationships. This interdependence imposes *constraints* on all their constituents. *Organization* can mitigate but not remove these constraints which tend to become more demanding and sometimes even more contradictory as the scale of organization rises. This places a limit, though usually not a predictable one, on the possibilities of organization.

3. Open systems cannot, by definition, be 'wholes' if this is taken to mean systems wholly independent of their surround. But in so far as any open system acts as a whole in relation to its surround it is useful to distinguish the *internal relations* which enable it to do so from the *external relations* which it thus sustains. It is thus both legitimate and necessary to move freely from the consideration of a system as a whole to the consideration of it as part of a larger system; it is equally legitimate and necessary to realize that its constituents may also be constituents of other systems.

4. Systems are thus *tools of understanding* devised by human minds for understanding situations, including situations in which human beings appear as constituents. They are not *arbitrary* constructs. They must include the minimum number of relationships needed to constitute the situation which is to be understood. But this is defined by its relevance to the *concerns* of some human minds.

Thus in one sense all systems are human systems since they are distinguished by human minds and judged to be acceptable by their correspondence with human standards. The seriousness of this limitation – that systems are human constructs – is a philosophical question not to be pursued here. Philosophers of science are less ready than they were to assume that even their concepts of natural science give us direct knowledge of objective reality. Positivism has passed its heyday and more modest assumptions have taken its place.

This book, however, is concerned with human systems in a narrower sense. It is concerned with human beings as systems and with systems in which human beings are significant constituent parts; that is to say with human societies and organizations and with ecological systems in which the behaviour of human beings and societies cannot usefully be studied without taking into account the mutual influences exerted on each other by the human element and its milieu.

I shall first describe two now familiar mechanisms which regulate a wide class of individual organisms, including man, and which we have learned to imitate partly or completely in technological artefacts. Then I shall look at the process of biological evolution which has developed in the organism of these regulative powers. For the whole of organic life on the planet possesses the characteristics of an open system. Immensely varied as its forms are, they share the capacity for self-maintenance and self-renewal by exchange with their milieu, and indeed they form each other's milieu to a large extent. And this is even more true of the specific species and populations of species, including man, which have from time to time appeared, developed, and perished in the long story of biological evolution.

Biological evolution, however, though it throws some light on the evolution of the human species and may in due course explain our disappearance, has not much to tell us about how and why we think, feel, and behave as we do during our still recent and possibly transient appearance on this long-suffering planet. Human history runs at a tempo much faster than biological evolution; personal history at a tempo faster still. To understand human history or the course of a single human life we need concepts additional to the concepts of biological evolution – concepts much older and more familiar than the body of theory which has been developing so rapidly since Darwin and Wallace formulated their theory of biological evolution. Societies and human beings can also be said to evolve. Socio-cultural evolution is a fact of societal and personal life and though it lacks a comprehensive theory, it cannot be reduced to or subsumed by biological evolution.

Social and cultural evolution is, however, no less open to systemic analysis than biological evolution is, and indeed much more fruitfully. For it is already clear that if the human race – or at least its more 'developed' societies – is to survive the impasse into which biological evolution has led it, it needs to exercise more regulation than simple biological controls will provide. Whether it can do so is an open question; no evidence yet points to a favourable outcome. But the analysis is none the less necessary and urgent, if only to offer a chance of understanding the biological predicament and thus the possibility of responding to it with any chance of success.

So the chapter on biological evolution leads naturally into the consideration of ecological systems and on into the ambivalent part played by the development of human consciousness not only in human adaptability but also in developing those human standards of the acceptable which so greatly affect, for good and ill, the regulation of human societies and of individual human lives.

CHAPTER 3
REGULATION, ORGANIC AND TECHNOLOGICAL

Until the scientific attitude of enquiry became part of the consciousness of educated Western people, order in every field tended to be taken as given and usually as God-given and thus something to be accepted with wonder but without investigation. And this was particularly so with human bodies, with human persons, and even to some extent with human institutions. But so soon as wonder was supplemented by enquiry two biological questions asserted themselves.

It took little more than casual observation to notice that whereas snakes and lizards showed activity roughly proportionate to the heat of the ambient air, the more highly developed animals, including man, maintained a virtually constant internal temperature despite extreme variations in the temperature of the atmosphere. They had a repertory of devices for doing so. Some were behavioural and easily noticed. They huddled together, they erected their hair or feathers to form a partly insulated climate around them, they shivered, developing superficial heat by the motion. Some devices were less obvious. In extreme cases they would restrict the circulation of blood in superficial tissues, risking peripheral frostbite in order to preserve the constant temperatures required at deeper levels. The French biologist, Claude Bernard, in mid-nineteenth century was so greatly impressed by the advantages gained by this class of creature that he coined a famous phrase. 'The stability of the internal milieu', he wrote, 'is the condition of free and independent life.'

Few statements, true in their original context, have been equally true in so many others as that famous comment of Claude Bernard's. It has its obvious counterpart in human emotional life, as anyone knows who has ever felt panic or lost his temper.

And yet it is a paradox, for it is only half true. Warm-blooded animals are not free and independent of their external milieu. They depend on it for food, air, water, and a host of other necessities. Yet because they can preserve a stable inner climate, they have a far greater range of interaction with the world around them than creatures such as snakes and lizards which pass from an active to a torpid state with every transition of sun and shade.

Bernard and others later, notably Cannon, explored the means by which such organisms maintain a stable state of inner temperature and a host of other relations such as the proportion of salt, sugar, and other constituents in the body. But stability does not necessarily mean stasis; and throughout the period biologists were faced with a different kind of stability which was the opposite of static, one in which the stability of certain parameters was combined with growth and development.

From its inception in the union of two cells the organism proliferates into a complex pattern of interdependent organs, built from cells which become highly differentiated to suit the function which they are to fulfil. From the fertilized ovum to the newborn child, to the adult, to the senile, the form of the organism changes spectacularly. Yet at every stage its parts maintain the relationship needed to sustain the whole at that stage of its development.

It seemed that the adult individual *must* exist, fully formed, however small, in the initial cell. Some biologists even claimed to have seen this homunculus in the male semen. (They might as well have seen it in the ovum but in those days most biologists were male.) The theory of preformation, however, could not be confirmed, and biological growth and differentiation remained a total mystery even in principle until the 1940s.

A further strangeness was pointed out by the biologist, Driesch, in the 1890s. A sea-urchin embryo, if divided sufficiently early in its career, grew into two complete though rather small sea urchins. The cells which would have developed into one organism responded to the mutilation by producing two instead.

In retrospect the implication seems clear. Every cell must be saturated with information about what was to be created. But even Driesch did not dare to suggest such a hypothesis. It would have seemed the height of anthropomorphism. Men did indeed use blueprints; but cells –! Instead he postulated a goal-seeking *force*, an entelechy, as he called it, immanent in the cells, which pushed developing cells in the direction in which they were to go. Energy was the only explanation which was then considered scientifically respectable, as a source of hypotheses for why things happened as they did.

He got off no more lightly for disguising information as a force. Forces should not pursue 'ends'. Teleology at that time was still a dirty word. His fellow biologists were far more concerned to revile him for a vitalist than to offer alternative hypotheses to explain what he had demonstrated.

Later experiments confirmed the two basic facts suggested by Driesch's experiment. Some tissues, though not all, if transplanted sufficiently early, would develop in the manner required by their new location. What would have become an eye, for example, would become normal skin. But after a critical and early date it would have become specialized for its original role and would realize that so far as it could, even though transplanted. It would develop into an eye in its new location however inappropriate, an eye anatomically adequate but functionally useless, since it lacked the necessary neural connections with the brain.

Thus by the beginning of this century biology had identified the two aspects of regulation which have so greatly dominated information technology during the last four decades. One was the preservation of a constant state by internal adjustments, despite external changes which would otherwise have disturbed it. The other was the unfolding of a developing form not imposed by external forces, capable of maintaining itself throughout its development and possessing a limited power to modify its development in response to context, a power which usually diminished rapidly in the course of development.

The first, the preservation of a constant state through internal adjustments, was the earlier to be studied and is still the better understood. Thermostats had been in use for years and Watts governors for decades before the 1930s. But it was the development of automatic pilots in that and subsequent decades which produced what Norbert Wiener was to call the science of cybernetics. This originated in careful analysis of what a human helmsman actually does and showed that the signals on which he acts can be specified and imitated by a machine, though they are more complicated than is immediately apparent.

The helmsman has a compass, a course, and a rudder. He derives the information he needs neither from the compass nor from the course, nor even solely from a comparison of the two. He needs to know not only the deviation of the ship's head from its course but also the rate at which it is deviating and the rate at which that rate is increasing or abating. Given these, he can calculate the amount of rudder movement needed to correct the deviation without generating an excessive deviation on the other side of the course. Some deviation there must be, since countless forces apart from his own rudder movements are for ever changing, however marginally, the direction of the ship's head. But he enjoys two conditions which are very seldom enjoyed by other controllers. He has a continuous and immediate input of information about one of the three critical variables, the amount of the deviation, and almost immediate information about the other two, the two rates which can only be observed over time. Further, he has one instrument of control, the rudder – only one, so he has no difficult choices between alternative methods of control, and one so powerful that so long as the ship keeps moving through the water he can offset any normal divergence. He also has a course set from elsewhere which it is not normally for him to question.

It is worth noting that if another ship puts him in danger of collision, the entire picture changes. The course ceases to be binding. It is for him to choose another course – any course – which will avoid collision. The criteria of good helmsmanship change. A miss is as good as a mile but even a light collision may mean a lost ship. The helmsman is no longer governed by a course to be held but by a limit to be avoided; and this is something to be achieved or not achieved. Much control in biological and human systems consists not in holding courses, still less in attaining goals, but in eluding threats. And the mechanisms and criteria of threat-avoiding responses are radically different. This difference is important and constantly ignored. I shall often return to it.

The outstanding characteristic of cybernetic control is the simplicity of the information on which it depends. All kinds of forces act upon the ship's hull but the helmsman has no need to measure or estimate them individually. He is concerned only with their resultant sum, including the force which his rudder has itself contributed. And this resultant is virtually always under his control. Happy man! Steering is a skill to be learned but it can be made explicit and imitated by a mechanism. The control of human systems, individual or societal, is very seldom as simple as steering a ship at sea, even apart from the fact that the course, which is the base of the whole exercise, is seldom unitary, often unspecified and, even when specified, sometimes unattainable.

The second problem of biological control, the maintenance of stability within a growing and developing form, though similar, is more complex and is still much further from being completely understood. The course to be held is a course of most elaborate development. It involves carrying out a complicated serial program. The word is new to science; only since the 1940s has 'information' become a definable and measurable variable and thus an acceptable member of the scientific universe. And only with the development of the computer have the possibilities of storing, retrieving and 'processing' information opened vistas of possible achievement with no agreed limitations. Once it was accepted in principle that any logical process which can be fully described could be embodied in a program and realized on a computer, the basic problem of biological development appeared to have been solved, subject only to discovering within the cell a set of variables complex enough to code all the instructions needed for making a biological man. And within a decade of the problem being so posed it was solved by the discovery of the structure of DNA associated with the names of Watson and Crick.

To discover the elements in which the code is written is not to break the code. There remain plenty of unsolved problems, such as the varying degrees of flexibility enjoyed by different tissues at different ages in dealing with different problems set by accident or disease or by the ingenuity of research scientists. But the new metaphor swept the board, as the metaphor of biological evolution had swept the board a century before. Information processing became an acceptable form of explanation for all forms of growth and development, even where neither the information nor the process were clearly describable.

So today the two basic problems of biological regulation are deemed to be solved, at least in principle. Whether the problem be the maintenance of an order which external forces might be expected to disturb or the development of an order which external forces would not impose, the explanation is to be found in principle in information which is either coded in the gene or learned by experience. For the organism which is programmed to develop includes a capacity for further development by 'processing' its own experience, including the experience in which as a social creature it is bathed from birth onwards by a babel of communicating others.

Unhappily, the parallel between biological and technological regulation breaks down at the point of real importance. Whence come these internal standards of order which is to be sustained or created by the system's own activity, rather than imposed by its surround? Biologically, the answer is familiar, if not as clear as it is supposed to be. They have been developed by trial and error through the blind process of biological evolution, supplemented, as is now admitted, even at nonhuman levels, by ecological processes, including sometimes transmitted learning. What is the technological parallel?

There is no *technological* parallel; for the process of standard setting, whether biological, behavioural, or social, is not a technological process. There is, none the less, a parallel and not an obscure one.

At least two blocks of high-rise low-income apartments, one in America and one in England, have been destroyed by explosives within thirty years of their erection. No one would live in them. They were dens of crime and vandalism. They could not even be taken down in situ. Yet we may be sure that technologically both their erection and their destruction were well-controlled operations. They were planned in advance with correct anticipation of physical cause and effect. Actual progress was checked against planned progress at every stage to make sure that everything went 'according to plan'. The only trouble was that the plan was wrong – or became wrong through social and cultural changes which were not anticipated. So, ultimately, did the biological program for making a dinosaur.

Many technologists are beset by an underlying contradiction of assumptions, though most of them manage to live with it astonishingly well. On the one hand technological men can do anything they want to do. The resources of technology have no predictable limit. Yet on the other hand technologists are not taught to concern themselves with values – these omnipotent animals have no business to have any wants except the biological urge to survive. Technology has nothing to say about *what* to want. Hence the extravagant efforts to derive their most bizarre aspirations from the urge for survival. In fact, of course, human cultures set and change the standards of order to which societies aspire. And human cultures are more than mere rationalizations of biological urges. They have a life of their own, as is attested both by human history and by cultural anthropology. The standard-setting process which defines for individuals and societies their idea of order and thus sets their control systems is a cultural artefact modified for each of us by whatever degree of personal artistry we may possess. And for the student of human systems the cardinal point of interest is the *evolution* of these manifold sets of standards, far more than the more familiar processes by which they regulate the systems in which they emerge. Technology has even less bearing on the first (evolution) than on the second (regulative processes) but both are of central importance to anyone who may have to manage or assist in managing a human system.

And that, of course, means everyone – partly because each of us is held responsible to some extent for managing the human system called himself;

and partly because each of us in our capacity as a member of other systems has the responsibility which falls equally on every member to accept the demands of interdependence, that equality of responsibility which, as I have pointed out elsewhere,[1] is the only form of equality which is anathema to our egalitarian age.

The examples I have chosen to explore in this chapter are examples where the standards of regulation are either built in biologically or supplied from some so far unexplored source and internally accepted. Of course not all regulation is of this kind. Form, as already exemplified, may be imposed wholly from without. It may be a mere resultant. And even where there is present some element of internal standard setting, it is always affected, and sometimes wholly offset, by external pressures. Such is usually the history of ecological systems in so far as they achieve enough stability to earn a name – those ecological systems among which human systems are such a bizarre and, until recently, such an unusual element. So it is useful next to turn to these before we consider the possibility that human systems might in the future, as they sometimes have in the past, develop internal standards which are neither self-defeating nor unacceptable. For it is the development of these standards, not the mere machinery for keeping them, which is central to the management of human systems.

Footnote

1. G. Vickers, 'Equality of Opportunity', *Futures*, February 1979.

CHAPTER 4

THE EMERGENCE OF ECOLOGICAL SYSTEMS

The evolution of life on earth is chiefly the subject matter of ecology and ethology. The theory of biological evolution with which Darwin and Wallace startled the Western world in mid-nineteenth century is only part of it and for the purposes of this book a relatively unimportant part; for adaptation by mutation and natural selection is a slow process, especially for a species whose generations turn over so slowly as our own. We shall have to meet the crisis of the next thirty years with such genetic equipment as we have.

Species far simpler than man have been learning to cope with each other in their shared environments by behavioural adjustment, sometimes mutual, sometimes complementary, as well as by changes of physical form ever since life began to colonize the planet; and this learning had become transmissible in many species long before men magnified their powers of communicating and storing communications in the way which so uniquely defines them. This does not mean, of course, that the theory of biological evolution is unimportant. It is vastly important, both practically and ideologically. Practically it is essential to the conservation of all the living resources which support us. An important recent study by the International Union for Conservation of Nature and National Resources[1] has pointed out how dangerously grain breeding and pesticides have depleted the gene pool of those cereal species on which we so completely rely, directly and indirectly, for our food supply and how critical is our dependence on those that remain. Ideologically the theory of biological evolution has been important in masking all the factors other than competition which combine to produce symbiosis, both within and between species, and thus reducing the conventional picture of life on earth to a zero-sum game, which was a travesty even of the Victorian society in which it emerged. Darwin and Wallace should not be blamed for this; every new theory expands beyond the field in which it was first developed, often despite the protests of its founders, and is confined only when it meets an intellectual frontier sufficiently developed to resist it. Darwin even observed that in a cooperative society a highly competitive individual might be singularly ill-fitted to survive. And T. H. Huxley, Darwin's protagonist, as we shall see later, was as deeply opposed to the 'social Darwinists' as he was to the doctrine of special creation. But few shared or even noticed the doubts of these great minds; and the huge picture of 'species' developing in an 'environment' obscured the countless pictures of populations developing in shared and specific habitats, of which the whole picture is in fact composed.

Yet these smaller pictures define the systems which are most significant for nearly all forms of life, even today and even including man. They are, of course, subsystems from some points of view; they share the planet's atmosphere though they may have their own climates. None the less their diversities are far more conspicuous than the features they have in common, even for most of their human inhabitants and still more for the others.

From the Arctic tundra to the Kalahari desert the planet offers a wide variety of habitats, even on the lesser part of it which is not covered by the oceans. And all but the most fearfully inclement of these have been colonized by life, nearly always including man. In each of these life is sustained by systemic relations, each species contributing something to the others if only to the control of numbers or the disposal of carrion. And ecologists, counting the numbers of each species over time in a particular habitat and observing their interaction, can form some idea both of the manner in which this form is sustained and of the degree of its stability. The form may well bear the mark of a dominant species. A redwood forest is largely composed of redwoods. English sheep walks, when they existed, reflected the dominance of creatures which destroyed all living vegetation except that which could regenerate itself from buds at ground level. None the less no species could exist in isolation; and generally speaking, the more numerous the species, the greater the chance of stability.

Such then are living systems. But when do they become human systems? Human beings have shared the Amazon jungle with its other fauna for many millenia without making much difference to the jungle, to the other fauna, or to themselves. Yet no one would call the Amazon jungle a human system.

We use the expression 'human system' in two contexts. We use it when we are speaking of human societies, their forms of governance and the ways in which each acts as a whole in relation to its surround. We use it also, more recently but probably more often today, of ecological systems so dominated by man that the whole system becomes, or aspires to become, a human design. Both meanings are of crucial importance and they are radically different. I shall pursue both in later chapters. In this chapter I am concerned to describe the basic ecological pattern within which both forms of human system have evolved; for all human systems in both senses are subject to the same ecological constraints. It is worth noting at this point, however, that T. H. Huxley,[2] in one of his last published essays, insisted with passion that a human society is as different from any other form of society as a garden is from the Amazon jungle. A new selector has set itself up with new criteria of acceptable order and new means of imposing it – though one no less bound by the natural laws which govern growth, survival and decay in the wild. These natural laws limit the alternative orders which he can possibly impose; and will reimpose their own order so soon as the gardener ceases to intervene.

There is no guarantee that an ecological community will reach and keep a stable form, whether on the scale of the Amazon jungle or of the habitat beneath a single paving stone. A stable ecology, where it exists, may be destroyed by changes in the natural environment, whether as sudden as an earthquake or as slow as a glaciation. It may be destroyed by the arrival of a new colonist, as in Australia with the arrival of the rabbit, or by the cumulative effect of the habits of an existing one, as, for example, the gnawing of bark by forest deer may pass the rate of regeneration and affect the habitat on which the deer depend. There are, however, certain inbuilt factors which tend to check most trends before they become irreversible.

The most obvious check on the multiplication of a species is limitation of the supply of food on which it lives, or other essentials such as suitable breeding sites. No such limits prevent the disappearance of a species, and countless species have disappeared from particular habitats and even from the planet, even before their rate of decay was speeded by the enhanced destructive powers of man. None the less there are factors which work in this direction also. The smaller the population, the more abundant, proportionally, the resources on which it lives, and, possibly, the less rewarding it becomes to the species which hunt it. Other controls are inbuilt and many are doubtless unknown. The Hudson's Bay Company was aware for many decades of an eleven-year cycle in the number of pelts both of Arctic hares and of the lynxes which prey upon them, and attributed it to a self-regulating process by which, as hares became scarce and harder to find, their predators diminished in numbers and gave them time to recover. It has since been discovered that the fluctuation in the number of hares is due not mainly to depredation by the lynxes but to a fall in the fertility of female hares as their numbers increase. The cause of this has not, I believe, been identified but it may well be due to the tendency found in all female mammals, including the human, to abort conceptions spontaneously when the female is not carrying a supply of fat sufficient to carry her young as well as herself through the whole period of gestation and lactation. It has been estimated[3] that half of all human conceptions are aborted very early for this or kindred reasons, usually without the mother's knowledge. But here we have reached the level of biological, rather than ecological regulation.

The relation of different species in an ecological system is partly hierarchic and partly complementary. The bottom level of the hierarchy is made up of vegetable species and their aquatic counterparts which alone are able to turn the sun's energy into living substance by a direct act of photosynthesis. Since solar energy is, so far as we know, the only substantial source of energy to reach our planet, this vegetative layer has always been and still remains the sole source of life on earth. The herbivores and carnivores raise on this base their pyramid of parasites and predators, culminating in that ultimate parasite and predator, man.

The picture is, in fact, more complex than this. Many vegetable forms could not spread and flourish, some could not even exist until insects were available to pollinate them and birds to distribute their seeds. The herbivores dung the pastures they graze. The carnivores help to some extent to control the numbers of the herbivores, often by culling the old and sick. The equation is far too complex to summarize, even were I competent to do so, but its details are not relevant to this book. The only point to be made here is that though the complementary relations are important, the hierarchic ones are crucial. The vegetables could get on without the herbivores or even the birds and insects, though not so well. The herbivores could get on without the carnivores. Everyone could get on without – man.

Everyone? We must except only the few species which he has made dependent on himself for his convenience and the bacteria and viruses to which he plays host.

No one 'manages' an ecological system (with the very qualified exceptions to be explored in the rest of this book). Commonly its subsystems respond or submit to its changes with no understanding of their causes, even when these are caused by themselves. If the system attains any measure of stability for any length of time it is because stability is self-selecting. An unstable system is by definition in continual change and so remains until it happens on a stable state or breaks up altogether. Its subsystems, on the other hand, especially where these are populations of social and highly developed animals, show some of the characteristics of self-regulation. They learn and transmit basic skills, notably in finding food and avoiding death. These include techniques for collective defence (like herds of musk oxen) and offence (like packs of wolves). They accept the leadership of self-chosen leaders (as deer do). They enrich their repertory of behaviour by ways of shaping their environment to themselves (building nests, making burrows) no less than by adapting themselves to an environment taken as given. A beaver lodge is not only a complex structure in itself but also depends on maintaining its water level by a form of dam building, which is perhaps more similar to human engineering than anything else in the economy of nonhuman nature.

Highly developed animals are not even wholly without invention, perhaps less so than we realize because the occasions on which it can be reliably observed in natural conditions by a human ethologist are bound to be rare. Few can have been so richly rewarded as the one[4] who actually observed a monkey wash for the first time a yam it had dug up and, presumably finding its improved taste worth the additional labour, adopted the habit, which spread first to its family group, more slowly to a few other members of the species and then, after passing some critical point, suddenly to universal acceptance by all his species on the island and later with curious speed appeared in other islands apparently far beyond any obvious means of communication.

The incident is worth recording because it is one of the few examples in the nonhuman world where a technological change seems to have been adopted for purely aesthetic reasons and – perhaps on that account – with no serious predictable side effects.

None the less the picture of regulation which emerges from a study of ecology is of a form almost entirely resulting from external pressures rather than designed from within. Nor is this picture substantially changed by the emergence of human beings on the scene until a remarkably late stage in their brief history.

Footnotes

1. *World Conservation Strategy*, International Union for Conservation of Nature and Natural Resources, Glaind, Switzerland, IUCN, 1980.
2. T. H. Huxley, *Evolution and Ethics and Other Essays*, London, Macmillan, 1894.
3. J. Tanner. *Foetus into Man*, Cambridge, Mass., Harvard University Press, 1978.
4. I cannot trace the original research on which this often quoted finding is based.

CHAPTER 5

THE EMERGENCE OF HUMAN SYSTEMS

Archaeologists, anthropologists and historians have put together a picture of the development of human societies on earth and of the physical environments in which they have developed in the three dimensions quoted in the Foreword – economic and technological base; political and legal institutions; and ideological assumptions. I have already explained why I am unwilling to believe that the second and third generate no life of their own sufficient to influence their own development and that of the first. But it does not seem to me useful to try to assign degrees of importance to any of them, except perhaps in the context of some particular time and place.

What we actually know of these developments is particulate, derived from the study of particular societies at particular times. They vary with the physical conditions of the habitat. No other species, so far as I know, has learned to colonize such an immense range of habitats – from Alaska to Tahiti; and the way of life of each society has been affected, socially and institutionally as well as economically and technologically by the conditions which nature has imposed. This is still true, despite the superficial similarity which the industrial culture of the West has spread across the cities which dot the planet like a chain of Hilton hotels. There are, none the less, important similarities between all these developments, notably their sequence. The general trend has clearly been from a relatively mobile life based on hunting and food gathering, to a more settled and more densely populated state, based on agriculture and husbandry, which in turn has been increasingly dominated by still more densely populated urban areas, supported by industries which expanded as they became able to rely on ever wider areas as markets and sources of supply.[1] With every increase in density and productivity came greater differentiation of wealth, power and function and consequential changes in institutions and ideologies.

The movement has not been wholly one way. There are man-made deserts in the Middle East and in North Africa where pastoralists move their flocks and herds from one scanty pasture to another, over land which once supported agriculture but is now too poor to farm. In Scandinavia the substantial minority of still pastoral Lapps move with their herds of reindeer over a circuit which has supported them from time immemorial. There are large areas of the earth's surface which cannot be cultivated but which can sustain herbivores seasonally if not continuously. Such areas might increase and become more economically important than they are now, and they invite a characteristic pattern of human life. But the pattern of regression has not yet set in on any large scale and could do so only as a companion and sequel to apocalyptic catastrophes about which I will not speculate here. I will only stress that the sequential change from scattered small human societies to an overcrowded and ever more industrialized planet will not necessarily – systemic thinkers should say cannot – continue for ever and that our economic and technological way of life is already being affected not by present change in our environment but by our own anticipation of changes which the future may bring.

There is nothing surprising in this, for as I have already observed, no system can tolerate indefinite linear change in one of its elements. Moreover, the general picture conceals many economic and cultural cycles of much shorter duration which ran their course and passed away. The merchants of Manaos grew so rich exporting natural rubber from the Amazon jungle that they adorned their city with an opera house built of Italian marble, designed and shipped out to be assembled in the heart of that great rain forest. Within a few decades monkeys were swinging from the chandeliers of the deserted building, while the booming rubber industry was being supplied by Malaysian plantations grown from Brazilian seed. Today Manaos flourishes again – as a duty-free entrepôt market for air travellers from the world's other continents.

The stages of economic development are sometimes classified by the use of the word 'post', which emphasizes the impression that they are successive. They are in fact cumulative. We do not live in a post-agricultural world. We depend on agriculture as much as we have ever done, and as a species we meet our needs ever less adequately. The numbers starving in the world today are not only higher in total than at any previous time in human history, they are also higher even as a proportion of the world's growing population. The Brandt Commission in 1980[2] estimated the world's destitute at 800 million, or one in five of a population of four billion. Only forty-five years earlier, the historian H. A. L. Fisher,[3] had estimated roughly the same class at 150 million, or less than one in twelve of a world population then estimated at two billion. An intermediate estimate by the World Food Congress in 1974 put the figure at 400–500 million and showed that the trend was worsening at far more than a linear rate.

These estimates assume that the industrialized world is free both from starvation and from the danger of starvation. In fact it is free from these dangers only so long as its political units redistribute their collective income on a scale which is already arousing resistance; and further, only in so far as each political unit is able either itself to grow or to buy in the market enough food for its collective needs. Neither condition is assured, as I shall seek to show later and as T. H. Huxley forecast for Britain in a prophetic essay published in the last decade of the nineteenth century.[4]

Similarly we do not live in a post-industrial world. The most optimistic technologists are the last to picture a world in which technology has withered away. A civilization which mined the ocean bed and used the products to build cities in space would surely not merit the title of post-industrial.

Yet the prefix 'post' is not meaningless. It means that something has been left behind – not the activity which it describes but a way of life which was once associated with that activity.

That is true of the transitions from a wandering to a settled way of life and from a predominantly rural to a predominantly urban way of life. There is as yet no sign of a post-urban way of life or of a way of life in which work for a wage does not constitute the predominant title to a place in society – unless the present mass unemployment be regarded as at least the precursor of such a change. But even if it is, it gives no clear indication of the way of life (if any) which might take its place.

The sequence of development in the other two segments of human life, the institutional and the ideological, is much less clearly marked, or rather has oscillated more often than the other. Its rate has been affected by its physical milieu, and so, it would seem, has been its content, though less directly. It has been observed that the climate of Greece is agreeable for human living but that its soil does not yield rich returns from intensive cultivation. North of the Alps, on the other hand, the forests of the Rhine and the Danube required heavy labour to clear but repaid intensive effort. This may have contributed not only to the different rates at which civilized life developed north and south of the Alps but also to the difference in its character.

But to me the most striking development of human societies is not so much in their use of tools as in their use of words, concepts, rules, and standards of obligation. These are found at a high degree of development even in societies which are notably backward in economic and technological development.

This is apparent from a study of the most primitive societies still open to us. Driberg[5] who spent many years administering a small East African tribe, has left us translations of their songs, spells and curses. One of the most moving is a curse upon a girl of the tribe. A stranger, lost in the desert, had been succoured and sent on his way as custom required. The discovery after his departure that he had seduced or been seduced by a girl of the tribe was an unbearable outrage. The man was followed and killed. The girl was sentenced to banishment, which meant death in the desert from hunger and thirst. The curse which pronounces this sentence, except for one burst of anger and disgust, is in a tone of sad inevitability. It falls into two stanzas. The first recites all the obligations from which the girl is set free. The second recites the corresponding claims which she no longer has on her tribe. No other words I know so tellingly define the factual and psychological realities of social interdependence in a human system. No other social creatures evolve such ethical imperatives. Few human societies achieve them today. Yet technologically the society which Driberg administered was at a very elementary stage of development.

The violent reaction to this particular act is strange to us, though not beyond our comprehension if we conceive ourselves within the culture of a desert tribe, fiercely endogamous, to whom strangers of another race were unusual phenomena, raising conflicting responses – on the one hand, the threat of the unknown; on the other, the appeal for help against the all too well-known hostility of the desert. The interest of the story lies in the clear enunciation of the mutual rights and duties by which such a society and its members survived.

And not only such a society. The members of today's societies, and not least its Western societies, are at least as interdependent as the members of the tribe studied by Driberg. Until recently it would have been easy to identify acts which were regarded as so powerfully symbolic of disloyalty to these core values that the offender could only be extruded by banishment or by death. Such spontaneous self-regulation was familiar in the American West no more than a century ago even without due process of law. There have been changes in the demands of membership and in the degree of alienation involved in the breach of any of them. But the quite contrary notion that personal independence and social interdependence are compatible without limit is a cultural product of the last two centuries. This idea was never logical and is increasingly discredited.

Another useful example of the preservation of order through mutual obligation is described by Max Gluckman[6] in a study called *The Judicial Process Among the Barotse*. The Barotse are a small African tribe, living at the time of his study by a simple form of agriculture untouched by modern technology. But their sense of justice was highly developed and greatly offended by the legal procedures which their British administrators imposed on them. These, seen by the British as protection for the accused, appeared to the Barotse as mere obstacles to the understanding of a case.

Among the Barotse everyone took part in the judicial process. No voice was too junior, no evidence too remote to be admitted. For the essence of every such situation was that order, that prized collective tribal possession, had been violated and the object of the exercise was to restore it to its habitual unquestioned place. The wife-stealing, the cattle-stealing, or whatever had precipitated the dispute, was probably a mere symptom. The cause might be found in a family dispute originating with the moving of a boundary stone generations before.

English lawyers had no difficulty in understanding and sympathizing with this logic, for they too used it – in children's courts. Even the most sinister act if committed by a child was to be considered first as a symptom of disorder in the only area of life, family life, where the breach of order could still be treated as a mere symptom directing attention primarily to the treatment of a social disorder. Happy Barotse! Order among them still had something of the sanctity of biological order; of health as opposed to disease.

Many social anthropologists have gone to great lengths to find ecological explanations for human cultures. Marvin Harris,[7] for example, shows convincingly that the pig is a highly unsuitable domestic animal in dry environments and argues that the religious taboo imposed on it by both Judaism and Islam is a mere reinforcement of a natural ecological imperative. It may be so; but what of the ban on wine-drinking so prominent in Islamic but not in Judaic or Christian communities? The hills of Moslem Morocco stand bare and eroded. The hills of Christian Spain across the strait, geologically identical, are terraced, cultivated and green to the summit – with vines. How can the same ecological imperative erode the hills of Morocco, blast the huge wine industry which the departing French left in newly autonomous Islamic Algeria, fertilize the adjacent hills of Spain and make one type of Spanish wine, sherry, a cultural symbol in England?[8] Must there be one explanation for everything? May not culture be an influence as well as an outcome? Does speech and example never initiate and never persuade?

Or consider a more sophisticated modern example – the structure of credit by which the world's national and international exchange of goods and services is carried on. Technologically, it is relatively new and has a fascinating history. Psychologically, it is one manifestation of a structure of self-expectation and mutual expectation which has been a major factor in human societies from the earliest times. Those who during the banking crisis of the 1930s were concerned with maintaining the financial system on which the trade of the West depended, despite the collapse of the trust on which it rested, were well placed to see the impotence of the technology when its psychological base was shaken, and to appreciate the nontechnological means by which the psychological base was reconstructed.[9]

But I am concerned not so much to disentangle the manifold sources of culture as to explain what I conceive to be its nature and function. This, as I shall assert, has two aspects, ethical and epistemological, and the two are intimately connected. If men are to communicate and cooperate, they must share some common assumptions about the world they live in; and they must also share some common standards by which to judge their own and each other's actions in that world. History records great changes in both, and periods of great confusion in both, none greater than the present; and changes in either have affected the other in different degrees. But there is a limit to the degree of divergence possible in either dimension. The shared epistemological assumptions must correspond sufficiently with reality to make common action effective. And the shared ethical assumptions must meet the minimal mutual needs which the members have of each other. The social injunctions of the Ten Commandments are to be found in the law and custom of all the settled societies of which I have heard, because some security of such mutual and complementary rights and duties is necessary for collective life. Where either shared assumptions or standards have not been attained, as in countries which still allow the vendetta, or where shared assumptions and shared standards are breaking down, as in so many Western societies today, the threat of instability or worse is implicit in the situation.

Until recent times this structure of self-expectation and mutual expectation depended on and constituted the accepted concept of order. One of the greatest changes of the modern world is the substitution of roles created, assumed and relinquished by contract for the earlier concept that roles were derived from and legitimized by an accepted concept of order to which all owed allegiance.[10] The device of the contractual role has opened vast new scope for design and innovation in human order but its bonds are more selective and weaker than those imposed by accepted social order, such as are constantly exemplified in the plays of Shakespeare, dominated as these are by the themes of loyalty and treachery.

The area of personal human rights has been correspondingly enlarged, to include many which have seldom been shared by societies before our day. Many readers will regard the story of the banished girl as no more than an example of dogmatic social tyranny. Yet there are areas of consensus both on the understanding of situations and on the judgement of actions which cannot be reduced below certain limits if a society is to survive. And history will disclose whether and where those limits have been passed, if our intelligence fails to forecast them aright or to devise means to keep within them. It is no accident that all the revolutionary regimes which have emerged in the last sixty years have taken it as their first need to engineer the consensus on which they depend.

Footnotes

1. This familiar division obscures the astonishing difference which history has emphasized between societies which combined animal husbandry with hunting but not with agriculture, and those in which agriculture and animal husbandry developed together. The largest empire recorded in human history – larger in area than that of Rome or Britain – was put together by nomad hunters and pastoralists from Mongolia under Genghis Khan – at an estimated cost of more than 30 million lives. The nomad pastoralist combined wealth with mobility in a way never again approached until modern times.
2. *North-South : A Programme for Survival.* Report of the Independent Commission on International Development Issues under the chairmanship of Willy Brandt, London, Pan, 1980.
3. H. A. L. Fisher. *A History of Europe,* op. cit.
4. T. H. Huxley. *Evolution and Ethics and Other Essays,* op. cit.
5. J. H. Driberg. *Initiation and Nine Other Poems: translations from poems of the Didinga and Lango Tribes,* Waltham St. Lawrence, Golden Cockerell Press, 1932.
6. H. M. Gluckman. *The Judicial Process Among the Barotse of Northern Rhodesia,* Manchester, Manchester University Press, 1955.
7. M. Harris. *Cannibals and Kings,* Glasgow, William Collins, 1977.
8. I owe this illustration to Mr Philip Stewart, of the Commonwealth Forestry Institute, University of Oxford.

9. The reference is to an agreement commonly known to English-speaking banking participants as the 'standstill' which was first concluded in 1932 for six months, but which, regularly reviewed and occasionally modified, lasted for more than twenty years, though it was, of course, in abeyance during the war years.
10. In describing the modern world as a transition from status to contract, Maine, I think, did less than justice to the fact that in the matter of human relations the main effect of the change was to change the origin and increase the flexibility of the role, rather than to reduce dependence on role playing, which is surely no less great whether the role and its corresponding status and responsibilities are allotted by contract or by custom or in any other way.

CHAPTER 6

THE PECULIARITIES OF HUMAN SYSTEMS

The human race has clearly developed in a way radically different from any other species. For the purpose of this book we need not go back into the depths of time. Let us go back no further than the earliest date at which we can form some fairly comprehensive picture of the state of our kind on earth, say the second millennium BC. Neither biological evolution nor major climatic change divides us from the human beings who then shared what is now our habitat. If we could revisit them, we should find in them only cultural differences to understand and allow for, if not to overcome, as anthropologists do today when they make contact with peoples of culture other than their own – or as we ourselves do when we meet for the first time members of a subculture radically different from our own even within our own national boundaries.

Yet cultural differences would have distinguished each of those early societies from the others, as they distinguish all those societies from our own.

What should we find in common between all those peoples and between them and ourselves, yet without parallel in the history of the other species? Four features seem to me outstanding – *communication* by language, fostering *cultures* sufficiently shared to support what *government* each society needed; and *war*, endemic or epidemic, between the societies thus distinguished. We have no reason to doubt that the members of every society which occupied our familiar earth forty to fifty centuries ago communicated by speech as freely as we do, shared a common culture sufficiently to remain at least as viable and cohesive as we are; governed themselves as effectively and sometimes more democratically than we do (remember the Barotse, page 37); and, as societies, fought each other no less fiercely. In this chapter I will briefly explore these four distinctions.

1. Communication

It is widely but mistakenly supposed that communication consists primarily in sending messages; and this delusion has been fortified by recent technological advances in doing so. In fact nearly all the problems of communication lie at the receiving end. Communication takes place only when someone receives some message which is meaningful to him; and this meaning may or may not bear any relation to what the sender was trying to convey.

If it is to bear any meaning at all, it must be capable of interpretation by some code familiar to the receiver; and if it is to have the intended meaning, the sender must know the code and shape his message accordingly. And this is so even if he is trying to deceive. Moreover, what I have called a code is far more complex than that word implies, for it is, at least in verbal communication, indefinitely expansible, shaped as well as changed by use. A Western anthropologist learning the language of a simple people finds many words in his own language which have no counterpart in the language he is learning and which he cannot even explain except by describing a whole unfamiliar culture. (How much explanation would be needed, for example, to explain the meaning of the word 'bank' to a member of a society which had no money economy?) But equally his mentors will find many words in their language which not only lack counterparts in his but which are explicable only in the context of beliefs and customs which he does not share or even know.

Nor is this limited to the relation of different languages. The meaning of any word is the ever changing sum of all the meanings which are currently given to it. Makers of dictionaries know this, because it dictates the way they make their dictionaries. Other people usually forget it because they cannot be fully aware of the limitations attending their own experience. It is easy to call a spade a spade; but only someone intimately familiar with the use and the feel of a spade in all contexts and conditions knows what a spade *is*. (Who else would know the difference between a 'good' spade and a 'bad' one?)

It follows that the more uniform the experience of members of a society, the more fully they are likely to share their common language and the more rich it is likely to be. We need not delve into the remote past for examples. It is sobering to reflect that even in the West two hundred years ago it must have been rare for two people to discuss anything which was not directly familiar to them both (the weather, the crops, their neighbours . . .). Perhaps the same is more true even today for a majority of Western populations than 'intellectuals' are likely to assume.

I find it surprising that we have no accepted word to describe the activity of attaching meaning to communication or the code by which we do so, a code which is constantly confirmed, developed or changed by use. I have for many years referred to this mental activity as 'appreciation'; and to the code which it uses as its 'appreciative system'; and to the state of that code at any time as its 'appreciative setting'. I call it a system because, although it is tolerant of ambiguity and even inconsistency, it is sensitive to them and tries to reconcile them. I describe my assumptions about it in the next chapter.

Languages have developed even over the last five thousand years; and since printing made the written word more available and literacy correspondingly increased, more individual users of any particular language have no doubt increased the richness as well as the breadth of their acquaintance with it. On the other hand, languages have fractionated as a result of diversification of experience as well as through the growth of specialized fields each with its own community of discourse. There may well have been an increase in the number of people who in some if not all fields of discourse cannot understand each other, though they speak the same language.

None the less the phenomenon of language remains a human constant, linking contemporary human beings not only with each other but also with countless and diverse human beings in the remote past and dividing them from all other species known to us.

Of course we share with other species a vast volume of nonverbal communication. Indeed this probably plays a larger part among human beings than among other species, because every act done by a human being is interpreted by other human beings and so becomes a communication. Even the bomb dropped on Hiroshima was more important as a communication of power and intention than as an act of destruction.

The example of the atomic bomb reminds us that communication can take place at many levels. The levels are ascending levels of trust and shared appreciation, needed to make communication at that level possible. They usually overlap and coexist but it is useful to distinguish them.

The first level of communication is *violence* – the riot, the bombing, the arson which increasingly defiles so many societies today. Violence cannot help communicating; it erodes trust and evokes response both to contain it and to abate it. But it is not directed to any specific communicative end, so it can be distinguished from *threat*, the conditional 'do it or else –'. We can distinguish between threats which are illegal, such as the kidnapper and the hijacker; those which are legalized, like the threat of strike action in Western industrial countries; and those which are extra-legal, such as the threats by which nation states seek to protect their 'vital interests'. But all alike involve trust only to the extent that the threatened needs to believe both that the threatener can and will carry out his threat unless the condition is fulfilled and that to fulfill the condition will avert the threat.

The next level of communication is the *bargain*. Here we are today almost necessarily limited to fields within which there exists an authority capable of enforcing the obligations undertaken or conditions which make its breach too expensive to contemplate. States still make treaties but so many have been broken since 1914 that they can hardly be regarded as more than (at most) expressions of present intent.

Bargaining involves a greater measure of shared assumption. Each party needs to be confident that the other regards the situation as one of bargain, not battle – the attempt to negotiate an exchange on terms acceptable to all the parties. Each must believe that the other parties can and will carry out their undertakings if agreement is reached. Each is free to make not merely an acceptable bargain but the best bargain he can. But equally each is free to withdraw from the negotiation. At the next level, we may put the giving and receiving of *information*. Here the receiver must not only trust the giver's competence and reliability, he must also be assured that the giver's appreciative system corresponds sufficiently with his own to ensure that what is received fits the receiver's needs. Even if it does, it will to some extent, however small, alter the setting of his appreciative system. So the giving of information slides into the activity of *persuasion*, where the giver actively seeks to change the way in which the other perceives some situation and thus to change the setting of his appreciative system more radically.

This process may be mutual and may thus become *argument*, each party striving to alter the other's view whilst maintaining his own. And this may rise to the level of *dialogue*, where each seeks to share, however hypothetically, the other's appreciation and to open his own to the other's persuasion with a view to enlarging both the approaching mutual understanding, if not shared appreciation.

I spell these levels of communication out because the current Western culture, especially, I think, American culture with its addiction to the adversary process, seems to be increasingly unwilling to envisage even the possibility of human communication at any level above confrontation or trade off.

The working of a human system would be impossible without a degree – and in modern societies a very high degree – of functional distribution of authority, supported by the corresponding and complementary pattern of trust. The functionary has a discretion to act within an allotted level of authority; and those who allot the authority must also accord the trust or replace the functionary by one whom they can trust. This is the concept of authority which Chester Barnard[1] formulated long ago and which remains, I believe, its best definition. The minister trusts his driver to drive him to the airport, leaving to the driver all the manifold decisions involved. And the driver needs to be able to trust the minister to exercise his discretions responsibly at the conference to which he is flying, because the minister has been vested with that authority by the accepted processes of the society to which both belong – even though the driver as a citizen may be deeply opposed to the policies of the minister's government.

At a slightly more complex level the professional adviser places himself at the disposal of whoever he is advising, offering supportive action or whatever he believes to be to the benefit of the receiver but using any authority which he may have by reason of some special competence only within the field of authority to which that competence extends. That is, in brief, the professional relationship.

Once again, the statement of what is needed contrasts so grossly with what is currently encountered that many contemporary minds may reject it as absurd. Of course the necessary levels of trust and responsibility may not be realized and are not realized in many societies today. But it they are not be realized and are not realized in many societies today. But if they are stability and quality to which it aspires, the society will dissolve or fragment or fall back to whatever level of organization will suffice to preserve its minimal requirements. The government of totalitarian states is designed to impose and maintain an appreciative system at least sufficiently shared to give the society its minimal coherence. They may fail. Societies based on Western democratic principles expect their numerous subsystems to generate sufficient consensus to be governable and to maintain it through change, however abrupt, whether originating from without or from within. They may fail too.

The limits to the stability of Western democracies are set, as I believe, by the extent to which they share an appreciative system or compatible appreciative systems and by the aptness of those systems to interpret their contemporary experience, especially when its pattern is changing. But since I use the term 'appreciation' primarily for the activity of an individual mind I will use the more common and wider term 'culture' to describe the shared basis of appreciation and action which communication develops within any political society.

2. Culture

The word culture basically means the activity of tilling soil (as in agriculture) and is also used of the management of some other living systems such as bees. Applied to human beings, it connotes activity deliberately designed to 'improve' body or mind. Physical culture was a common expression earlier in the century. Less generally it connotes the products of such activity. This use is increasing as activities in biological laboratories become more familiar. To many today culture will suggest a population of bacteria in a test tube – a sombre example of the power of communication and experience to shape each other.

But at the beginning of the century the unqualified word in a human context meant the ability to appreciate the 'higher' activities of the human mind, especially artistic creations in all media and, less directly, the body of creative work to be appreciated. The mind was regarded by implication as a seed bed which cultivation could make both more fertile and more richly stocked.

Culture was thus something which could exist in greater or less degree. It was also a narrow term, reluctant to include the domain of science and capable, even as late as 1959, of fuelling the fierce debate about the Two Cultures between Lord Snow and Professor Leavis.[2] The concept of culture was more akin to the concept of civilization than of education. The earnest captain of the Beagle, on the voyage which carried Darwin to his enlightenment, brought back to England three children from Tierra del Fuego, and returned them several years later as missionaries of civilization, equipped not only with an English education but also with broadcloth suits and chamber pots. And even up to this century the colonizing West was prone to regard its ways of life, thought and feeling, that is, its culture, as a package necessarily more 'advanced' and therefore 'better' than those of the less developed peoples which it dominated.

In the meantime anthropologists were establishing the term 'culture' in its wider sense. Different societies had different ways of life and thought, ways which had an inner coherence not obvious to the outsider who had not immersed himself in them so deeply as to see them from within. They involved a set of accepted relations of people with each other, with 'authorities' and with their environment. The piecemeal introduction of Western ways, monogamy no less than gin, might be deeply disruptive. The West had much to offer but also something to learn and already much to regret. This awareness coincided with Western loss of confidence in its own culture, following the first and, still more, the second World War. The pendulum swung the other way and it became as unseemly to refer to one culture as better or worse than another as to refer to one of its members as being more or less cultured than another.

In fact we cannot afford wholly to dispense with the dimension of more or less 'cultured' when comparing one member of a society with another or wholly to abdicate our judgement of a particular culture (including our own) as better or worse in some particulars than another or than itself at some earlier stage. We need and we have criteria for making such judgements; indeed, an embarrassing combination of them. For at every level, from the personal to the planetary, we judge human systems both by their stability and by their quality, and the two criteria often conflict.

The expression 'ways of life and thought' is, of course, exceedingly wide, and necessarily so. To realize its dimensions we have only to look first at what happens to a human child from birth to maturity; and next at what can happen to a society with the passage of even two or three generations.

The newborn infant has virtually no powers of discrimination. (Professor Gorn has written, 'We spend the first year of our lives learning that we end at our skin; and the rest of our lives learning that we don't'.) It has no means of interpreting incoming experience except physical pain or satisfaction, to which is added very quickly the distinction between the familiar and the unfamiliar. It has no guidance for action except a few innate responses. Two decades later this same creature, physically mature, has developed culturally along several dimensions which can be recognized, though the variety of his possible states is vast. If he is fortunate he will by then have developed what Erikson[3] calls the 'virtues' or 'strengths' of childhood and adolescence – hope, will, purpose, competence, and fidelity. He will have learned to trust his world and himself, to sustain action competently in achieving chosen or accepted purposes, and to accept the constraints involved in his freely chosen commitments. Erikson claims that his schema has validity across different cultures. It has, of course, a Western flavour with its emphasis on individual freedom, though a welcome emphasis on the fact that 'freely chosen' commitments involve constraints no less binding than conditioned ones; perhaps much more so. But even within a single culture the individual may have attained these strengths in very different ways and degrees.

The trust which supports him may be strong or weak and may repose in a 'world' much smaller or wider than that of other members of his society – perhaps wholly in a dissident group united in attacking the culture into which he was born. His commitments may be wide or narrow, strong, or weak, and his sense of commitment may or may not correspond with the net of interdependence in which by then he is involved. Above all, his 'interests' and his corresponding span of awareness may vary enormously in character, diversity, and intensity.

It is these interests, or, as I shall call them, concerns, with their associated commitments and constraints, which give to his character such quality and coherence as it may come to possess. They are the unpredictable product of his interaction with the culture in which he grows – his contribution to it and its to him, for good and ill.

If we turn our attention from the individual to the society into which he is born and follow it over a period of a few generations (as I do later in this book) we see its culture transmitted by and through the transient generations and changing in the process. The rate of this change is important in its own right, apart from its content and direction. For there is a limit to the rate at which new generations can assimilate change, a limit set partly by the rate at which these generations turn over. This rate is perhaps the only rate of change which is, in effect, slowing, rather than quickening, as life expectancy rises.

Over the span of the generations (less than 150) which separates us from the early world, the rate of cultural change among most societies remained for a long time so slow as to be barely noticeable during a human lifetime. Generally speaking, the more rapidly they developed, the sooner they broke up. The rate began to speed with the development of technology, multiplied with the use of thermal energy, and in the West in the last two centuries has gathered speed at an exponential rate, with the cultural and other results which I examine in the rest of the book. It may well be that, despite the latest phase in the technological revolution, which claims to have so greatly enlarged human powers of control, the difficulties of control will exceed what any culture can mediate even before other and more obvious limitations are met. But these questions I will leave until later. I am concerned in this chapter with the basic peculiarities of human systems and their implications; and in this context two further differences need to be noticed here – the capacity of human societies to govern themselves (until now) at a level of complexity far higher than that attained by societies of other creatures; and the violence with which they so frequently interact with each other.

3. Government

The examples already given show that the government of human societies is not dependent on the degree of their technological development. Societies as simple as those studied by Driberg and Gluckman are at least as capable of self-regulation as any modern Western society; indeed much more so. Nor are they examples of dictatorial rule. The really simple societies we know work with a degree of democratic consensus unknown to our complex industrial societies, and for good and obvious reasons. The life experience of their members is far more similar; the disproportion of wealth, power, and function is far less; the environment in which they live is far less disturbed by their own activities; and in consequence past experience is a better guide to the future and correspondingly more valued. Today's Western democracies do indeed represent the closing phase of a widespread revolution against dictatorial government by a minority; but the political conditions which excited this revolt were as far from those of primitive society as they are from the new conditions which the revolt has ushered in; indeed much further. I shall be concerned in a later chapter with the extraordinary delusion which has dominated the Western world for two hundred years, equating individual liberty with universal peace.

I am concerned here only to identify government as a human constant, a level of regulation which, even in simple societies, far exceeds anything achieved – perhaps even anything needed – by societies of other social species.

There is, none the less, a vast contrast between the level of regulation needed and achieved by societies such as, for example, the Barotse and the industrialized societies of the modern world.

I shall be concerned later to identify the minimal conditions which must be satisfied to enable a developed society to survive in the contemporary world. They are primarily cultural, rather than technological. They require from societies, interest groups and individuals an ability to reset their appreciative systems, their standards of what to expect, what to attempt and what to put up with, to an extent which our kind has not previously achieved or needed. Moreover, their increasing lack of self-sufficiency involves them increasingly in each other's fates, though not, I think, quite so universally as is sometimes assumed. All their inter-societal exchanges distinguish them from those of other species, in kind as well as volume; but one needs special attention. This is the unique and remarkable phenomenon of war.

4. War

War, however widely defined, occurs so far as I know only among men. No other social species bands together to attack other populations of its own kind or to defend itself against such attacks. This phenomenon cannot be attributed to technology for it is endemic from the earliest times. On the other hand, it has from the first eagerly seized on and greatly stimulated technology. The first smelters of metal made swords before they made ploughshares.

The nature of these armed conflicts varies immensely. They may be interruptions of what is otherwise the peaceful symbiosis of adjacent groups, like the periodic wars described by Roy Rappaport in New Guinea.[4] They may be forays in search of plunder or slaves, or mere adventure, like the dreaded Norse raids on the coasts of England and Ireland in the ninth century of our era. They may be simple assertions of dominance, demanding at least acknowledgement, possibly tribute, sometimes subordination.

Equally they may be assertions of independence, the refusal of some constituent society to remain part of a larger whole. Finally they may be – or might have been until very recent times – essays in colonization in which the previous occupants of the area were subordinated or expelled, assimilated or exterminated. It is too soon to say that the days of the last are over but its object can no longer be achieved in the same way without widespread disturbance, if not world war, for reasons pursued in a later chapter. National ownership partitions the world. Frontiers are fortified by all the legacies of the colonial era.

Examples of all these forms of war fill recorded history from the earliest to the latest times; and they are not confined to 'uncivilized' peoples, either as agents or as victims. The Athenians decided in democratic debate to slaughter all the males of the neighbouring island of Melos (which had been on the losing side in the Peloponesian war) and to enslave the women and children in the service of an Athenian colony to be planted there. The Romans did the same to an already defeated Carthage to exclude the possibility of its recovering power. The settlers in Tasmania exterminated the aborigines much more recently and even more completely, since the slave trade was no longer either legal or profitable. Yet in the homelands of the countries involved homicide was a relatively rare crime, socially detested and punishable by death.

Moreover, this form of collective struggle remained an accepted form of political action throughout the world until the carnage of the First World War revealed the extent to which technology had increased its costs in life and treasure and the uncertainty of its outcome; and armaments today claim a larger share of all national budgets than they have even done before – except in the one happy country (Austria) which has been disarmed by the will of its recently hostile neighbours.

It has even degenerated during the present century. J. R. Seeley, writing in the 1870s in his classic *Ecce Homo*, cited as an achievement of Christian morality that war was no longer endemic between all states not united by an express treaty of peace. A declaration of war was needed to terminate the normal status of peaceful coexistence. Even in his day, his complacency applied only to the established states of 'Christendom'. And in the century since he wrote, most of his hopes have been drowned in blood. But his comment is still useful as a record of the view of war taken by a well-informed and humane English historian only a century ago.

The constancy of war throughout recorded history – one of the few constants to be found in it – demands to be understood, especially by anyone seeking to place the human species in its ecological context. The present pattern of sovereign states not only reflects the results of wars but was held universally to justify them until the last few decades. Indeed it is widely so held even today.

Of course we 'understand' how wars happen to the extent that we can usually assign both 'reasons' and 'causes' for particular wars, often a tiresome variety of them. I have already cited the most common. We also know that it usually takes only one combatant to make a war, at least in the view of the other; and we are familiar with wars in which each side claims, often with justice, to be only 'responding' to threat or aggression – a familiar example of the power of positive feedback to destabilize a system. There remains an uneasy contrast both between collective and individual human violence and between the collective violence so often practised between organized human societies and the absence of any comparable relations in other species.

Two conclusions can, I think, be tentatively drawn. One concerns the systemic nature of societies organized for war. Once we have admitted that new characteristics emerge at new levels of organization, we have no reason to expect that the behaviour of an army in the field or a terrorist gang or any other group organized for war, will reflect what would otherwise have been the behaviour of its consistent individuals. It need not surprise us, for example, that at Christmas 1914 some Allied and German troops disturbed their respective commanders by meeting between the fortified lines to share a common Christmas dinner. An unpremeditated change of role abruptly changed the situation as experienced by both parties. Less dramatic examples are quite common, for example, in wage negotiations and similar adversarial proceedings. The participants are even expected to retain some awareness of their role as human beings and its responsibilities. This is manifestly most difficult if not impossible in martial roles, but the pursuit of it is often resumed so soon as the status of combatant is given up, as by those who become prisoners of war.

The other conclusion emerges if we consider war not as an instrument of coercion but as the lowest level of communication. Except in extreme forms of genocide on whatever scale – the physical destruction of an identifiable population – even war is more effective as a threat than as an act. It is usually intended to influence decision, to secure acquiescence in some demand or even unconditional surrender. The acquiescence is of course 'unwillingly' given but it is, none the less, willed by the loser. Recent history shows repeated examples of mistakes made by an attacker in estimating not the physical impact of his attack but its influence on the behaviour of those attacked, especially on their willingness to submit.

The concept of war as the residual instrument of foreign policy is, of course, as old as Clausewitz. Over the last century war or its equivalent – any threat of unacceptable harm – has become increasingly widespread as an instrument of policy and ever less residual. This should not surprise us, though it is, of course, a sombre index. In an ever more interdependent world ever smaller minorities can threaten unacceptable harm to their neighbours. And in an ever less integrated world ever fewer constraints and commitments restrain them from using what power they have. Moreover, it is usually much easier to organize in order to do collective harm than collective good. The trend does, of course, call in question the possibility of a governable world or even of governable societies of current size and complexity, but it is no less understandable for being unwelcome.

It also illustrates the tendency of communication to degenerate. Lower level communication drives out higher levels as depreciated currency drives out good currency. A few men communicating with bombs can soon reduce to their own level the rest of a society which would otherwise prefer to use words. The reverse process is much more difficult, as all experienced negotiators know. Happily it is not unknown. Whether it will be strong enough to reverse today's decline only time will show.

Footnotes

1. Chester Barnard. *The Functions of the Executive*, Cambridge, Mass., Harvard University Press, 1938.
2. C. P. Snow. *The Two Cultures and a Second Look*, New York, Mentor, 1964. (The original lecture was given in 1959.)
3. E. Erikson. *Insight and Responsibility*, New York, W. W. Norton, 1964.
4. R. Rappaport. *Pigs for the Ancestors*, New Haven, Yale University Press, 1968.

CHAPTER 7

APPRECIATION AND ACTION

Before turning to the present and future states of the human systems which most concern us, I need to add a statement of the assumptions which I am making about the working of individual minds and policy making bodies. For these assumptions, though they seem to me to be necessary implications from experience, are not in my view fully accepted among our current cultural assumptions and indeed are in danger of getting buried in the interests of a simpler ideology, more convenient to the technological handling of information for purposes of control and decision.

1. *Concern*

The activities of a human mind, when they are more than innate or conditioned responses, seem to me to originate in some *concern*. I do not think that these concerns can be arranged in a hierarchy quite so rigid as Professor Maslow has proposed, since concerns in the upper range of his hierarchy are sometimes given priority over those in the lower range by cultural imperatives for which he does not, I think, sufficiently allow. Consider, for example, the frequency with which traditional Japanese culture required its members to vindicate their honour by suicide, or the fortitude with which outstanding characters sometimes preserve their humanity through the horrors of penal labour camps. None the less his hierarchy clearly describes an important factor affecting the priority and variety of human concerns. We may expect that societies with increased security and leisure will develop more varied concerns than those which must labour unceasingly to keep alive, while remembering that security and leisure may be abundantly provided for some individuals even in poor societies and that many societies, poor by our standards, found time for rich ritual and for the building of immense symbolic structures.[1]

The response to a concern is to construct an inner representation of the situation which is relevant to that concern. I have already exemplified the immense diversity of situations which may be thrown up by the test of relevance to different concerns. An example in the institutional field is the water engineer who sees his fellows in all their various occupations primarily as generators of sewage. Conversely a representation called to consciousness by one concern may awaken another.

In fact we seldom need to do more than update existing inner representations, since our concerns, personal, social, and institutional, and their corresponding representations of the situation relevant to each, are usually continuing or frequently recurring and are constantly reinforced or challenged by the stream of human communication in which we are continually bathed.

I have called this pattern of concerns and their simulated relevant situations 'an appreciative system'. I regard an appreciative system as a work of art, both personal and social, one that is constantly revised or confirmed by the three needs. First, it should correspond with reality sufficiently to guide action. Second, it should be sufficiently shared by our fellows to mediate communication. Third, it should be sufficiently acceptable to ourselves to make life bearable. It is thus a mental construct, partly subjective, largely intersubjective, that is, based on a shared subjective judgement, and constantly challenged or confirmed by experience.

The first and most critical result of such an appreciation is to classify the situation as one that must be accepted or simply enjoyed; match signals are as potent as mismatch signals and still, happily, more frequent though less noticed. Alternatively, the situation may be classified as one that human action could change or is needed to preserve. A major change over the centuries, vastly speeded in the last two hundred years, is the increase in the range of situations which are held to invite and allow designed change by human action.

If – and only if – the appreciative mind classifies the situation as one which human agency could possibly change or needs to preserve, then – and only then – the concerned mind devises possible responses and evaluates them with the aid of criteria set by other concerns. A 'problem' begins to emerge. 'Solutions' are sought. Action may or may not follow.

I labour these points because our technological culture, dominated by 'problem solving', tends to take problem setting for granted. It is, I think, essential to remember that without concerns there would be no problems and that without criteria (which often conflict) there would be no solutions.

Every culture includes an appreciative system which must be at least sufficiently shared to guide collective action, to mediate communication, and to give the society which generates it enough self-confidence to survive. And this interpersonal artifact is sustained and changed by transmission through the series of personal appreciative systems which it develops and supports in succeeding generations.

2. Ethic

What then of the criteria by which these representations are judged? These develop as part of the appreciative system but they deserve special mention in any study of the control mechanisms of the human mind because, as I have already stressed, any internally generated control depends on the existence of standards with which actual or hypothetical experience can be compared, and which are themselves confirmed or changed by use. These standards are the basis of all discrimination – factual no less than ethical or aesthetic. I am particularly concerned here with the standards which need to be shared by any society if it is to remain stable – that is, to cohere sufficiently to act together for at least the purposes needed for its survival. I will comprehend them by the word ethic, used in its widest sense.

When we look back over the historic span which I have chosen, we find human beings only in societies of limited though varying size, often with sharply defined boundaries. In preagricultural times these had obvious upper and lower limits of size; for a human community cannot endure unless it is composed of an aggregate of families, even though the aggregate be small and loose; and in hunting and pastoral economies it could not exceed the size which could be supported by the area over which it could range in a day. Agriculture and, later, increasing industry, extended the upper limit of density and made possible the accumulation of wealth and the differentiation in distribution of wealth, power and function. Subcommunities and subcultures emerged but boundaries remained.

I have already argued that the basic force which holds these groups together is a set of shared expectations about each other and about the world they share. I will examine in more detail later how this is reinforced, notably by the self-expectations of the individuals who grow up with the constraints and commitments of a particular culture and come to internalize some version of it. This sense of obligation I comprehend under the word ethic. Its contents may be diverse, ranging from the most trivial formalities, such as forms of greeting and styles of dress (important forms of communication, reassuring or the reverse), to the more basic commitments and constraints which support security of life and property. But I am immediately concerned not with the particular content of such codes but with their ubiquity among human societies. Ethologists report no such patterns of behaviour among any other species. Many species do, of course, develop 'pecking orders' and have ways of enforcing and occasionally changing them; and very occasionally they develop role functions such as 'lookouts' to protect a grazing herd. But they show nothing comparable to the net of accepted rights and duties which marks the most simple, at least as much as the most complex and modern, human communities. A modern Westerner is at least as liable to give unintended offence in another culture, not least a simple and traditional one, as its members may give to him. The sense of obligation based on mutual expectations and self-expectations is another constant shared by human communities simple and complex, contemporary, or of remote antiquity, which is not shared by any other species.

3. *Reason*

What then of reason, that preeminently human quality? I would not question for a moment that our ancestors possessed 'reason'. But the word has become so limited and confused that I cannot use it without definition. Four or five centuries ago it included virtually all I have subsumed under appreciation and ethic as well as any resultant process of decision. For many today it means no more than the process of logical deduction.

Under appreciation I have included the power of representing to ourselves situations relevant to our concerns and comparing these situations with standards defining what we should expect them to be and, if this be different, what we should like them to be. Even where these exercises do not invite overt action, they involve understanding, which is also an activity. To appreciate a situation we need to understand how it arose and to what it might lead within all the contexts relevant to our concerns; and this involves at least three mental activities which it is useful to distinguish if only because two of them are so often ignored.

One activity is the much prized capacity for logical deduction, to which the word 'rationality' might well be confined. A second activity is the capacity for *contextual* understanding, the recognition and manipulation of figure and ground with which we may include the creative power of inventiveness and design, whether of scientific hypotheses or technological innovations, or social or organizational structures. I will call this intuition. A third mental activity, applicable wherever other human beings are concerned, is the power to represent to ourselves their subjective states, a power which often misleads us but which we cannot escape. For most of the vocabulary with which we explain to ourselves other people's actions has meaning for us only because we have experienced the thoughts and emotions which we attribute to them. I do not know what fear or anger mean to another person but if I had not experienced them myself I could not even guess, however closely I had observed their symptoms in others.[2] This capacity I will call empathy.

Rationality, intuition and empathy are all recognizable aspects of the activity of a human mind. Reason may be an even more ample term, but it cannot be less. I will use 'reason' in this sense in my list of the abilities which distinguish human systems from other living systems.

Footnotes

1. Avebury, southern England, laid out in the third millenium BC, is on the scale of Versailles or central Washington. Avenues of megaliths, some weighing 40 tons, stretched for miles. The rampart round the central enclosure, more than half a mile in circuit, rose 60 feet above the bottom of the dyke which its excavation made. The men who made these things, with reindeer picks and wicker baskets and levers, were fed by the labour of others who had also to feed themselves.
2. A friend once confided in me that she was not sure she knew what other people meant by the word 'fear'. It did not seem to correspond with any similar experience known to her. Was she defective in some way? Could I explain? I couldn't.

CHAPTER 8

THE BONDING OF HUMAN SYSTEMS

Human beings are not only social but also acculturable creatures. At the extreme limits of our historical vision into the past we find them living in societies united by cultural bonds – common ways of perceiving, thinking, valuing and acting.

The elements of this cultural bonding are relatively clear and agreed. They are, first, the mutual expectations generated between the members of a society endowed with human powers of appreciation and communication, expectations which are reinforced by the powers of all to express their approval of conformity and their disapproval of deviance. In closely knit societies these powers of approval and disapproval are very great, and they are used with an intensity proportionate to the extent to which the conformity or deviance is held to be a matter of public concern.

Powers of approval and disapproval are usually reinforced in matters of public concern by formal acts of the legislature, judiciary, and executive, in so far as these powers of government have been developed and distinguished; and there is a constant interplay between formal and informal acts of regulation,[1] the formal acts serving sometimes to record, sometimes to initiate cultural change or to confirm cultural continuity; and there is usually some disparity between the two. The informal regulators are, of course, far the older. In traditional societies the distinction was often blurred or even lacking; and even when it was present, the formal regulator relied for its powers of enforcement always in some degree and sometimes wholly on informal sanctions. The Icelandic assembly which served as both legislature and judiciary had for centuries no formal powers of enforcement at all. Yet disputants often thought it worth while to fortify themselves by its judgements.

Until less than a century ago the power of 'sanctions' to 'enforce' laws was greatly exaggerated, even in accepted theories of jurisprudence. The only truly coercive power exercisable even by the most extreme dictatorship is the power to kill, to imprison, and to expropriate, and even these are at least as potent as threats as they are as changes of state. Communication governs human societies to an extent which can hardly be overestimated and is usually grossly undervalued.

The power of these pressures depends immensely on the extent to which they are internalized and become accepted as expectations which the individual entertains of himself. This in turn depends in part on the degree of the individual's consciousness of self, a dimension known to most human beings, especially contemporary Westerners, both by direct experience and by inference from communication with others, even though by its nature it defies the kind of analysis which we can only make as observers and to which the natural sciences have attached so great a prestige.

Both mutual expectations and self-expectations, whether they are fortified by society's formal rules or not, may be further confirmed by the injunctions of religion. In the now largely secularized but formerly Judaeo-Christian West this word has acquired such a narrow meaning that it needs some further examination; for its basic assumptions and unanswered questions are important to an analysis of human systems.

All the world's great religions include both a metaphysical view of the world in which individual men find themselves (including their own nature) and a moral view of the way in which they should conduct themselves in such a world; and the cogency of the morality is presented as a necessary implication of the metaphysics. Some critics have reversed the causal chain and asserted that the metaphysical view of the world associated with particular religions has been developed to support the assumptions and injunctions of particular cultures. To me there seems to be overwhelming evidence that patterns of moral obligation and patterns of metaphysical belief have developed independently in human societies but that each has powerfully influenced the other, though in varying degrees. It is easy, for example, to describe the moral development of republican Rome with virtually no reference to its metaphysical beliefs; but no one would expect to do the same with Jewish history over the same period.

It is also noteworthy that though the great religions make radically different metaphysical assumptions about the nature of the world and the legitimate aspirations of human individuals, they are much more closely at one in their moral codes. The metaphysic of Buddhism and its concept of the proper goal and hope of an individual is profoundly different from the

Judaeo-Christian. But the eightfold path which the Buddhist is enjoined to follow is essentially the same as the Judaeo-Christian path.

This seems to me further evidence that a society's moral code is not dictated by its metaphysical beliefs, though it is greatly influenced by them.

If this is so, we might expect that the changes which the natural sciences have introduced in our conception of the universe we live in would have influenced but not determined the culture and especially the ethic of the societies which it has affected; and this is indeed what we find. I describe later as optimistic, determinist and materialist the ideologies which I associate loosely with the names of both Adam Smith and Karl Marx; and it is easy to see in these attitudes the influence of science and technology exploding in what seemed to be the infallible service of man. But at the end of the century that great evolutionary scientist, T. H. Huxley,[2] described the task of mankind as the duty to create, in opposition to the state of nature, the state of art of an organized policy, capable of continually maintaining and improving itself. Moreover, he regarded the effort, though noble, as doomed to ultimate failure. The cosmic process would resume its sway. 'Evolution,' he wrote, 'encourages no millenial expectations.'

Today the dawning realization of ecological limitations leads many ecologists to call for an 'ecological ethic', a sense of obligation to preserve the planet, even at the cost of contemporary sacrifice, as a habitable home for man. And for many this is coupled with a sense of obligation to share the planet's resources more equally between the world's political societies and between the individuals in each.

These moral imperatives do not derive 'rationally' from the facts. Hume pointed out long ago that it would not be 'irrational' for him to prefer the destruction of the rest of the world to a pain in his little finger. And science has long insisted that it is impossible 'rationally' to derive an obligation from a fact, an 'ought' from an 'is'. But this tells us more about the limitations of our concept of rationality than about the origin and cogency of our changing set of cultural values. The ecological threat is seen by some as a cogent reason for securing what they need at whatever cost to those who are thereby left in want of it; by others as an equally cogent reason for sharing what there is with all who need it. The difference is not an antithesis but the contrast between different positions on a spectrum which identifies the individual with a narrower or wider group and extends his concern to a more distant or less distant time horizon. There may be – I think there are – built-in limitations to the extent to which individuals, and still more societies of individuals, can extend both their sense of social identity and their effective awareness of future time. But we do not know what these limits are or how far they can be extended by cultural development. There is indeed a relationship between what we define as an actual state or situation and what we define as what 'ought to be'. Both are human artefacts, for we can get no nearer even to 'reality' than the mental representation which we make of it. We know by no means all there is to know about how we make the first, what is, still less the second, what ought to be. But we know that we mentally represent what is largely, if not entirely, by its perceived relevance to what we think ought to be.

Finally, although these ethical and conceptual standards are the basis of what I have called a common culture, I would emphasize again that they are mediated by appreciation and communication, human abilities which make it possible for human beings *up to a point* to understand and accept both cultural difference and cultural change with time. The implications of those words 'up to a point' will be a major theme in the rest of the book.

Such then I conceive to be the binding forces which give coherence to a society – first, the expectations entertained by each member of all the others especially on matters where each needs to rely on others; second, the formal constraints and imperatives of the society's governing political institutions; third, the constraints and imperatives which flow from its shared religious beliefs (in the wide sense already described); fourth, the internalized imperatives embodied in each individual's standards of self-expectation, an inner regulator which may deny or confirm or add to the other three; and fifth, embracing all the others, a shared appreciation of matters affecting the group and the individual's relation to the group in all matters essentially relevant to its continuance. The *result* of all this is a sense of belonging which is at least strong enough to make bearable the constraints involved in membership and at best sufficient to make membership an enhancement of the individual's personality.

It is no longer possible to regard a modern political society as a single cultural entity except for a few, usually important, purposes. It consists of a mass of subcultures some of which, such as membership of a scientific discipline or a profession, may establish more obvious links with fellow members in other political societies than with others under the same political allegiance. Indeed I find it convenient for some purposes to regard even individuals as subcultures of one. None the less any political society, like any other system, requires a sufficient sense of community to act as a whole to at least the minimum extent which its situation requires. And this requirement of a sense of community, contrary to widely and deeply held beliefs, is growing much more exacting, rather than less so.

The bonding of a society is evoked as well as revealed by the context in which it is tested. In Britain this bonding has been conspicuous in two world wars, although some critics argue that it was also weakened by both, especially by the first.[3] Both wars involved the effort to avert a perceived threat; and as I have already pointed out, the need to avert a perceived threat is different from and usually more cogent than the aspiration to attain a more desired state. German socialists were amazed in 1914 that British working men, instead of starting a revolution, flocked into the armed forces in such numbers as to render compulsory service unnecessary for a year.

The same sense of solidarity was even more marked in Britain during the Second World War, when the country achieved by 1941 and maintained a degree of economic and social mobilization not attained even by Germany until the latter part of the war. This combined the centralized direction of policy with diffused implementation to a degree seldom if ever attained by any totalitarian state. Nearly every civilian had a part-time, usually unpaid job, locally organized (such as watching for fires) in addition to his or her full-time work. The agricultural plan was implemented and monitored by local committees of farmers. Rationing of food and other materials was universal and so fully observed that black markets were virtually unknown. The production of luxuries ceased and the distribution of necessities was regulated with a firmness and accepted with a readiness which had no parallel before or since. The demand for all this was made obvious by air raids, submarine attacks on shipping, the economic and human demands of war and, especially before the entry of America in mid-1941, the sense of maintaining a virtually solitary struggle.[4] But demands are not necessarily met merely because they are obvious.

The cogency of aspirations, as distinct from apprehensions, was exemplified in the social legislation of 1946–1951. I shall be concerned with this in greater detail later as an example of changing standards of aspiration extending over more than a century. It is also worth recording that food rationing in Britain was increased in severity for some time after the war ended, as part of the Marshall Plan to relieve famine in Europe.

Large-scale responses to the need for regulative action are not unknown, but those which I have cited took place in a particular society at a particular time and they were closely associated with the high degree of consensus generated by war. It is conspicuously lacking in the same country thirty years later.

Yet it remains too obvious to ignore that even in peace – or the current state of less than total war – the dependence of the individual on the political state of which he is a member has increased to a degree at least comparable with that of the tribe studied by Driberg. The state – the Western 'democratic' state – plays a part without precedent in the regulation of internal as well as external relations. Internally it is expected to maintain the infrastructure of power, transport and all the physical and social structures of a crowded urban community; to redistribute income in cash and kind through health, welfare, education and other social services; to maintain full employment, stable money and a rising standard of living; and also to maintain its traditional functions of preserving order and enforcing law, both civil and criminal. Externally it is expected to preserve peace and a viable political and economic relationship with the other governments and peoples of the world, including an international monetary system (which as I write is lacking for the first time since gold was first minted).

This combination of expectations, though absurd, is fortified partly by the experience of two hundred years of Western ascendancy and partly by aspirations bred from three critiques, those of Adam Smith, Bentham and Marx, of the price which was paid for that ascendancy. One result is withdrawal of confidence from those chosen to deal with the situation, a withdrawal which of course makes them even more impotent than they would otherwise be. The bonding of contemporary Western societies is threatened as never before.

Footnotes

1. A. V. Dicey, in his classic, *Lectures on the Relation between the Law and Public Opinion in England*, (London, Macmillan, 1905) traced this mutual interchange through the nineteenth century. He was puzzled that he could find no honoured and famous names to account for the growing socializing trend which he detected in his own day – none at least to compare with those on which his own individualist assumptions were based.
2. T. H. Huxley, *Evolution and Ethics and Other Essays*, op. cit.
3. P. Fussell. *The Great War and Modern Memory*, Oxford, Oxford University Press, 1975.
4. The heroic and even more solitary struggle of the remote Finns, first against the USSR and then against Germany, is sometimes forgotten by those whose experience was confined to the beleaguered island of Britain. Unhappily the two remaining combatants were in no position to support each other directly.

CHAPTER 9

FOUR DIMENSIONS OF INSTABILITY IN HUMAN SYSTEMS

The relationships on which mankind depends fall into four groups – first, the relations of person to person; second, the relation of individual persons to each of the societies, large or small of which they form part; third, the relation of these groups to each other; and fourth, the relations of all of them to the resources of the planet on which they all depend.

These categories overlap to some extent, especially the first, the relationship of person to person, which permeates them all. For all human relations involve the interaction of persons; and even in the interaction of the largest societies the persons representing them often affect each other significantly for good or ill even though they are divided by role, culture and conflicting interests. (The personal relations of understanding and mutual trust between Lord Halifax when Viceroy of India and Mahatma Gandhi are a familiar historical example.) None the less it is useful to distinguish the four categories in seeking to understand the multiple instabilities which beset the contemporary world.

In the chapters which follow I will explore them and their interrelations so far as space permits. I want at this point only to summarize them in the briefest manner. I will focus on the culture which I know best and most directly, that of Britain, though I believe that what I have to say has some general application, despite the great cultural differences which divide even the countries of 'the West'.

The relations of person to person have been weakened by a narrowing of the area of mutual expectation so assured that it can be taken for granted by all those who are likely to meet and interact. This is partly because of increased mobility, including immigration; partly because of a weakening in the acceptance of agreed social roles; partly by the secularization of the culture and the associated eclipse of the ethical dimension; and partly by a heightened sense of individual consciousness. All these may have been partly offset by the increased exposure of all to one-way communication and to the reduction in outward signs of class and other distinctions, such as styles of clothing and speech. But on balance the tacit consensus which united Britain a hundred or even only fifty years ago seems to me to have been notably weakened. A further weakening of national consensus can be attributed to the corresponding rise in the dominance of loyalties to subsystems, notably occupational, which have become far less subject to constraint by general social bonds.

The relations of person to person cannot be clearly separated from the relations of person to group since all human relations except war (in whatever form) take place between persons who have some acknowledged group relations. Here the weakening of the bond has been largely due to the multiplication of groups making rival demands on their members, to the loss of traditional and accepted orders of priority among these claims, to the distrust of all such claims. Group bonds have also been weakened by the extraordinary belief that the world can accord to its members increasing freedom from constraints, but still be sufficiently orderly to survive.

The most important factor in the weakening of relationships has been the universal emergence of the nation state by a process almost wholly of fractionation and by the continuing pressure towards fractionation so manifest today. Thus the problems of stable relations between human systems today focus chiefly on the relations between nation states and the internal relations, within each of them, of the increasingly numerous organized groups and subcultures of which each consist. At each level, difficulties are accentuated by differences of culture, sometimes unsuspected and seldom fully understood, which limit, obscure or even destroy the possibility of communication.

PART II

Western Systems Since The Enlightenment

CHAPTER 10

REGULATING POLITICAL SYSTEMS: THREE DECAYING HOPES

To appreciate the three critiques mentioned in Chapter 8, which are associated with the names of Adam Smith, Bentham and Marx, as they have developed in the West over the past two hundred years, we need to take a summary view of the concepts of political regulation. It would, of course, be an impertinence to attempt any comprehensive review of these momentous movements in the space of a chapter, but it seems to me valid to extract from them the contrasting elements which are relevant to this book.

The first, and for long the most potent, was Adam Smith's vision of the market as an automatically self-regulating system. It seems strange to me that writers on the history of systemic thought seldom, if ever, begin with Adam Smith; for the free market is the largest, oldest and most fully developed essay in human self-regulating systems of which we have any knowledge and its history is sufficiently long and well documented for us to trace its development and the emergence both of its limitations and of its competitors. It is also highly modern in concept, for it relies wholly on the exchange of information.

According to the theory, a rise in price alerts suppliers to a shortage in the supply of something effectively demanded and at the same time promises increased reward for those who supply it. The supply rises, the shortage is abated, prices fall and entrepreneurs respond to other demands which have become more rewarding. The pursuit by buyers of the cheapest way to satisfy their changing wants automatically evokes the response by producers and sellers which is best calculated to provide that satisfaction, since it is also the way to maximize their profits. An unpredictable variety of wants evokes its own satisfaction by a process far more sensitive than any which could be comprehensively planned. Like the helmsman watching the rate and direction of deviance of the ship's head, the entrepreneur need not identify all the separate forces which occasion the deviance. The deviance itself, in this case the rise or fall of price, is sufficient to tell him where to intensify and where to reduce his effort. It is a message from his collective master the Consumer.

Thus stated, the theory, in the perspective of the 1980s, seems almost too naive to be useful. It assumes so much that has long ceased to be true. But it was not always so. It was a revolutionary concept that men should be equally free to satisfy their own wants in a world so designed that each could prosper only by excelling in satisfying the needs of other people. And it had implications extending far beyond the field of economics. A famous orator, in the passionate debate which led to the abolition of duties on grain imported into Britain, declared that the principles for which the Anti-Corn Law League was fighting were expressions of divine law. God had made the regions of the world with their diverse climates and resources to be complementary, not competitive. The Wealth of Nations was not a quantum to be fought for in a zero-sum game. It was indefinitely expansible by the cooperation of men. And this cooperation, marvellous to relate, did not depend on the altruistic care of each for others. A hidden hand ensured that each could enrich himself only by enriching others. The dazzling prospect of universal economic affluence, fortified by the dawning promise of science and technology, put politics into the receding background. The Prince Consort, opening the Great Exhibition in London in 1851, declared, 'Nobody who has paid any attention to the peculiar features of our present era will doubt for a moment that we are living in a period of most wonderful transition which tends rapidly to accomplish that great end to which all history points – the realization of the unity of mankind.'

These men were neither stupid nor insincere. They were dazzled by a new prospect which threw all others into the shade. It had been stated as early as 1760 by a French economist, Mercier de la Rivière, in words which reflect its inadequacy more clearly today than they did then. 'Humanly speaking the greatest happiness possible for us arises in the greatest possible abundance of objects suitable for our enjoyment and in the greatest liberty to profit by them.'

The unity of mankind was to be achieved through a Great Commercial Republic. It was to be self-regulating as well as self-exciting. But it depended on political conditions which required deliberate creation and enforcement. It required a world where contracts were equally enforceable by all and against all, and it needed to be fortified by a high degree of trust both by bargainers in each other and by all of them in the conditions which they assumed, notably the stability of money both internationally and intranationally. It assumed a market (including a labour market) in which both buyers and sellers were so numerous that variations in price were an outcome beyond the influence of any one of them. It assumed unlimited abundance of resources, so that nothing need influence the changing course of price signals except the relation between current supply and current demand for finished products. It assumed that the wants of consumers were beyond the manipulation of producers. I am not concerned here to assess the merits and limitations of the free market or its role in the world today. I am concerned with it only as an outstanding example of a human system which was designed to be self-regulating and which still plays an important part both in the regulation of human affairs and in the shaping of human ideologies and expectations.

Marx believed, no less than Adam Smith, in the possibility of a self-regulating human system; indeed he regarded it as ultimately inevitable: but his diagnosis was fundamentally different. Concerned with the inequality of distribution which he saw in his contemporary system, rather than with its increasing productivity, and identifying this inequality with the unequal distribution of property, he pinned his faith on the abolition of private property in the means of producing wealth. This, he was convinced, could not be done peaceably (except, conceivably, in a few societies). A violent revolution followed by a dictatorship of the proletariat was the inevitable road. But the goal was a state of automatic regulation as free from political interference as the goal of Adam Smith's. Freed from the causes of dissension implicit in private property, political government would involve no more than the administration of things.

The doctrines of Marx and of Adam Smith, though at daggers drawn, have much in common. Both are deterministic. Both are optimistic. Both are materialistic. Both anticipate that the state will ultimately 'wither away', though in different ways and for different reasons. And both reflect the assumption that human beings, if freed from the inequalities imposed on them by their inherited political and social institutions and relieved of want by the radiant promises of science and technology, will have no conflicts which 'reason' cannot resolve. In all these respects they reflect the ideology of the Enlightenment.

Both have changed greatly since their inception. Both have revealed limitations. Neither has yet been justified by history, though in this century Marx has won more recruits than Adam Smith and the Communist world now far outnumbers what can still be called the capitalist world. But both facts and ideologies have so changed that the old labels can no longer be confidently used. What is common to both is an enormous extension of the third political philosophy, mentioned earlier but not yet explored, the philosophy associated with the name of Jeremy Bentham.

Bentham published his *Fragment on Government*, the first statement of his position, in 1776, the same year in which Adam Smith published *The Wealth of Nations*. He was concerned with the power and with the criteria of good government. He insisted that the criterion of good government was not the aggrandisement of the state, still less of its rulers, but the happiness of its members – the greatest happiness of the greatest number. It was a principle at least as old as Marcus Aurelius but none the less daring in a world where Bourbons still ruled France and London provided subjects for the drawings of Hogarth. It was daring also in its aspirations; for Bentham believed in the power of legislation to shape a society's institutions and even its culture. He is the spiritual father of all social engineers though he would probably reject with passion any responsibility for the social engineering which today marks both the Communist and the non-Communist world – and all its intermediate forms. He is the most explicit originator of the proposition that the shape of a human society is a proper object of human design.

Through almost the whole of human history, as I have already mentioned, social order has been regarded as given and usually as God-given. This did not negate the possibility of social mobility by individuals. This could occur, at least as early (in England) as the sixteenth century, by Royal favour, by successful trade, or by buccaneering – or sometimes by a combination of all three. But the structure itself was commonly regarded as being almost as remote from man's control as his biological order. Scholars could write Utopias; but these approached realization only when propounded by successful revolutionaries.

The earliest serious attempt in England to create a social order is probably that recorded by Christopher Hill[1] in a book called *The World Turned Upside Down*, which consists largely of quotations from tracts and broadsheets published between 1640, when Cromwell's army attained sufficient control to abolish censorship of the printed word, and 1660 when censorship was reestablished on the accession of Charles II. The landed gentry who initiated, organized and won the revolutionary war, had clear and modest notions of the political rights which they wished to establish. But the rank and file of their army contained many whose imaginations roamed much more freely. I know no heresy, political, economic, social or religious, propagated by the 'counter-culture' in the headiest days after the Second World War which is not to be found in the revolutionary outpourings of those twenty years three centuries before. Yet no extensive measures were needed to frustrate them. None of these revolutionary outpourings gathered critical mass; and the bourgeois revolution rolled duly on to its remarkably successful conclusion in 1689.

None the less that revolution, restrained though it may seem to us now, was the culmination of a human design. A country which had killed one king, Charles I, driven out a second, James II, and engaged a third, William III, by something remarkably like a contract[2] could not fail to be seen as engaged in a major act of political design. And the complacency with which the inheritors of its benefits enjoyed them during the century which followed was not much greater than the interest and often admiration with which they were observed by exponents of change elsewhere in Europe.

But to the English it seemed a once-for-all affair. Few centuries in England have been more conservative than the eighteenth. It was not until after the American and French Revolutions and in the intoxicating atmosphere of the Enlightenment that the European mind began to accept the idea of human order as a continually developing design, the supreme though never to be completed work of human art. Fundamentally this view was to prove deeply at variance with the determinism of both Adam Smith and Marx. But the inconsistency was to be long concealed, for the self-regulating economy of Adam Smith did indeed need legislation to create and maintain the conditions for its existence and so did the creation and management of the revolution which was to lead to the classless society, even though it needed violent revolution as well. Moreover, even the potentially *dirigiste* implications of social engineering were masked by faith in the potency of the extending franchise. It is true that few if any of the politicians who voted for the Reform Act of 1832 realized that universal suffrage was implicit in the new criterion. (The 'greatest number' would surely insist in time in having a definitive say in what constituted their greatest happiness.) Yet it was implicit and the concept helped to give to representative democracy an element of 'automatic' regulation similar to that implicit in the free market. Did not politicians bid for the support of voters by a process essentially similar to that by which producers sought the support of consumers? In politics as in business the customer was king – and was always, by definition, right.

What has emerged two hundred years later in both Communist and non-Communist countries is a society regulated as never before by the deliberate decisions of centralized institutions and by the proliferation of rules governing the interaction of men with each other and with their institutions. In non-Communist countries the change is eloquently marked by the vast increase both in the number of government institutions and their staffs and in the volume of legislation. The attempt to stem this tide of centralized regulation, current, as I write this, in Britain, America, and to some extent elsewhere, is a testimony both to the force of the tide and to the ideology which it threatens.

In mid-nineteenth century the British Government had only twelve departments,[3] of which four were wholly concerned with external relations. (The Foreign Office, the Colonial Office, the War Office, and the Admiralty.) The Home Office was responsible for a mixed body of internal relations, including law and order. The only executive departments (apart from the Services) were the Post Office and the Inland Revenue. The Treasury, responsible for balancing the budget, claimed a say in all matters of policy, internal and external.

By 1953 there were about thirty departments of Government, the majority of them large administrative establishments employing from several hundred to many thousands of civil servants.[4] By 1969, after some years of intensive efforts to merge Government departments, there were still nine departments which did not exist in any separate departmental form sixty years before (Transport, Power, Housing and Local Government, Overseas Development, Technology, Economic Affairs, Employment and Productivity, Civil Service, and Welsh Office).[5] In addition, there were public agencies providing public services at the expense of the public, sometimes of the users and often both; and the local authorities, whose responsibilities had steadily increased. In 1976 the central Government employed 2.3 million people; this combined public sector employed almost 30 percent of the total labour force.[6] In that year, total UK Government expenditure was £58,481 million, that of the local authorities £16,792 million, and that of the public corporations £5,270 million; that is, the public sector disposed of some 65 percent of the gross national product.[7] The Government was responsible for redistribution in kind through the provision of services, such as health and education, the benefits of which fell in a pattern largely unrelated to the pattern of their users' contribution.

This gigantic machine operates, I think, more efficiently and less corruptly than far smaller public organizations have operated in the past. Yet it does not generate the confidence, still less the pride, which it might seem to deserve either among its beneficiaries or even among its providers. Indeed, as already mentioned, it is currently attacked as an overgrown if not cancerous development by a volume of opinion large enough to dominate a government.

The reason, I think, is the current disappointment of these three hopes, the market economy, utilitarianism and Marxism, separately and in any of their combinations. The area of automatic regulation by the market has manifestly shrunk to a point where it is inadequate to provide the minimum regulation needed even in the purely economic field. Equally, such transfer of wealth and power as has taken place from the haves to the have nots has not of itself eliminated problems of political regulation or even curbed the concentrations of greater power in fewer hands, though the dominant power holders today are corporations, unions, and pressure groups and their leaders, rather than rich men. And the residual hope that *deliberate* human design would supplement or even take over from a given social order, the product of history, has revealed its limitations so sharply as to hide even its own substantial but insufficient achievements.

But the two hundred years which have seen the rise and fall of these hopes have seen other changes, partly generated by the hopes themselves. The problems of political regulation which confront the world today are incomparably greater than those of two centuries ago. The most conspicuous change is in the dominant form of political societies themselves. It is useful to remind ourselves of these in however summary a fashion.

Footnotes

1. Christopher Hill. *The World Turned Upside Down*, London, M. T. Smith, 1972.
2. The wife of William of Orange became queen by right of succession; but her husband was not content with the status of a mere consort. England had no reason to regret that it made an exception in his favour.
3. Llewellyn Woodward. *The Age of Reform*, London, Oxford University Press, 1964.
4. S. Stout. *British Government*, Oxford, Oxford University Press, 1953.
5. J. A. Cross. *British Public Administration*, London, University Tutorial Press, 1970.
6. *Annual Abstract of Statistics*. London, HMSO, 1982.
7. Ibid.

CHAPTER 11

THE EMERGENCE OF THE NATION STATE

The most conspicuous type of human system today is the autonomous nation state. These, numbering about 160, divide dominion over the world's four billion people, the whole of its land area and an increasing area of its seabed. They vary in size of population from hundreds of millions to tens of thousands, and in resources actual and potential from immense abundance to gross deficiency. The autonomy even of the strongest of these nation states is qualified both by their dependence on some resources available only from outside their borders and by their cultural solidarity. Few of the categories we use embrace so wide a variety of members. Yet as a category it is of paramount importance and it is likely to remain so.

Most of these states were created during the last two hundred years and especially the last fifty years by the collapse of ten empires – Spain in South America, Portugal in South America and Africa; Austria in Europe; Turkey in Europe and the Levant; Holland in the Far East; Britain and France in Africa and Asia; Belgium, Germany and Italy in Africa. In addition four were formed by Western peoples colonizing the remaining areas of the world where the native inhabitants were too weak and too few to constitute a significant cultural force. Only two – Germany and Italy – were formed by fusion. Germany has been again split more radically than before by the fortunes of war, whilst Italy has barely yet forged an entity strong enough to dominate its former constituents. Most of the fissions have taken place with the aid of war and all have been approved and often actively supported by Britain, even whilst building her own empire on the grounds that 'free' men can only live in a 'free' country.

This principle was formulated as the principle of self-determination and rested on the assumption that the smaller group, thus 'self-determined', would 'govern itself' by processes of representative democracy which had been absorbed by the Western world with the force of a revelation, largely during the eighteenth and nineteenth centuries.

This principle of self-determination is still at work to promote further fissions among these states – even some of the smallest. For the coherence of the emergent states has depended on subtler historical and cultural continuities within them and often crossing their boundaries, continuities to which the much older word 'nation' is more appropriate. Some of these national continuities have emerged again after long periods of quiescence even within states which were formally created at a much earlier date, like the national consciousness of the Basques. Some national continuities have persisted through long periods of dismemberment, like the nationhood of Poland, or from periods before the concept of the state was clearly defined, like the Armenians.

The principle has also tested the assumptions which underlay the concept of representative democracy. These have not survived this test very well. Many even of the smallest states are governed by dictatorships, usually provided by the Army as the only well-organized force in the country. Others, even the largest, have become progressively less governable as more and more special interest groups have developed power and the will to use it in their own interest, irrespective of that of other constituents in the system. Among these special interest groups economic class interest has a dominant but increasingly confused place.

The only impressive exception to the fissiparous trend has been the Soviet Union, embracing a number of nations within its own borders and several powerful and industrially developed states within its sphere of influence if not control; a new form of imperialism the future of which I will not try to forecast here.

It is fashionable to decry the importance of the nation state as being a new but already outmoded form of organization, too large for some of its problems and too small for many others; a barrier to 'rational' organization and a breeder of war. The criticisms are valid, but the problems remain. There has always been an ultimate focus of authority, be it tribe, empire, feudal lord or nation state.[1] The tiny tribe studied by Driberg was as autonomous as Britain or USA – more so, indeed, since its autonomy rested on a stronger inner coherence.

The tendency towards indefinite subdivision is perfectly understandable in systemic terms. The fission of a political entity turns intrasystemic strains into intersystemic conflicts, and the second may or may not be both more bearable and more negotiable than the first. Factual interdependence is welcome only so long as psychological interdependence makes it so.

Beyond that point it is easier to regard it as external constraint, a subject for bargain, even for battle but not for welcome, least of all as personal enrichment.

The trend towards fission is not inherently self-limiting though it is self-defeating. It has been monstrously magnified by the individualism of the Enlightenment. It was further fuelled by the antisocial trend of the 'scientific management' of organizations as first proclaimed by F. W. Taylor; and it reaches its ultimate absurdity at the level of the individual and often divided self, which I examine in the next two chapters.

I will return later to examine in more detail the extravagances of individualism and the relation between personal liberty and social order in an overcrowded world consisting largely of human relations. Meantime let us recall that from the earliest beginnings of recorded time, belong-ing to a political society has been a basic element in the nature of social, cultural man. It remains true that the pattern of belonging has grown bewilderingly complex. As MacIntyre[2] has pointed out in his *Short History of Ethics*, in the society mirrored by the Homeric poems the word we translate as virtue (arete) meant the successful performance of a defined role, whether king or shepherd. Society was structured by well-defined complementary roles, performance in which was judged by equally well-defined criteria and which seldom conflicted with each other. It is not surprising that in such societies the obligations of membership were seldom questioned and the rights of membership highly prized. Today's politico-fiscal units, all formally nation states, are supported in very varying degrees by traditions of nationhood carried over from earlier days. But few if any of them have the political coherence of earlier and simpler societies. Few Western political societies have even the degree of coherence which they had seventy years ago.

The right of self-determination has its counterpart in the right of free association. Political societies have of course always included subsystems, often powerful foci of loyalty. Social and occupational subdivisions were common and the two were usually linked and distinguished by varying degrees of power and prestige, which were reflected in their influence on the government of the societies which included them. And in Europe, if not elsewhere, the higher class divisions sometimes transcended national frontiers, as did the academic and the religious establishments. But during the past two hundred years such subsystems have vastly extended in both variety and power. Among those which are presently potent, chiefly within the borders of a single state, the most conspicuous have been the trade unions, an expression which, in Britain at least, includes most professions including all levels of the Civil Service. They have organized themselves to exercise both political and industrial power; and at the time when I write this they are embarrassed to the point of fission by developing inconsistency between the two objectives.

But trade unions are only the most conspicuous example of a strong drive towards the creation of multiple single-interest groups. As these groups develop, conflict is bound to be generated both within each group, since no single interest can be wholly homogeneous, between one group and another, and between each group and such general interest systems as exist, since no single interest can be wholly indifferent to all the others.

By general interest systems I mean societies possessing governments to which is accorded the ultimate legitimate power of regulation, and also their subsystems of local government however much devolved. A Swiss commune, a New England township, even an English parish council are general interest systems in this sense, no less than their state governments, and are equally required to take decisions involving the choice between different courses which satisfy disparate interests in varying degrees. A national government, for example, has no built-in priorities which determine whether a few marginal millions of resources shall be given to or lopped off from education or transport or defence; and local governments have similar problems within their more limited scope.

The distinction between general interest and single-interest associations is not so sharp as the words imply, because even general interest groups have limitations, constitutional or practical, which exclude some fields from their regulation, whilst even the most blinkered of the single-interest groups must sometimes admit more than one criterion into their calculations. But the distinction is none the less important if only because of the different formal definition of responsibility which each involves. The two can even be seen in conflict within a single government organization. For nearly all governments are organized in departments for action within a specified field, and these are to this extent single-interest organizations, whilst nearly all important policies involve action in several fields. It is not easy to reconcile the machinery for functional action with the machinery for policy making, and efforts to do so form a substantial part of the history of recent political organization. None of these efforts has yet been wholly successful.[3]

Footnotes

1. Though not always a unifying force, the sharing of secular and religious authority in Europe from at least the time of Charlemagne seems to me to have been remarkably useful in mitigating universal claims by either church or state.
2. A. MacIntyre. *A Short History of Ethics*, London, Routledge & Kegan Paul, 1967.
3. The most promising experiment of which I know was begun by the Canadian province of Ontario in the 1960s. The heads of all func-tional ministries were excluded from the Cabinet. Cabinet members, all 'without portfolio', presided over committees of functional ministers. They had no power to impose a settlement. Any dissentient could take his case to the full Cabinet. But the move was calculated to change the ambitions of politicians, making them aspire to Cabinet positions where important policy was made rather than to the more conspicuous roles associated with leadership of an executive but functional department. I do not know the present status of this experiment. It could only succeed over a period of time long enough to influence the behaviour of a new generation of those who would become senior statesmen. Seen in that perspective, it seemed to me possible that it might chart a successful middle course between two British experiments neither of which had adequately achieved its purpose. One of these was the 'Overlord', chairman indeed of Cabinet committees but no match for his colleagues, the heads of the great spending departments, who were also by tradition in the Cabinet. The other was the mammoth functional department which internalized some of what would otherwise have been Cabinet issues but did nothing radical to reconcile the divergent scope of policy making and departmental action.

CHAPTER 12

THE EMERGENCE OF THE AUTONOMOUS INDIVIDUAL

In the previous chapter I pointed out that politically autonomous states have multiplied during the last two hundred years, largely by acts of fission initiated by what were previously parts of larger systems; and that this process of fission is still continuing. Something similar has occurred over the same period at the level of the individual. The quest for individual autonomy has developed to a degree unknown before even in the West. The result has been, I think, more loss than gain.

The autonomy sought alike by states, groups and individuals is basically the same. It is freedom from the obligation to accept as given the decisions of other groups and other individuals. Submission to natural laws is still accepted as inevitable, though grudgingly, since technology has found so many ways to escape their most unwelcome effects. But submission to the judgements of others has become almost synonymous with weakness and subservience.

On the face of it this seems a singularly inept response to the obvious situation and trend of our time; for the dependence of men on each other is clearly greater than it has ever been and is obviously bound to become greater still. Each individual depends on others more and more for the basic necessities of life as well as for nearly all its amenities. Each therefore depends more on others for the faithful performance of their roles and should expect that their dependence on him and the faithful playing of his role will be correspondingly increased. This interdependence is further increased by the multiplication of human numbers and by the shadow of scarce resources. The shadow of scarcity far precedes the impact of actual scarcity and is cast by the increase of costs, which may itself imply no more than increased effort to achieve the same result. Even if OPEC did not exist, the cost of extracting oil from the bed of a stormy ocean would far exceed the cost of pricking the Pennsylvanian soil for it only a little more than a hundred years ago.

None of this will surprise a mind attuned to the simplest elements of systemic thinking. Every organization (system) imposes constraints on its constituents as well as conferring enablements; and no constituent can long enjoy the second without accepting the first. Citizens who enjoy the complex infrastructure of a modern state – physical (roads, power); social (education, health); judicial (the law, the courts, the police); pay for them not only in cash by direct and indirect taxation but also by accepting the constraints which all of them necessitate, such as the discipline of safe driving. And most of those who try to enjoy the benefits without paying the costs will find themselves in trouble.

The price mounts with the benefits. Not only are roads today incomparably more expensive than they were a hundred or even fifty years ago, they are also far more crowded and make greater demands on the patience as well as the skill of those who use them. No doubt every system can support a certain number of parasites and predators among its own constituents. And the greater its self-confidence, the higher it can afford to raise the threshold of its tolerance of deviance. But an upper limit there must always be.

Why then the widespread reluctance to accept the constraints involved in our way of life whilst insisting on a set of enablements never dreamed before? There are, I think, several reasons which need to be widely understood.

One is unfamiliarity with systems thinking. Gregory Bateson[1] thought that systems thinking is itself 'counter-intuitive', a form of thought not naturally congenial to the human mind. I am not persuaded that this is so; but it is certainly counter to the Western technological culture of the last two hundred years, in which success has been so closely identified with the attaining of a given 'end' by the most economic means. I have suggested elsewhere[2] that systemic thinking could and should be taught and practised in primary and secondary schools, so that the young at the threshold of adult life would be familiar with the concept of regulation and of the manifold costs and benefits inherent in any systemic reorganization.

The success of technological culture by its own standards has also helped to confirm in the Western mind the absurd beliefs that there is a technological fix for everything and that this need have no costs other than the spending of resources in carrying it out.

A more subtle but equally important factor (already mentioned) is that the mutual relations of persons in a role-playing relationship are mainly not reciprocal but complementary. Parent and child, teacher and student, doctor and patient, do not have identical expectations of each other. Their expectations are complementary. So are those of workers who perform different operations in industry. The difference does not always imply a difference of status or dominance. The three shifts in traditional 'long wall' coal-mining depend heavily each on the one before but none of the three is superior in status. And even where difference of status is involved, responsibility for action, and usually also competence for action, is distributed in a manner unrelated to status. The designer of a new machine depends for its realization on skills which he is unlikely to possess to anything like the same extent as the fitters in the toolroom. The pilot of an incoming plane obeys the directions of ground control as promptly as any new recruit obeying orders on a parade ground, but he does not feel like a servant. There are still services in which people feel it is ennobling to serve. And even where one party goes to another for the sake of his special skill, the role of the expert is not necessarily the dominant role. Solicitors call those who seek their services 'clients'; but the clients regard themselves and are regarded far more as patrons.

None the less past history has attached immense importance to the concept of equality and corresponding distrust to any relationship in which, for whatever reason, overtones of dominance and superior status attach to one side of the relation rather than the other. The attitude is understandable for there are indeed rights and responsibilities which are both identical and reciprocal and they are rightly regarded with special sensitivity. These are the attitudes such as honesty, respect, and compassion which are regarded as due to human beings as such by other human beings. They have often been ignored or underrated in the past. They need special protection. But they are not all that is involved in the performance of role or even the most important part.

It would be misleading, however, to ignore the fact that complementary relations often necessarily involve an element of dominance in the role of one party. What at one level is a matter of policy decision becomes for other levels a datum to be accepted. And whatever is done to ensure that 'lower' levels contribute their advice, especially on aspects which are clearer to them than to those with the actual responsibility for decision, that responsibility cannot be wholly devolved. This, in today's context, provides two further reasons why decisions today are less readily accepted by would-be autonomous subordinates.

One reason is the fact that as interdependence widens and intensifies, decisions are required in fields which habit has not yet made acceptable. Planning is a case in point.

Another and more serious reason is that authority can no longer claim the legitimacy which tends to follow success. On the contrary, all persons in authority – policy makers, planners, administrators, legislators, teachers, scientists in the human and social fields, and even technologists – are increasingly seen by those who should be their beneficiaries as dealing with problems which they do not understand, with problems which they cannot solve, or as exercising powers of which they cannot predict the outcome. Many of these problems are in fields which until recently no one expected 'authorities' of any kind to control, but that does not abate the loss of confidence generated by their failure to control them now. Conspicuous examples are inflation, unemployment, the fear of war and the disappointment of dreams of ever increasing affluence. I shall be concerned in the last part of this book with the very limited possibilities offered by an overcrowded earth to its human systems to revise their contemporary pattern in a way compatible with their survival.

The mistrust of complementary relationships is fatal to the effective performance of a role by either party and hence to the effective working of any organization, since all depend on the trust by each in the faithful role playing of all the others. This resistance to reliance on role, or even to the playing of role, has developed as a protest against inequality of status in those organizations into which people are born, notably the nation state, or from which they cannot in fact opt out. Resistance to role playing is at least equally acute in those large organizations for business, politics, educational, or other purposes which individuals join voluntarily but from which they cannot later exclude themselves without loss of some kind. (The 'self-employed' person becomes an exception, as is so clearly implied by this extraordinary name which has become attached to his position.) Nothing could be more fatal to the working of any human system. The fact that resistance to role playing has grown as the need for it has increased raises the question whether we are indeed biologically incapable of supporting organizations on the scale on which we have now come to depend, especially in a future where their costs must become both greater in total and more widely spread. But such speculations are fruitless except in so far as they focus anxiety on the most critical threat of our age.

The trend has another equally serious implication in its effect on the individual. Although it does not necessarily lead to anomy and alienation, it has a bearing on these modern psychological disorders which is worth exploring. If organizations cannot make up their minds acceptably, why should individuals hope to do better? The human psyche is also a system and one not designed for isolation. The exploration of that I will defer to the next chapter. I will close this one by a very summary examination of the recent history of human thought concerning the relation of man and society.

This focused largely on political society before the great organizations of trade and industry claimed attention as another branch of social organization. I have already observed that for most of human history, social and political order was regarded in the West as given and usually as God-given. Since it became an acceptable subject for human analysis, a very wide variety of speculation has been expressed about it; and this has naturally been closely associated with speculation about the individuals who were thus ordered.

For Hobbes man was an animal so aggressive and destructive to his own kind that the emergence of order could be due to a surrender of some personal autonomy for the sake of self-protection. Even the threat of the Leviathan state was preferable to the threat represented by his neighbours. I think Hobbes was right in his belief that if put to the extreme test most human beings will prefer tyranny to anarchy. But his views were too sombre for the age ushered in by the Enlightenment. For Rousseau, men were corrupted only by their institutions. If not so perverted, they would find full satisfaction in participating in that baffling abstraction, the General Will. Marx also put the blame on institutions in the wider sense, the institution of property. And for Adam Smith, as I have already noted, the market was not only a better regulator in its own field than any conscious device but also a very comprehensive one, a view which was to expand still further as technology made good its promises of the abundance of 'objects suitable for our enjoyment'.

These, however, were by no means the only or perhaps the dominant view of political institutions in the West in the nineteenth century. The traditional power structure was being altered in ways which excited enthusiasm even more than resentment and in some countries widespread satisfaction. In Britain the extension of the franchise was a change of both practical and symbolic importance and the country's political institutions were a source of pride. A responsible executive, an elected legislature, and an independent judiciary seemed to many to have solved the age-old problem of making power accountable without emasculating it. And J. R.

Seeley,[3] a well-informed historian writing in the 1860s, could enumerate with pride the large-scale inhumanities which had been eliminated by what he called the Enthusiasm for Humanity and attributed to the influence of the Christian ethic. Moreover, the legislature increasingly assumed the role of designer as Bentham had encouraged it to do and expressed the society's collective humanity by a century of legislation developing from the first controls of the conditions of labour to the massive assault on Beveridge's 'five giant evils' which was expressed in the social legislation of 1945–1951.

To put it in another way, not contradictory but at least complementary, the distribution of wealth in cash and kind has become a highly political, rather than an economic, issue and has virtually monopolized the political attention of that 'greatest number' to whom politicians are now responsible. Nor has it satisfied them. Those Britons who remember the years immediately following the First World War and can compare them with the years immediately following the second, will compare with pride the second response with the first. The social legislation of the second period was widely felt to be an achievement deserving satisfaction and pride. Yet it did not yield, either to its providers or to its beneficiaries, the abiding sense of fulfilment which might have been expected; and through the 1970s it fell into disrepute sufficiently striking to be reflected dramatically at election times. No doubt this was due partly to the fact that it led the public to expect from governments more than governments can do – or at least more than governments can do without greater cooperation by the governed than they dare ask for or would expect to get. But whatever the cause, and despite great efforts to present its benefits as 'rights', the acceptance of which did not reduce the citizens' 'autonomy', it produced in the public mind neither a comfortable image of the state nor a comfortable relation between the state and the citizens who were its beneficiaries. The main cause, according to the late Professor Robson,[4] was that the culture of the society did not change as fast as its institutions. A Welfare State can function successfully only in a Welfare Society.

The attitude of the citizen to the state has reverted almost to the position of Rousseau. The United Nations has produced declarations of Human Rights and Children's Rights not merely to protect them from the tyranny of the state but also to enshrine as rights the aspirations born of two decades of prosperity. No one outside the Communist world has produced Declarations of Duties defining the wider responsibilities which have fallen on the governed by the simple increase of their systemic interdependence with each other and which alone can create the rights so glibly asserted. Responsible writers still define 'liberty' as freedom to do anything which does not interfere with the freedom of another, knowing full well that no one can do anything without impinging on countless others for both good and ill. Futurists from Skinner in *Walden II* to Toffler in *The Third Wave* depict a future in which individuals enjoy a life unstructured by anything but their own whims, a state of community without consensus which no epoch has ever enjoyed and which few would desire for themselves or others unless they were in acute reaction against an era of most rigid regimentation – which they certainly are not.[5]

Or are they? I have argued that interdependence inevitably brings its constraints as well as its enablements. Have the changes of the last two hundred years – and especially of the last sixty years – been too violent and far reaching for two generations to absorb?

It may be so; for the major characteristic of our time is that the environment of every human being, especially in the industrialized West, has become far more an environment of men than an environment of 'nature' and correspondingly an environment far harder for would-be autonomous men to bear with equanimity or to manipulate without conflict.

We can discern three major stages in the concept of 'adaptability'. In the first, human societies supported themselves by adapting to the natural environment which was available for their support, as other creatures do. In the second, they began to adapt that environment to themselves and thereby changed the relatively constant factor by reference to which they had defined their own successful response. Thereafter every change would require further change and ever faster change because the world, constantly changed but never 'mastered', still less controlled, would pose an endless series of new questions, demanding further adaptation, not merely in the environment but in the society which would not let it alone long enough to learn to live in it. But as this process developed, empty space filled up, multiplying men became each other's environment and each society tried to adapt the others to its needs as they had formerly adapted the forests and the prairies. Of course the natural resources are for the most part still there though their rate of erosion is increasing and in many cases approaching critical levels. But apart from this, an even more rapid change has led to their being more closely incorporated in would-be autonomous human systems. Everyone exists only by the grace and favour of other men, some in the same society, some far removed; all linked –

though by no means united – by the fact that nearly all are vital parts of someone else's environment.

So it is possible that the passion for individual autonomy does indeed signal a valid sense of threat from human dominance little different in kind or degree from that from which the Enlightenment claimed to set men free.

The fact remains that people have to learn to live if they can in a world in which they form each other's environment to an extent never known before. And this raises two problems which have not yet been solved and which may be insoluble but which are fundamental to the continuance of human life on earth. One is the problem of sustaining a sufficient degree of personal autonomy without foundering in a sea of alienation and rival pursuits of the new ideal of authenticity. The other is the problem of creating a sufficient community of culture to support such an interdependent world without weakening diverse existing cultures so much as to make nations, classes and even individuals even less comprehensible to each other than they are now. I conclude this part of the book with notes on these two threats to the future level of human systems and indeed to their continued existence.

Footnotes

1. An opinion expressed at a conference held by the Wenner Gren Anthropological Foundation in 1969, in a paper which so far as I know has not been published.
2. G. Vickers. 'Education in Systems Thinking', *Journal of Applied Systems Analysis*, vol. 7, April 1980.
3. J. R. Seeley. *Ecce Homo*, (first published London, 1866) London and New York, Everyman Library, vol. 305, 1908.
4. W. Robson. *Welfare State and Welfare Society*, London, Allen & Unwin, 1976.
5. Professor John Buchanan, in his presidential address to the American Anthropological Society, added his authority to the belief that a society can be sustained by a transient sequence of largely informal single-interest groups. Neither he nor the other authorities he quotes seems to realize that human systems are sustained not by the pursuit of successive goals attainable once for all or even by the once-for-all avoidance of specific threats but by the increasing regulation of relationships varied by changes, sometimes designed, more often unconscious, in the standards of relationship which are to be deemed acceptable.

CHAPTER 13

AUTONOMY, ALIENATION, AND AUTHENTICITY

The demand for greater personal autonomy does not spring from any increased sense of ability for responsible choice. On the contrary, the excessive weight of personal responsibility which Western, and perhaps especially British, society attached to the individual up to the beginning of this century has been immensely abated. Criminals and sinners have largely become patients and victims – sufferers from psychopathological states which are themselves usually attributed to the defects of society. On the other hand, as already noted, society, seen increasingly as a man-made system, is correspondingly regarded as responsible for any individual human defects which can be attributed to it. In consequence the focus of moral indignation has shifted from individuals as such to the society which they constitute and especially to those individuals who have public roles to play in that society. As Michael Polanyi [1] pointed out in many of his writings, there is plenty of moral passion around, perhaps too much; but it has been displaced – 'inverted' is his description – from the individual on to society and its representatives.

This could not happen in a homogeneous society; and even in societies as heterogeneous as those of the West today it can only happen partially and by grace of that tolerance of inconsistency which so happily protects the limited human mind. It divides the critics of a society's mores into two camps. On the one hand are those who recognize, however imperfectly, that these mores are a collective work of art to which they have the duty as well as the right to contribute. On the other hand are those who can see society only as a limitation on their self-hood and mistrust or reject any standards which are attributable to it. The first, that social mores are a collective responsibility, is much the older tradition and much the less offensive to the conformist. In consequence the intensity of the conflict which arises when social norms are challenged depends not only on the importance attached to the norm which is being criticized but also to the attitude which is attributed to the challenger.

Not every culture is yet regarded as a collective work of art to which any member has a right and duty to contribute; and all societies draw a line somewhere to define the limits of the debatable, though it is a line which many change with time. But where a member's deviance by word or deed is recognized as intended to be criticism or contribution, he is usually acknowledged, at least in principle, to be exercising his autonomy in a legitimate way, even though it be shocking and offensive to the majority. Individuals who campaigned for equality of civil rights in America in the 1950s were usually accorded this status, if only in principle and they certainly deserved to be.

Such 'principled' protests may be of four kinds. They may insist, as did the proponents of civil rights, that rights already acknowledged in principle are not being accorded in practice. Second, they may insist that acknowledged rights should be replaced by others regarded by the proponents as more just, as for example did the British Parliament when it extended the suffrage to women. Third, they may insist that matters which have hitherto been regarded as needing public regulation should be left to individual judgement, as did the British Parliament when it abolished restrictions based on religious conviction and later ceased to penalize homosexuality or suicide. And fourth, they may insist that areas previously left to individual judgement be publicly regulated, as the British Labour Party aspires to abolish the citizen's right to educate his children privately.

Of course changes of law do not usually effect immediate and corresponding changes in the culture but they provide clear-cut examples of the process of change, often linked with the name of some 'deviant' who promoted them. For example, many causes combined to favour the abolition of slavery in British dominions but few people would be satisfied with an explanation which wholly omitted the name of Wilberforce.

The four kinds of deviance which I have described are continually at work in the much larger area of a society's culture which is not regulated by law but is, none the less, powerfully affected by the other bonding forces described in Chapter 8, notably the pressure of all those forms of public influence to which the dissenter is sensitive.

When 'principled' deviants promote their courses by illegal methods, as they increasingly do, they compromise their status as legitimate contributors to their culture, since they are at least trying to exercise a power greater than their society's constitution allows them. At one extreme of this spectrum we may place the decorous Welsh proponents of the disestablishment of the Church of England in Wales, who early in this century drew attention to their cause by going to prison for refusing to pay rates due to the Established Church. Gandhi did something similar a few decades later by his technique of peaceful disobedience. From them a continuous spectrum runs through protests of varying degrees of violence to revolutions with or without civil war and so to the urban guerrilla movements which are a feature of our time. However, even at their lowest level guerrilla movements are distinguishable from the other form in which individual autonomy may be asserted, that is, rejection of all social standards.

This alternative form finds an absolute antithesis between the freedom of choice claimed by the individual and the claim of society to establish *any* rules or norms of judgement for its individual members or any of them. I have already pointed out that this assertion is incompatible with life in an interdependent world and that its emphasis today may be due to a dawning sense that the freedom of individual choice, which has been loudly acclaimed as an achievement by the industrial West, may in fact prove to be its first casualty. I want in this chapter to explore some of the more extreme expressions of this second claim and their inevitable results; on the one hand, alienation from every society which claims its members' loyalty (as all to some extent must do); on the other hand, the replacement of the old ideal of an individual as a well-integrated character by the ideal of chaotic self-expression in the name of 'authenticity'.

This can best be done by selecting some extreme cases.

The Marquis de Sade is a classic example of a man who claimed autonomy in the second sense. He claimed explicitly and proudly to have rooted out everything in his nature which might interfere with his 'enjoyment'; and he identified his enjoyment with the satisfaction of whatever passions happened to move him in any particular circumstances. It is noteworthy that even the Marquis de Sade claimed that his personality was a self-made work of art. Rival criteria might have been imposed on him by the standards of his society or of religion, or even by some inborn standards other than those which he chose to cultivate. He gave his name to a type of conduct and personality which is widely loathed and regarded as a vice or a pathological deformity, and which few wish to emulate. But there is no doubt that *he thought* he was exercising autonomous choice; and those who study such characters have to explain the deliberate quality of their acts as it appears to them.

Several other types of persons who have claimed autonomy in the second sense have appeared in West European literature in the last two centuries. The most recent is existential man as he appears in some of the writings of Sartre and other existentialists (though not of Camus). Accepting individual choice as a fact of experience but finding no source for its criteria except the norms laid down by a given society for its own convenience, the extreme existentialist can find no basis for authentic action except the purely arbitrary. Sartre portrays a character who kills a total stranger simply to prove that he is capable of 'authentic' action. To one who has drawn so total a division between self and society it is natural that 'playing a role' should symbolize the opposite of free – and therefore authentic – choice. Yet the concept of role playing has been essential to all the human societies of which we have any record and its erosion by the concept of authenticity over the last two centuries has played a significant part in defeating both their government and their capacity for self-government.[2]

Moreover, as the existentialists discovered, if society is wholly discounted as a valid source of ethical criteria, it becomes impossible to find any 'authentic' alternative, at least above the level of the Marquis de Sade.

A third type, created by Diderot[3] during the latter part of the eighteenth century, accepts role playing as essential to maintaining a human society but views society with its bundle of roles as a worthless and contemptible creation. The individual who wants to be his authentic self can do so best by exploiting his society through the many opportunities open to the role player (who must by definition be trusted to some extent and therefore given opportunities for fraud). The character who thus glories in being an authentic con-man is called Rameau's Nephew. Diderot, though he left this manuscript long unpublished, does not treat his character with the severity we might expect; on the contrary, he gives us leave, in Lionel Trilling's[4] words to 'take him to our hearts'. No doubt he felt that the *ancien régime* on which the nephew preyed deserved nothing better than a predator.

In the middle of the nineteenth century Nietzsche was to extol another model of authenticity. His Superman was indeed to make himself at the cost of the world which he would dominate. The shackles of morality were not for him.

Freud also described society as providing a valid reason for individual human discontent, rather than as the field in which individuals might become human. But although Professor Rhinelander,[5] in his analysis of the 'models of man' which thinkers have offered us over the last century, classified Freudian man as driven rather than swayed by any human choice, I think we must allow him a measure of autonomy in that he can to some extent change himself by bringing his hidden drives to consciousness. Even so, it remains to be explained how he chooses to reconcile the conflicting demands of biological urge and socially introjected inhibition. Ego psychology today allows the self something more than a mere broker's part in reconciling the demands of its 'three hard masters'.

Some have unkindly found room for authentic choice even in the conditioned man depicted by B. F. Skinner – or at least in one of them; for who will decide how the rest of the world shall be conditioned? Either Professor Skinner escapes his own net and becomes a Nietzschean superman or some process of mutual conditioning and self-conditioning must exist and await an analysis which Professor Skinner has not yet given us – but which is, none the less, part of our direct experience.

All these types are marked by their authors' inability to find any criteria other than suspect social rules for the ethical criteria which they use. There is a far longer and larger set of traditions which allows these norms a valid ontological status and finds it either in the will of God or in the nature of the cosmos or of the world, or even in human nature. One of the earliest is to be found in the Hindu scripture, the Bhagavad Gita,[6] in which at the beginning of a dynastic battle, the warrior Arjuna questions whether it is right for him to fight in a battle in which he may well kill many respected kinsmen. The god, Krishna, disguised as his charioteer, points, amongst other reasons, to his duty as a member of the warrior caste, to fight when fighting is required and to leave the outcomes to Karma. The argument runs as it must have run in thousands of American homes during the days of the Vietnam draft, except that Krishna's arguments seem to me even weaker than those which were available to proponents of doubtful wars on countless occasions between the two dates so vastly removed in time and circumstances.

The effort to distinguish 'just' from 'unjust' wars beset the Christian church for centuries and was renewed on an intercultural stage in the attempt, extended over forty years first in the League of Nations and later in the United Nations to reach an agreed definition of aggression. That was a fruitful debate in that it reduced the concept to four irreconcilable forms, each dependent on its own set of assumptions.

In the Bhagavad Gita Krishna prevails, not by the logical force of his arguments but by silencing objection when he revealed his divine nature.

This situation, the clash of moral values, is of course the stuff of tragedy and tragedy can exist only when recognized and accepted values conflict. The Greek tragedians developed the theme obsessively. European and American history supplies endless examples. The clash may be between two civic loyalties or two religious loyalties, or between a civic and a religious loyalty such as the one which led Sir Thomas More to execution. But there is an important though subtle difference between two views of 'the right'. In the one the right path is defined by the fiat of authority. In the other, the authority's decision, however much respected, must be confirmed by the inward assent of the individual conscience, that is to say by those criteria which proponents of this view believed to be innate but capable of development in the individual psyche and capable, in the course of their development, of criticizing the authority which was developing them.

This belief in the individual's inherent power to distinguish between good and evil, especially in specific contexts, or at least his duty to try to do so – has not been undisputed even in the Judaeo-Christian West. Mediaeval churchmen argued with deep seriousness whether the will of God was good by definition or was good because a good God could not will other than the Good. For Aquinas, the human reason unquestionably included the power of ethical as well as factual and logical discrimination. At that level the argument may seem unreal to us now; but it is real enough when it reappears at the level of human authority. Exponents of Natural Law found its source in the nature of things and notably in human nature. The framing of codes of international human rights testifies to the view that whatever differences may legitimately exist between cultures, there are some fields in which human beings are believed to have – or sense a desperate need to create – rights as human beings. This renewed concern with Natural Law may be regarded as an exercise in discovery or invention or design but it seems to be potent, if not always for good. It found dramatic illustration in the Nuremberg trials and perhaps even more in the later trial of Eichmann. Eichmann was not excused his lack of autonomy because he was acting only under orders. On the other hand Hitler was not excused his policy merely because it was an exercise of autonomy.

The concept of Natural Law is finding its way back into human consciousness very slowly and uncertainly but sufficiently to attract the attention of jurists. The concept of natural justice has never been wholly eclipsed and is also a subject of livelier debate. For example, the principle that an accused person should be allowed to speak in his own defence is accepted in most contemporary systems of jurisprudence as 'natural', that is, logically implied by the concept of justice.

The real situation seems to me relatively clear. The ethical dimension is a cultural and therefore an intersubjective creation. It is, none the less, universal in scope though not in content because human beings are never found outside the influence of some culture. Different cultures may vary so widely in their ethical imperatives that it is hard to find any common denominator. Some more than others nourish a half-acknowledged admiration for the freedom of the ethical anarchist; but even this is mild and shallow when compared with the cogency of the culturally admired type. And even between two divergent cultures, members of the one can usually understand the structure of the other when it is explained to them, even though they may compare it unfavourably with their own.

Ruth Benedict,[7] for example, in her classical study of Japanese culture, explains the enormous gulfs which separate it both from the American and to a less extent even from the Chinese from which it so largely sprang. For example, according to her analysis, an act of benevolence done to another by one who is under no obligation to him is likely to be felt as a burden, even an outrage. For it leaves the beneficiary under an obligation which he may have no means of repaying, still less any wish to repay. It is an unfamiliar attitude to most people bred in the Judaeo-Christian tradition where the obligation on the recipient to repay *to the giver* what is freely given is not normally felt as a burden; but it is not at all incomprehensible. Indeed, extreme examples of the giver who will not receive are recognized and resented in Western cultures also.

The ethical dimension as an intersubjective cultural artefact, is a structure of largely tacit standards slowly built and changed and more quickly eroded by the activities of human lives. These are themselves partly shaped but not wholly determined by the conditions which a society must satisfy to keep alive. But they are also active agents in their own growth and change as well as in their resistance to change. This ambivalent effect makes the course of history hard to predict, but not hard to understand.

Consider an example already given. At the beginning of the century few men and not many women in England thought that women should be entitled to vote. The demand that they should, however widely rejected at first, raised to the level of conscious debate what had before been an almost unexamined assumption. The debate was passionate and inflamed until the outbreak of the First World War. After that war women were accorded the vote without rancour and almost without debate. Their participation in the war effort had changed the perception of their social role in the minds of both men and women. But it is at least debatable whether this would have changed attitudes to women's suffrage to the same extent if earlier assumptions had not already been shaken by the agitation of the prewar years.

Similarly if we ask why attitudes embodied in British social legislation in 1946–1951, especially as regards unemployment insurance, were so free from the intense passions generated by the first mild and tentative moves of the Liberal administration between 1906 and 1914, we can attribute it partly to changed perceptions of class derived from two world wars and the intervening depression. But we cannot dissociate those changes from the endless discussion of them which filled the interim period. The shift of political power to Labour may explain the course of the legislation but it does not explain the change of perception which over the period had emerged in the population, irrespective of party, and especially in the generation which had acceded to the seats of power.

Surely people would not spend so much time seeking to persuade each other if they did not have some ground for thinking that communication has an effect and usually a mutual and enduring effect on all who take part in it.

The presently inflamed awareness of conflict between self and society and between one subculture and another, including the intensified but exaggerated care for the autonomous self, seem to me to be inevitable expressions of the common refusal to face that fundamental aspect of systems theory that I have stressed so often, namely the fact that organization necessarily constrains as well as enables and that every extension of the enablements is bound to extend the constraints more widely also. This it is which limits both the rate at which change can be initiated and the rate at which it can be absorbed without disaster. It may also – indeed it almost certainly must – place an ultimate limit on the level of organization which can be attained by the human species, at least as now biologically constituted.

The position is, in fact, far more complex and more forbidding than has so far been described. For I have frequently used the term 'society' to cover any unspecified human system, primarily one of the autonomous politico-social entities which now divide between them the domination of the planet. But in fact, of course, each of these is a complex of subsystems arranged not only hierarchically but in many overlapping networks, most of which have some common components. It is useful to ask whether it is possible to imagine any system comprising the present human systems on the planet which could conceivably have enough stability to earn a name or even to preserve its present human constituents. I shall not try to answer that question; but in later chapters I will list what seem to me to be the main difficulties.

Footnotes

1. M. Polanyi. Notably in *Beyond Nihilism*, Eddington Lecture, Cambridge, Cambridge University Press 1960; and 'History and Hope', *Virginia Quarterly Review*, vol. 3, no. 2, 1962.
2. Lionel Trilling, in his *Sincerity and Authenticity*, has traced this trend over the past four centuries. Oxford, Oxford University Press, 1972.
3. D. Diderot. *Le Neveu de Rameau*. English translation, Harmondsworth, Penguin, 1974.
4. L. Trilling. *Sincerity and Authenticity*, op. cit.
5. P. H. Rhinelander. 'Is Man Incomprehensible to Man?', Stanford Alumni Association, 1973.
6. *Bhagavad Gita*. English translation. London, Murray, 1931.
7. R. Benedict. *The Chrysanthemum and the Sword*, London, Secker & Warburg, 1947.

CHAPTER 14

THE DECLINING FORCE OF MEMBERSHIP

A recurrent theme in earlier chapters has been the eclipse of the individual's sense of belonging in so far as this involves acceptance of the commitments and constraints which any membership requires. I have stressed the logical inconsistency of this aspiration to enjoy the benefits of membership whilst avoiding its constraints and commitments. In this chapter I will explore a little further the subjective aspects of what I am calling a sense of belonging. They are today obscured, at least in England, to an extent which would have been hard to credit a century ago.

The simplest form of belonging is familiarity with a place. The stream of visual input 'fits' the expectations which previous experience has constructed to receive it. Although we are less conscious of 'match' than of mismatch signals, they are still happily the more frequent and not the less informative. They reassure us both of the constancy which we expect in the physical world and of the reliability of the model of it which our previous experience has constructed.

But much of our input is from a different source – the human world – and it is differently interpreted. For its regularities – and irregularities – are imposed by men and it is intensely important to us to understand them and to draw the right conclusions from them. I have already stressed that all human action is also communication. We need to feel at home in the human world, no less than in the physical world; and we can do so only if we can build up reliable expectations of it and make reliable interpretations of it. We do so largely from our own experience.

This then is the first dimension of 'belonging' which I need to distinguish. Its two halves have very different impacts. To explore unknown country in a trusted team of explorers is very different from dealing with untrustworthy people in a familiar place. The distinction is usually masked by the assumptions which we unconsciously make about strangers, unless they prove to be wrong.

Qualitatively, these sets of relations which place us in the physical and the human world differ in three further dimensions. They may range from the most prized to the most hated. They may range in their assurance from the most uncertain to the most assured. And they may range equally widely in the extent to which they are regarded as inevitable or as possible and proper subjects for change (or sustainment) by human action.

These three qualitative judgements are to some extent related, especially the first and second judgement, about value and certainty with the third, a judgement about changeability. What is regarded as 'the way things are' is accepted as part of life's 'givens'. Climatic differences are accepted; but barriers against migration are and will increasingly be resented. Similarly the uncertainties of the natural world – droughts, floods, even earthquakes – can be lived with if they occur sufficiently often to be embedded in folk memory if not in personal memory as part of the way things are. Uncertainties due to human agency, on the other hand, are much less readily acceptable even where they cannot be withstood. The depopulation of the Scottish highlands was seen as the result of landholders' decisions, not as an 'Act of God'. The dividing line is not always clear. Bankruptcy is not seen as an employer's act (though it may reflect on his competence). But liquidation to avoid bankruptcy is so seen; still more, redundancies to avoid liquidation. These are acts of an employer, not of his creditors. The human mind, or at least the Western mind in its present state of education, seems to be inadequately equipped for understanding degrees of human responsibility. This is perhaps not surprising in a culture which has become so unwilling to include the concept of responsibility in its model of the individual human mind, though not in its model of human institutions.

In a world where so much of each individual's milieu consists of his fellow men and their doings, his sense of belonging must increasingly depend on the extent to which he accepts and trusts this milieu. And where the human milieu is increasingly institutionalized this trust must include his institutions. Furthermore, in a world where his own status increasingly depends on his employment by one of these institutions, he needs not merely to accept and trust them but also to find within them, or within one or more of them, some major scope for significant life. Correspondingly, where this scope is felt to be lacking, he will himself feel impoverished as well as threatened. And so he does throughout the Western world today, though he is more likely to be conscious of the threat than of the impoverishment. This represents an astonishingly complete reversal of the hopes born in the Enlightenment. It illustrates the dialectic course of history and strengthens the argument of this book that the phase of cultural development associated with 'the West' is reaching an abrupt conclusion.

Condorcet, waiting for the guillotine, declared his faith that a day would come when the sun would rise on an earth of none but free men with no master save reason. It is the most succinct statement I know of those hopes amid the ruins of which we live today. And in the perspective of two centuries it is easy to see both why it was at the time so moving and why it has proved so inadequate.

Men, as I have already insisted, are not born free. They are born in total dependence on others. Nor do they become free, for by the time they have outgrown their physical dependence, they have become immersed in a sea of mutual and complementary responsibilities. The antithesis to servitude is not freedom but service and service may indeed be an enlarging and ennobling experience. Nor is reason a sufficient master to demand the service of a free mind, unless we seek its definition from Aquinas, rather than from Herbert Simon. But these were not refinements likely to appeal or even appropriate to the population of a France largely populated by small farmers and in revolt against the *ancien régime*.

The message of the French Revolution was not particularly welcome or welcomed in England, still developing the fruits of its own more modest revolution of a century before and more interested in the economic freedom of the entrepreneur than in the political freedom of his employees. None the less England developed during the nineteenth century a collective sense of belonging seldom found in a large industrial country in the course of rapid change. This tacit consensus endured long enough into the twentieth century to attract the astonished attention of an acute Continental observer, Adolph Löwe,[1] who spent the eight years between 1932 and 1940 in England between his exile from Germany and his final settlement in America. His description of it in his little book *The Price of Liberty* was a surprise to Britons at the time and awakens nostalgic memories now. For the problem to be explained is that Britain, after two centuries of what seemed successful development, has fallen into a psychological state closely comparable in aspiration, though not in faith, to that expressed by Condorcet. Organization as such, at least above the level of the face to face group, has become the enemy; and the very idea that belonging might be enlarging has become highly suspect and widely taboo. Service has again become identified with servitude.

Earlier I described the conditions needed for a coherent society as a set of memberships making reasonably consistent claims on each member and changing at a rate not too rapid to allow their members to adapt to it. In Britain, through the latter part of the nineteenth century and even up to the First World War, these conditions existed to a degree unusual in a large industrial country. So belonging was still a good word; and all its associated words – loyalty, responsibility, commitment – resonated with approval. It may be hard for many of today's generation to believe that there was a time when people generally accorded to their institutions enough legitimacy to support their authority and felt themselves not impoverished but enriched by doing so.

The main foci were at least six in number. Of course not all applied with equal force or at all to all the population and it is impossible even to guess their relative importance, but there is no doubt that each of them was important enough to earn a place in this summary catalogue.

One focus was religion, a term which even then was of very varying implications, both ethically and metaphysically, for different people but which was far too important to be ignored. Metaphysically, its importance lay, I think, not so much in the simplistic system of future rewards and punishments which led Marx to describe it as the opiate of the people, but in its provision of a focus for loyalty which could be allowed a dominant place without fear of dangerously weakening other commitments or of dangerously accepting a potential political tyranny. The second of these assurances was only fully won in the course of the century; perhaps we can safely date the 'privatising' of religion from the abolition of (nearly all) constraints imposed on all but professed members of the Church of England. But the power of religious faith as a binding force was not lost merely by its privatisation. It remained a largely common possession and it remained a support for countless individuals who had grown up with its assumptions and who were united in accepting a common personal loyalty to a supportive and ever present deity.

Ethically its influence was great, although I do not think that its ethic derived solely from its metaphysic. One central tenet which was – and is – of cardinal importance is the injunction to accept the essential humanity of others as the individual accepts his own – or was assumed to accept his own by the Levite who first made that famous generalization some thirty centuries ago.[2] It did not follow that everyone would always do so. The period abounds with examples of man's inhumanity to man; and the barriers of class were often unbelievably strong. None the less it was important to the coherence of society that the principle should be deeply embedded in the community's cultural aspirations.

Probably the most powerful and general focus of loyalty was country, a concept with a very rich content, historical, geographical, cultural and ethical. Service provided another powerful focus. Public service was more prestigious than private service, whether at the level of assistant secretary or of post office sorter. But private service enjoyed whatever prestige it earned. I recall one private firm, now a multinational, in which it was common for employees to enter their children at birth for employment when they left school. *Métier* was also a major focus, embracing all skilled trades as well as the burgeoning professions. Class had its powerful claims, closely associated with *métier* as well as with property, each class firmly defined as a subculture but admitting penetration by those who could and would absorb its special ethic. Class alienation was of course most marked by far in the realm of so-called unskilled labour which served the great labour intensive industries. Finally family, in a less mobile world of larger families with little organized support from elsewhere, served a function almost comparable to a Hindu or Moslem extended family. The coherences generated by these foci were marked, often by a self-conscious awareness; but they coexisted without sapping each other's validity, and usually with a substantial measure of mutual recognition and support.

It is common knowledge how much of these sources of coherence the same society has lost in sixty years. For many, not only of the younger generation, the very concept of belonging has become at least suspect, at worst a basic threat to prized individual autonomy. All forms of organization have come to be seen as impersonal powers, threatening to those over whom they are exercised and, still more, threatening to the individuals who enter their service and thereby become 'mere' role players, less than men. This applies especially to the state, which is often described as the antithesis to 'society'. The only exceptions are organizations designed for protest or battle against 'authority'. I have already emphasized that this is inconsistent with the survival of a system wholly dependent on the playing of complementary roles by individuals and subsystems. I am here concerned not with the consequent break-up or change of the system but with the impoverishment of its members. The social dimension has fragmented and partly disappeared, leaving the individual and the institution glaring at each other across the gulf which its disappearance has created. It used to be a criticism of employers that they hired only hands and brains, not people. Today, when most employers are desperately seeking to hire people, they are likely to find potential employees passionately anxious to hire out no more than their hands and their brains.

The ethical dimension has suffered accordingly. For the sense of obligation to others is dependent on feeling some common sense of belonging with them, and this is largely dependent on feeling also some sense of trust in them. The evaporation of loyalty and trust has diminished this sense of obligation to vanishing point. And with its decline the right to 'pursue happiness' (in the crudest material terms) has grown to dominance, whilst the duty to 'pursue goodness' (which actually was often attested by devotion as well as hypocrisy) has been so discredited that it cannot be acknowledged even where it is still felt. Few today admit that a cost benefit analysis of any importance relies on ethical judgement to weigh its costs and its benefits and even distinguish between a benefit and a cost or to admit the status of either. Still fewer would be prepared to acknowledge the ethical criteria for the ethical judgements which they in fact make.

It is easy to list contributory factors to this decline though vain to seek to distinguish causes from effects, since in systemic relations most factors function in both capacities. Some I have already mentioned. The multiplication of systemic relations in a contractual world can easily produce a situation in which the claims of each so weakens the claims of the others that conflict of loyalty degenerates into a vacuum of loyalties. These uncontainable conflicts are heightened by the escalating increase in the rate of change. The impact of both is increased by failure to understand the worsening of the situation in terms of growing systemic instability. This in turn is fortified by technological habits of mind which seek to carve up even the most complex systemic situation into a series of problems awaiting solution. Science, by identifying experience with observation, destroys the legitimacy of other forms of experience and adds to the isolation and loneliness of the experiencing self, a loneliness which would in any case be a natural corollary of the decay in the social and ethical dimensions.

An even more general factor, which I have already mentioned, is a fallacy in the philosophy of progress which has inspired the last phase of our cultural journey. This was the failure to distinguish between economic expansion and political betterment. There was indeed a connection between the two. To improve the conditions of human life called for more economic resources as well as better political institutions and more sensitive social relations. But none of these was a substitute for the others and none was a necessary consequence of the others. Moreover, linear progress in any was likely, as in all systemic relations, to breed its own limitation or reversal, but at different rates and with different consequences.

The net result of these predictable but unexpected changes was absurdly escalating expectations of what those 'in authority' should be able to do and corresponding mistrust of them when they failed to do it.

Absurd though it may be, Westerners have every reason for their contemporary loss of confidence in all who are seen to share any responsibility for regulating human affairs. Their contemporary lack of success is manifest.

Western men today are aware that they are threatened and aware that their leaders are as unable as are they themselves to reverse these threatening trends or even to understand them. The real weight of these threats is still not fully realized. It is easier to assume that they are temporary disturbances, which existing techniques of regulation will suffice to correct. I believe that this assumption is false. Our current escalating threats deserve and admit of more thorough systemic analysis than they usually receive, not least because such an analysis will disclose how much the limited scope of the governors is further limited by the limitations of the governed.

Footnotes

1. A. Löwe. *The Price of Liberty; a German on Contemporary Britain*, London, Hogarth Press, 1937. (Day to Day Pamphlets, no. 36.)
2. Leviticus, Ch. 19. verse 18. Curiously little attention has been paid to the fact that to a Jewish exponent of religious law some three thousand years ago it seemed natural to take 'love of self' as an exemplar for love of neighbour and almost to imply that it was a necessary counterpart. I can find no meaning for this kind of self-love except acceptance of self and of responsibility for self – for one's whole self, one and undivided. Few people have been more ready than the Jews to criticize themselves and each other, but this is no way inconsistent with accepting responsibility for the whole self and correspondingly for inescapable membership of the whole society. A happy people where such assumptions could be made! It is a far cry from our own in which love of self is regarded as a defect, however natural, barring the individual from achieving a desirable but supposedly unnatural 'love' of neighbour.

PART III

The Threat to Human Systems

CHAPTER 15

SIX ESCALATING INSTABILITIES

The threats which face the world today are all threats to the maintenance of systemic relations on which we depend. By a threat I mean that we are no longer maintaining these relations within tolerable limits and we have at present no means in sight for doing so. By tolerable I mean that current trends either threaten the life support systems of ourselves or of others whom we cannot ignore, or that the only forms of regulation open to us would at present be regarded as unacceptable by those who have power to block them. This second category reminds us that the definition of what is tolerable is partly subjective.

The relations involved are closely connected; they can be separately examined only with some degree of artificiality and overlapping. Neither they nor, still less, the means of regulating them are primarily technological; they are usually political, economic, or cultural. None the less technology has played a great part in their present disorder and has a great part to play in any plan for their better control. The relations thus endangered can be grouped into several overlapping categories, already foreshadowed in my earlier analysis of 'areas of instability' (Chapter 9). They include:

1. Relations between and within human populations. These in turn divide into relations within entities where a common government exists or is claimed, and relations between such entities. They also include:

2. Relations between human populations and their physical surround.

The first of these involves internationally the regulative mechanisms of political pressure up to and including war and of international exchange, with its ancillary mechanisms of money, credit and exchangeability of currencies. Unrequited transfers (or transfers not fully requited) are as yet barely of sufficient volume to rank as a significant international regulator except in so far as they take place within politico-economic areas of common interest such as the EEC and perhaps Comecon.

Within each political entity the same kinds of regulator are found in both political and social fields but with very different scope. In particular the field of unrequited transfer has so proliferated that its boundaries are almost indefinable. The state collects revenue through so many sources, direct and indirect, and redistributes it in cash and kind through so many channels that the concept of individual independence is little more than a historical memory. None the less it has its powerful symbol, employment for a wage, increasingly universal as the means by which individuals and families participate both in the productive and in the distributive process.

The second area of relationship is the relation with the physical environment. This includes all that familiar group of instabilities involving environmental pollution and change in the availability or price of resources, whether biological or inorganic.

Both sets of instability are, of course, made worse by the exponential increase in human populations, expected to more than double overall in present lifetimes, even on the most favourable assumptions of deliberate control. (War, pestilence and famine, could of course, check this trend.) I shall avoid referring to population increase as itself a 'pollution' but it is at present both a major stimulus to pollution and a major obstacle to most forms of pollution control.

I will briefly examine this tangle of unstable relationships under the headings of war, exchange and development, inflation, unemployment, concentration of power and wealth and environmental constraint. It is worth doing so if only to sharpen our realization of the suddenness with which they have broken into human consciousness and the total lack at present of any hopeful plan for abating them.

Before 1914, war, though mildly deplored in Britain, was still regarded as an alternative and sometimes necessary instrument of foreign policy. I have already described the honourable part which it played in liberating the constituents of those empires which had foundered in the century before 1914. Our present degree of terror and horror towards war is new, escalating since the Second World War and much more marked in some countries than in others.

Up to 1914 at least international development by the exchange of commodities and products was still regarded as a beneficent linear process without any obvious inherent limits. Faith in its complementary nature was qualified by the realization that competition, at least between industrial nations, could be a painful process and that Britain's earlier preeminence was not due to any inbuilt advantages which would always endure. But the division of function between the colonized world and its colonizers was still both marked in fact and unmarked in consciousness – or at least in the consciousness of the colonizers.

Inflation was no threat to a country which could borrow at 3 percent without a repayment date. Fluctuating employment was regarded as the main regulator of the market system, and the need to abate its worst impact on those who most suffered from it had only recently been accepted.

Inequality of wealth was to some extent offset by the continued growth of the total national product; and the emergence of trade unions as an industrial and political force promised redress to the inequality of bargaining power which was seen as the only flaw in the machinery of the 'labour market'. Inequality of power was seen as disappearing with the extension of the franchise, already nearly complete for males and focusing debate only on the major issue of votes for women.

Environmental limitation was still below the level of awareness. The deserts of the Middle East were a historical curiosity. The dustbowls of the West had not appeared. Even the squalor of cities was hardly yet an invitation to social and physical design. Most Western countries had a policy designed actively to encourage the growth of their populations, largely to support their relative 'strength' in war.

Thus the six threats which today discredit the ability of government to achieve its ancient goals of peace abroad and prosperity and content at home had no such effect at the beginning of the century. They were wholly contained within three comfortable faiths – that Western military power could police the world without tearing itself to pieces; that Western industry would continue to develop the world and to yield *and distribute* an increasing return sufficient to satisfy the demands both for continued material progress and for greater equality; and that the Western political system (with which there were then no serious competitors) would suffice to meet all foreseeable social as well as political demands.

Within two generations all three faiths have been shattered. Two world wars, both beginning in Europe, have discredited the Western international system in its own eyes and in the eyes of the world; have transferred world dominance to two nonEuropean powers incomparably more different in ideology and culture than those which formerly comprised the 'concert of Europe'; and have yielded results so grotesquely remote from those intended as to discredit war itself as an instrument of policy. The two world wars have at the same time left an endemic state of war far less controllable by a balance of terror than it ever was by a balance of power, yet so magnified by technology as to be a threat to human existence.

The industrialization of less developed countries has proved to be even less an automatic process than it was before their independence. Even the Western economic system, after two decades of recovered vitality and unprecedented growth, has run into what does not look like a merely temporary recession.

The Western political system no longer commands confidence in its powers as a social designer or even as a social regulator. Social democracy is so widely regarded as having failed that the title *After Social Democracy*, in Professor Dahrendorf's pamphlet of 1980,[1] requires neither explanation nor justification to most of its potential readers. A billion of the world's inhabitants have adopted Marxist regimes which are not democratic in the Western sense. Scarcely any have copied the Western pattern of economic and political development by private capital and biparty or multiparty representative government. And even in the increasingly vague area known as the West, faith in representative democracy wanes as the power of pressure groups increases.

In addition and no less suddenly, the realities of environmental limitation have become an obsessive concern, especially to minds which have not a vested interest in ignoring them. The resources endangered are no less biological than inorganic. (Throughout much of the world the most intractable shortage is of wood for burning.) The effect of pressure on resources is felt economically and politically long before they emerge as absolute shortages. The problems then posed are manifold and not chiefly technological. None the less they have a common characteristic – pressure on the patient earth and on its not so patient inhabitants.

Faced by these cataclysmic changes the political will and wisdom of the world is at present almost numb – and no wonder. Despite such will for peace as now exists armaments multiply under the pressure of positive feedback derived from several mutually reinforcing factors. International exchange and development operates in a world in which for the first time no international exchange medium has any material backing (such as gold) or even any individual currency backing (such as the U.S. dollar after Bretton Woods) for the confidence which it invites. Inflation excites most bitter conflicts between rival theories for explaining and controlling it; but underlying them all, though seldom acknowledged, is the sombre fact that no single country or imaginable consortium of countries today possesses the power adequately to control the volume of money and credit, except perhaps for any large enough and rich enough to seal its frontiers and go it alone. Unemployment has barely begun to reflect the effect of the next wave of automation replacing men by machines. Increasing concentration of power and wealth is one of the very few features common to all forms of polity and the reaction against it is equally widespread. Environmental constraint is the most conspicuous and intractable threat of all.

In the next two chapters I examine these instabilities in greater detail – first, those which threaten relations with the natural milieu; then those which threaten relations within and between societies. The two are increasingly interconnected. I shall be particularly concerned to distinguish the part which technology has played in creating them and the part which it might play in helping to control them.

I think the enquiry will also help to make clearer why the governed have so notably withdrawn their confidence from their governors, even though their major institutions and their major institutional role players are probably more competent and less corrupt than they have ever been before.

Footnote

1. R. Dahrendorf. *After Social Democracy*. Unservile State Papers, no. 25, London, Liberal Publication Department, 1980.

CHAPTER 16
UNSTABLE RELATIONS WITH THE NATURAL MILIEU

Our contemporary power élites may be divided into five classes – policy makers, executives, administrators, planners, and technologists. The first four are the names of functions rather than of offices; those who perform any of these functions probably perform them all at different times and in different proportions. Together they describe the main contemporary elements in the art of human governance, whether in the public or the private sector. It is understandable that they should lose prestige at a time when the governed have lost confidence in the governors, whether disappointment is justified or not. The technologist, on the other hand, has a different and more limited role and a far more impressive record in achieving it. In the course of this century he has surpassed all his previous achievements and has brought within the reach of most Westerners, and within the aspirations of most of the world, physical facilities and conveniences which were inaccessible even to kings a century ago. Why is he not the shining exception to the general mood of disillusion, the one power élite which still deserves respect, admiration and confidence?

In fact he not only bears a full share of the mood of general mistrust, he even focuses it. S. C. Florman,[1] in his engaging and well-documented book, *The Existential Pleasures of Engineering,* has described and criticized the powerful contemporary trend of thought which finds in technology the root of all evil in modern society. I shall be particularly concerned with the answer to the question why the technologist should be saddled with such monstrous responsibilities for our current ills and trusted so little to abate them. The reasons are, I think, more cogent than Mr Florman is ready to admit.

The answer requires us to examine the relation between a people's technology and its means of subsistence, and also between its technology and the other elements in its culture. The first is the easier. I have largely covered it in the first part of this book.

Whatever else it does, any population requires to maintain a viable relation between its numbers and the resources of its habitat. It has four, and only four, means of doing so. It can limit its numbers. It can adapt its way of life to the changing resources available to it. It can enlarge its habitat by colonization or conquest, or to some extent indirectly by trade. Or, lastly, it can find ways to get more from the same habitat, either by pressing more hardly upon it or by increasing the habitat's power to respond, or both. Technology has contributed in different degrees to these four forms of adaptation.

The control of population has been largely by abortion or infanticide, except for the contribution of inbuilt biological controls to which I have already referred. The major technological contribution has come in our time with the chemical control of fertility. The cultural effect of this technological change has already been enormous, but its demographic effect can only be slow by the time standards implicit in this book. Apart from the unpredictable impact of war, pestilence and famine, a doubling of today's world population is already in the pipeline.

The adaptation of food habits to resources has occurred historically at a great variety of speeds and for a great variety of reasons, not all of them technological. The lord of an English manor whose exclusive privilege it was to keep a 'dovecote' had a richer and more accessible source of animal protein through the winter than the peasants whose fields were gleaned by his doves. But the differential was imposed by culture (in this case politico-social structure) not technology – though a dovecote is a most efficient and economical technological structure.[2]

The bedouin, moving with their flocks and herds from one scanty pasture to another over what was once arable land, probably consume a higher proportion of animal protein than their predecessors in that earlier age. The whaling, sealing Eskimo lived – and lives – more exclusively on animal protein than the richest New Yorker, though vegetable protein now begins to reach him – in cans, as a luxury, from the South. The fact remains that to feed stock for human food on grain which could itself have been used as human food, wastes something between four-fifths and nine-tenths of the energy which could have been derived by eating the grain itself. Energy intake is not the sole measure of a good diet. But for whatever reason, it seems that animal foods have acquired a prestige value over vegetable foods, at least in those countries which practise both agriculture and husbandry or which have access to the products of both through an international market.

In theory the world's human food supplies could be multiplied with no change in technology by a redirection of consumption through subsidized markets or otherwise. And this would be of major importance to that one-fifth of the world's present population which is already hungry. These generalizations may some day become politically important. Meantime they operate largely to divert attention from the very different realities which structure each particular situation. The anchovies of the South Pacific are harvested by North American ships and ground into fish meal which is used as stock feed or manure almost entirely in the northern hemisphere. How much of the energy they stored in their life cycle ultimately sustains human or other life? What other life forms suffer from the strange and novel fate of the anchovies? These are proper questions both for science and for politics. But they are not questions for techno-logists – at least not yet. It has been, and it still is, the province of technologists to devise efficient means to catch anchovies; efficient machines to grind them up, and so on. Whether they have a contribution to make to understanding the effect of these interventions on the cycle of reproductive life on earth, let alone to controlling that cycle – that is another matter, and one to which this book seeks to make a modest contribution.

The third of the ways which I distinguished for enlarging a habitat is the way of colonization, conquest and trade. Its importance is obvious. It has had three phases – so far.

The first phase was the complementary exchange of products, usually of high value in relation to their bulk, of kinds not produced by the importing society or not produced in such quality. Such were the early exchanges of bronze and, later, iron artefacts and of Chinese silks and ceramics. The second phase was the production for export of plantation crops and minerals including fuels in undeveloped countries usually dominated by the importing country. The third phase is the competitive production of industrial and agricultural products, notably in countries of formerly colonial status.

The main agency in the transition from the first to the second phase was the revolution in transport, notably by sea in the form of the efficient, capacious, ocean-going sailing ship.

The products which these ships brought back were products of the lands which they visited and of the technology of the peoples of those lands. Chinese makers of ceramics did not import European technologies.

The value of their goods lay in the fact that they represented resources and technologies not available in the lands which sought them. This was the source of that faith in the complementarity of international trade, which as late as the 1830s imparted a religious fervour to some of the utterances in support of the Anti-Corn Law League.

It was, of course, the latest phase of a long history of international trade. Geoffrey Bibby[3] has summarized the astonishing extent of this by sea and land as early as the second millenium BC. He even argues persuasively that prior to 1500 BC a man could have travelled from Bombay to the Baltic on ordinary commercial transport and returned by the same route within two years, although after that fateful date many centuries would elapse before such conditions would recur. (1500 BC is the estimated date of the destruction of the Indus Valley civilization; the existence of this civilization had made seaborne commerce across the Indian Ocean a worthwhile commercial enterprise for Arab traders.) Trading exchanges brought transfers of technology, though until the eighteenth if not the nineteenth century I know of none except the technology of the plantation which moved from West to East, rather than from the more advanced countries of the East to the western outskirts of the known world. It remains valid, I think, to regard the wind-driven sailing ships which dominated the world's oceans for some centuries up to the second half of the nineteenth century as symbolizing the close of the era of colonization dominated by complementary trade but not by competitive manufacture. The main technology exported was the technology of the plantation, such as tea, indigo and, later, those explosive seeds of Amazonian rubber.

I have already stressed the importance of the fact that the colonial era – or at least the last colonial era – has closed. The whole habitable world is partitioned by frontiers which can hardly fail to grow more and more selective unless political force prises them open. Only trade remains as a distributive mechanism between them. And trade is limited by its need for reciprocity and by its dependence on international markets and international credit; limitations which are becoming increasingly obvious but not increasingly easy to overcome.

And so to the fourth way which I distinguished by how a population can enlarge the support which it derives from its habitat. It can increase the yield, either by pressing on the habitat more heavily or by enlarging its capacity to respond. The two are not always easy to distinguish in practice but their differences are hugely important and are disclosed by the passage of time even if they are not foreseen.

I have already traced the main changes. In the earliest of our human phases each human population, surrounded by abundant game and natural vegetable food available for the gathering, lacked only means to catch and to kill (and, at least with some vegetable foods, to grind and to cook). Technology supplied these means. The first result was an increasing catch. The next was a reversal, due to the scarcity of game. No further improvement of hunting weapons or skills could make the situation other than worse. A new, more intensive and often more laborious but more rewarding technology was needed, additional to the first (which still survives in the important fishing industry). This was the technology of farming and husbandry. Men could now be assured of their basic needs only by growing, breeding, feeding, watering and the rest of the farming cycle. The first result was more affluence compared with hunting and food gathering in ever more denuded areas. The next was impoverishment of land under increasing pressure. Forests were stripped. Deserts appeared. More intensive agriculture depended on irrigation, which in time increased the salinity of the soil. Technology was constantly challenged to respond to threats resulting from its previous efforts, including increased populations made possible by its own previous successes. It responded accordingly, more and more proud of its resourcefulness, less and less conscious of the effects of its increasing pressure on the patient earth.

I have already stressed that the familiar stages of human economic development are cumulative, not successive. The industrial epoch did not replace the agricultural epoch. It supplemented that epoch – usefully in so far as it encouraged more intensive but sustainable agriculture; harmfully in so far as it competed for agricultural land and indirectly increased the number of human mouths demanding to be fed and the intersubjective standard of what was a sufficient and acceptable meal. It also mortgaged the future in so far as it depended on and used up irreplaceable fossil fuels and committed areas of the earth's surface irreversibly to nonproductive uses. The second is almost as irreversible as the first. Even airport runways, if they can support the landing of jumbo jets, will not readily be reconverted to agriculture either by men or by those earthworms which Darwin made famous for their exploits in burying even the most resistant of men's discarded pasts.

So the historical situation poses a new question to the technologist. Can he get more from the habitat not merely by pressing more hardly upon it but by finding ways to increase its responsiveness even to lighter pressure? In practice the two are closely interwoven but in principle the distinction is, I think, crucial. Is there even in theory scope for another technological revolution comparable to the one which introduced the agricultural epoch and for the first time established the image of man as the guardian of a world which not only supported him in the present but grew more able, under his guardmanship to support him in the future?

No one, I think, need doubt that the technologist can still get a little more from the habitat by pressing even more hardly upon it. He can mine familiar materials in more remote places and in thinner seams and poorer qualities. As their price in consequence rises, it will become 'economic' for him to seek, devise and market alternatives. If he succeeds, shall we be better off? Better off no doubt by comparison with the absence of both resource and substitute. But the rise in price means greater effort for the same return, even if the rise is caused, as it usually will be, not by any absolute shortage but by the action of a cartel of producers. (There was no lack of oil in the ground when OPEC quadrupled its prices in 1974–1975.) The effort to get more of the same from a habitat which has less of the same is bound to be an ever less rewarding battle.

The effort to get more return for harder pressure in the field of biological resources is equally limited. The water cycle revolves in its majestic way without losing water, but the water available to particular men at a particular place is not thereby assured. Wood renews itself – if it is cut at a rate not exceeding its growth rate. But most of the world's woodlands are not so managed, not for lack of technological knowledge or even for lack of competent government, but simply through the imbalance of supply and demand. The International Union for the Conservation of Nature and Natural Resources (IUCN) report estimates that in Zambia the equivalent of 360 days of women's work per household is spent each year in gathering wood for burning from ever more remote sources. If these vanishing woodlands were replanted, if they were scientifically managed and effectively protected, what would the Zambian woman burn while they were growing? Or even after?

Even the 'green revolution' so widely acclaimed, has proved to fall only doubtfully into the category of increased responsiveness. These new grains do indeed respond wonderfully – to fertilizers. But the fertilizers must be manufactured and, usually, manufactured in countries other than those in which they are used and thus bought over international exchanges, usually by the countries which can least afford to buy them, especially as their price escalates with the price of the energy which their manufacture uses so abundantly.

These are all familiar matters; but they are peripheral to the major hope which the optimists have of technology. This is the hope of an ecological revolution which will leave our species in secure control of the planet; not for ever living from hand to mouth by increasingly mortgaging the future.

Technology does indeed offer us at the present time the prospect of many revolutionary changes. But I can detect in only one of them the characteristics which might qualify it to rank as an ecological revolution. This is the possibility, however remote, of raising the production of energy and matter by inexhaustible natural forces – notably photosynthesis – to a level which will provide a sustainable economic base for such of our species as then remain.

An economy is either sustainable or it is not. One of the merits of the IUCN report, 1980, already cited, is that it does not bury this inconvenient fact. Like other insolvent debtors, the human species is required not just to be a little less profligate but to balance its budget and keep it so. The unused possibilities of photosynthesis are immense. We cannot know how much more of them can be brought into use both by cultivating the natural process and by devising supplements for the direct conversion of solar energy into more convenient forms. We do know that this, plus the harnessing of the other natural forces – wind, tide and the gravitational force of water above sea level – are the sources of our income, in whatever form and however directly or indirectly they may be drawn on. All else is stopgap; and a stopgap is only a stopgap.

Other technological revolutions seem to stir the imagination more widely. They are indeed exciting; but even the most arresting seems to me to lack relevance to the basic issue of the sustainability of human life.

The most revolutionary to many minds, is the revolution in control and in the processing of information. But this would be significant for good only if it made men more governable – and for evil only if it made them less so. It will undoubtedly do both and my expectation that the second will exceed the first may prove to be mistaken. But at the best it can, I think, have only slight relevance to creating a sustainable economy. We do not need to save labour.

The nuclear revolution is even more spectacular and much more controversial. But here also the possible contribution to a sustainable economy seems to me to be far less than is commonly supposed, even on the basis of generally accepted fact. The present generation of nuclear reactors is manifestly stopgap if only because they use for fuel a type of uranium of which known reserves are no greater than those of oil even at current rates of consumption.[4] They continue to be built although no process has yet been devised for disposing of their radioactive waste or – even more threatening though seldom mentioned – for disposing of the obsolete reactors themselves after their relatively short service life of some thirty years. But there is no present reason to hope that they will ever attain the relatively benign status of a stopgap which stopped its gap and is gratefully remembered for a past service. Such servants are not easily dismissed.

The breeder-reactor promises a much more economical use of fuel but all the dangers and burdens of managing a plutonium economy. These dangers and burdens are not technological and cannot be solved by technological fixes so they are widely ignored. But they will not go away. It is useful to contrast the rapture with which railways were received from the first with the basic terror, anger, and mistrust inspired by nuclear power. The common man will tell you why.

The fusion reactor beckons from the more distant future, not wholly 'clean', especially if we remember to include its vast thermal pollution as well as its much smaller radiation pollution. But it is a distant and uncertain prospect. It has yet to be proved feasible even in countries of the highest technology. It cannot begin to fill the gap for many decades. Perhaps by then there will be no gap to fill. In any case there remains the question how far such high technology can be of any aid to that woman in Zambia and the billions of human beings whom she will then represent.

The most dramatic and least relevant of all the technological revolutions offered to us would seem to be access to 'space'. Cities in the sky may be useful in increasing the amount of solar energy to reach our planet in one form or another. But on what assumptions could they be expected to increase our living space? What will be the cost per head of providing each of their inhabitants with his far from enviable *Lebensraum*? Why should individuals who can secure such VIP treatment be willing to make use of it? And what possible difference will it make to anyone if they do? Except for their possible function as interceptors of energy and, of course, for their inexhaustible capacity for extending the arms race, cities in space seem to me totally irrelevant to the issues of which this book treats.

There remains the hope which attaches to the first of the four revolutions which I have mentioned, that is, a technological revolution which helps man to create a self-sustaining environment. This is one which should awaken the enthusiasm and claim the devotion both of technologists and of men generally. It will need to do so. For its success will depend on reversing a process which is deeply embedded in the consciousness of Western men.

Its success can, of course, only be relative. It will not easily reverse trends which are moving at exponential rates towards limits which, when crossed, will probably not be reversible. Even for today's destitute, already 20 percent of our species, they will be too little and too late; and by then that sinister figure will presumably be far higher. Yet, if the only delays to be expected were technological, they would be far less formidable than they are.

They are not only or even principally technological. They are political and cultural; economic (one aspect of culture) but not chiefly economic as we have understood that word in the West for nearly twenty decades. Before turning to these it is well to stretch the imagination as far as it will go, to place ourselves in the appropriate frame of time and space and human difference.

We measure in many millenia the span through which our species subsisted in small populations each in sufficient balance with its milieu to remain stable, given the huge areas of unappropriated land and resources. Even so, many failed to survive; but, far more important, they threatened the survival of even fewer of the species on which they subsisted.

We measure in only a few of those millenia, perhaps the last ten to fifteen, the slow transition to settled agriculture and in even fewer the growth of the first urban civilizations. None of these civilizations has had a continuity comparable to that of their simpler predecessors.

We measure in only two centuries the growth of civilizations based on thermal motor power; and already limitations are emerging in several vitally important directions. Each limitation can be met at least for some time and at least at some cost. But the times generally grow shorter and the costs generally grow higher and the refusal to pay them or even to recognize them grows greater. There may be a more stable state awaiting at least some of the world's societies but they have only decades in which to reach it.

Any movement towards it involves the regulation of relationships not only with the physical milieu but between and within the immensely varied societies of sentient human beings which today make up the human race. The regulation of these human and societal relations is not within the field of any technologist's competence. None the less technology profoundly affects and usually intensifies the difficulties of the regulative process.

Footnotes

1. S. C. Florman. *The Existential Pleasures of Engineering*, New York, St. Martin's Press, 1976.
2. The dovecotes to which I refer are the cylindrical structures often found in chalk country (and perhaps elsewhere) of which the inner skin is built of blocks so arranged as to leave a nesting place between every two blocks in every course of blocks. A central ladder can be rotated so as to give access to every nesting place. Ingress and egress is through an opening between the top of the cylindrical walls and the cap which roofs the structure. Such cotes, often built of chalk blocks, are common in the grounds of old houses on the chalk downs.
3. G. Bibby, *Four Thousand Years Ago*, London, William Collins, 1962.
4. W. Jackson Davis. *The Seventh Year*, New York, W. W. Norton, 1979.

CHAPTER 17

UNSTABLE RELATIONS IN THE HUMAN MILIEU

Even if the planet were to become tomorrow a single farming and industrial enterprise, managed by a team of human technologists for the benefit of its human fauna as a whole, its prospects would be sombre, unless the appreciation in the previous chapter is more radically faulty than I can find reason to hope. But the planet is not like that. It is an aggregate of very varied habitats, each colonized by a pyramid of the interdependent life forms to which biological evolution has given the chance of survival and which have developed ecological and ethological relations sufficiently stable to account for their existence today, though none of them is guaranteed its existence tomorrow.

Among these life forms our own, with its singular cerebral equipment, has taken off on that further evolutionary adventure which T. H. Huxley[1] described as the ethical process, as distinct from the 'cosmic process', to which of course it has also remained subject. I am in this book generally referring to Huxley's 'ethical' process as the cultural process, although the origin of the word 'ethology' reminds us that human cultures are not unrelated to the simple patterns of regulative norms which are characteristic of other species. Although this new and common biological development has given some common character to even the most diverse human societies and has no doubt set limits which are common to them all, the development of each has been particulate, a function of its own history as well as its own habitat, resulting in a work of art neither wholly individual nor common to the species but unique to the society which made it and which it made.

Even today what perishes or survives or changes under the pressure of threat or promise is not primarily a species or an individual but each of a number of more or less particulate societies, each dependent on its own relations within its own habitat more than on its relation with others. Even a society like Britain's, which has become highly dependent on international trade for the necessities of life, can achieve what it needs only by collectively accepting common constraints which are today beyond the capacity of its members to attain or even to identify.

All of these human societies are threatened directly or indirectly by the instabilities which I distinguished in an earlier chapter – war, 'development', inflation, and unemployment as well as by the instability of relations with the physical milieu. None of these is directly due to technology; but each of them is affected by it in important ways.

War

There is no need to argue the case that technology has made war more threatening without making it less frequent except possibly between states armed with nuclear weapons. (The ability of these to deter even conventional war is a hotly debated issue. It should be remembered that what we now regard as the 'conventional' procedure of bombing open cities horrified the world when it was first demonstrated at Guernica, less than a decade before the 'carpet bombing' of Hamburg and Dresden.) The wars of 'liberation', which marked the century before 1934, have continued and, as already detailed, several more empires have been liquidated, nearly all with some aid from war. But their constituents, now formally independent, have not for the most part developed as yet into stable states. Most of the world's armed conflicts, never so numerous before, are powered by fierce drives for partition, secession or fragmentation.

There are integrative trends which can be set against the general stream of fragmentation. They are of three types, of which the Soviet empire is by far the most apparently unified at the time I write this.

It is easy to list the integrative forces. They are political and military dominance, ideological affinity (however imposed or spontaneous), shared fear of a powerful neighbour, economic dependence or interdependence, sometimes fortified by the facts of geography or by a sense of religious or ethnic identity. I will not attempt to forecast the future of any of today's embryo empires or spheres of influence. But it is a manifest lesson of the last hundred years that economic interdependence counts for less and war counts for more than anyone at the beginning of that period would have hoped or expected. It remains an open question what will be the effect on human governance of the power to multiply the dissemination of information. Obviously the answer will vary with the society and with the number and quality of the disseminators. Equally obviously it will not be answered by technologists or technology except to the extent that the mere existence of the technology will promote its use for any purpose useful to its potential users (though not necessarily to the recipients of its product).

The Soviet and the American spheres of interest, and to some extent some of the others, show some alarming tendencies to proliferate under positive feedback. By far the most obvious and dangerous of these is the emergence of what President Eisenhower called 'the military-industrial complex', a self-exciting system in which defence departments, armament makers and research and development centres everywhere, not least universities hungry for research grants, stimulate each other in the endless pursuit of innovation in attack and defence, in addition to the stimulus provided by equally active potential enemies. Consider the weapons devised and used in the eighty years since 1900. Consider the weapons devised and not yet used, chemical, biological and nuclear. Consider the size of the world armament industry, recently estimated to have an annual output of 450 billion U.S. dollars. Consider, above all, the arms trade with its economic and financial, as well as its political implications. This is no mere adjunct of political power, to be used, kept idle or discarded at will. It is a semiautonomous force, potent though blind, a dominant expression of political philosophy and a major source of the technological research and the development which also maintains its momentum.

Development

The instabilities associated with international economic development are far harder to analyse though not to recognize. I have already emphasized the novelty of a world in which former colonial possessions have become autonomous, with no international regulation except the market, modified by the activities of multinational corporations (themselves naturally suspect as possible centres of 'economic colonialism') and intergovernmental regulation within the blocs of varying coherence to which I have already referred. A summary approach to this area of instability is to examine the Brandt report.[2]

The Brandt Commission faces explicitly the basic problem how a distribution system based solely on reciprocal exchange can possibly benefit any of its members by more than the value to others of what that member has available for export. Credit is manifestly useless unless it is expected to increase the power of the disadvantaged in the world's markets at least enough to make them trustworthy debtors of credits indefinitely long, if not developers heading for a credit surplus in the world's markets. And it must do so at a cost reckoned as acceptable not only by the governors of the credit-giving states (or of the national and international institutions which they control) but also by their productive organizations and by their workers who are also their electors. And it must do all this at a time when international financial machinery is not serving the needs or commanding the allegiance of most of the developed states themselves.

Some readers of the Brandt report will not be convinced that its proposed combination of unrequited and commercial credits would have the effect predicted for the various categories of underdeveloped countries. Others, accepting this, may doubt whether it would have the predicted effect on more developed countries even in the long run, still more in the short run where increased competition will not be offset by increased markets. Yet others, accepting all this, may doubt whether the financial measures proposed could be sustained without an unacceptable degree of inflation (though the Brandt Commission estimates that it could). But the most revealing part of the Commission's exercise is probably the way it spells out the political and economic costs of doing what it reasonably regards as the least that needs to be done to sustain international trade on a basis consistent with the further development of all countries. (The idea that some may be already overdeveloped finds no place in the Brandt report.)

It is still for history to show what the world's response to this call will be and indeed what is the most it can be. What is the most that can be hoped from international trade in a world of such diverse sovereign states as we now have, which has inherited little more international machinery than was appropriate to the days of colonial plantation economy?

What, for that matter, is to be hoped from it even by the less successful developed states where the rewards of labour in the widest sense have ceased to be related to its return?

The last reflection brings us to the third escalating threat – inflation; the unstable relation between incomes and prices. This controversy divides the most eminent economists. Noneconomists may be tempted to keep out of the fray. But I think some things of importance can usefully be said about it and that some aspects of it may even be more obvious to the outsider than to the professional, since it is easier for the outsider to notice and accept changes in what were valid assumptions less than a century ago. As always, a systemic viewpoint is essential.

Inflation and the standard of living

The word inflation is commonly used today for any worsening of the relation between incomes and prices or sometimes even for any rise in the retail price index. For example, pensions which are linked to the retail price index are often referred to as 'indexed against inflation'. This confuses several issues which it is essential to distinguish.

Four main causes operate, separately or together, to worsen – or sometimes to better – the relation between incomes and prices. Only one of these, the monetary factor, is properly called inflationary (or deflationary). The other three are physical, technological, and commercial. I shall be chiefly concerned with the monetary factor but I include them all because they all contribute to the uncertainty which still attends the efforts of human individuals and populations to meet what they have come to regard as their needs; and they all contribute to the not very satisfactory index which we call the standard of living and measure by the relation of incomes to prices.

Before world markets or even national markets became dominant, physical variables played a larger part than they do now; but they are still significant. The fisherman may work for days for very little or fill his hold in a few hours. So may the whaler. The farmer's return from a year's labour may vary vastly from one year to another although he works no less hard, perhaps harder, in the lean years than in the fat ones. The effort needed to get a ton of identical coal from two different pits may vary by several orders of magnitude for purely physical reasons. Even from the same pit the product of the same effort will vary from year to year, usually adversely, as faces work further from the shaft bottom, seams grow thinner and faults appear.

These physical factors can be diminished, offset or sometimes reversed by developing technology. Oil technologists have found ways to extract oil from the bed of stormy seas. I have already observed that as nonregenerable resources diminish, technological developments will often provide alternatives, but usually at prices which have become 'economic' only because of the escalating costs of the diminishing resources which they replace. The new resources remain far more expensive than they were when cheaper ones made them not worth working. In other words, more of something has to be got and given in exchange for them. Technology has also brought some risks of its own. Research and development may not pay off. Capital intensive industry may become obsolete before it has paid for itself, or may impose rigidities from which less specialized and complex technologies are free. These risks slide into the third sector, the market sector.

Here, even more than in the technological sector and far more than in the sector of physical limitation, development has brought both gains and losses which at their present stage are impossible to balance. Initially the opportunity to exchange surpluses and thereby make good local deficiencies must have been a tremendous advance in terms both of stability and of prosperity. World-wide markets magnify this advantage but they also bring problems of their own. As interdependence spreads, so may the impact of local disaster as well as local abundance. And, as already mentioned, markets as such, however wide their area, do not of themselves enrich those who have nothing to give in exchange, however much they may desire to buy. This thought brings us to the fourth area of instability to which this section is particularly directed – the financial area on which the market area depends.

It is well to remember that purchase and sale is still a form of barter, even though money and credit has so greatly amplified it. Every sale is an exchange of goods and services for money; every purchase an exchange of money for goods and services. Until very recently money itself was exchangeable for a commodity at a fixed rate. Barley, rice, rye, silver, and of course preeminently, gold have all served this purpose at various times. The last suspension of convertibility of sterling into gold occurred as recently as 1931 and dismayed dock labourers almost as much as bankers. (It had long been barely thinkable that sterling was not 'as good as gold'.) But the fact that a currency was backed by a commodity, even gold, did not guarantee it against inflation – or deflation. The commodity itself was subject to price fluctuations responsive to supply and demand. Sweden in 1918 and still more Spain three to four centuries earlier, when it was flooded with gold from its South American colonies, experienced their own versions of the inflationary situation colloquially known as 'too much money chasing too few goods'. There would seem to be no reason in principle why money not convertible into any specific commodity at a fixed rate should not serve all its traditional purposes at least as well as it did when backed by a commodity and possibly better.

There are, however, good reasons why money, whether so convertible or not, should in practice introduce into the human milieu, and especially into its market relations, instabilities which we cannot yet control and which may prove to be uncontrollable.

The first of these is that the money supply is exceedingly hard to measure.

The second is that the money supply is even harder to control – far harder than it was even a decade or two ago when it was more subject to control by a few central banks and far less dependent on the joint agreement and action of many autonomous and disparate authorities.

The third reason for monetary instability is that the money supply depends absolutely on the trust of those affected (which means everyone) both in the ability of all the authorities concerned to exercise this control and in the policy by which that control is guided.

For here again, as in so many areas examined in this book, the machinery of automatic control has broken down whilst the machinery of deliberate control has barely begun to emerge. And the realization of this vacuum, sharpened by bitter debate about rival policies of control, is eroding the public confidence on which alone depends the effectiveness of any control machinery and any control policy.

Moreover, the political pressure to inflate the money supply is very great and the economic results of doing so, by the time they are sufficiently obvious to demand action, are hard to reverse, and devastating in the capricious way in which they fall on different sections of the population. We have had recent examples in Germany in 1924 and, to a less extent, in China in 1948. But these were occasions when a monetary system positively disappeared. They are classical examples of a system driven by positive feedback past the point of no return.

There are intermediate stages in the progress of a monetary system towards its threshold of dissolution. Its first function to disappear is its function as a means of storing wealth. The British Government can already borrow money without interest in return for the promise to return an amount of unabated buying power. The next function to falter is its function as a unit of account. Banks and other institutions have already been driven to devise new forms of accounting to allow for changes in its intrinsic value. The third stage, failure even as a medium of exchange, appears when the catastrophe is much nearer. The last days of the German inflation abounded with stories of depreciation so fast that the would-be buyer found that money could evaporate in the time taken to get from a bank to a shop. But there is an earlier threshold almost as critical. The international trade of any country depends on the willingness of dealers in foreign exchange to buy its currency 'forward' at some price. The moment a currency's value up to three months hence in terms of some other currency becomes too speculative to be an object of purchase and sale, that country's machinery for import, if not for export, breaks down, unless supported by highly abnormal international emergency measures.

The fact reminds us that in talking about money and credit we are talking about specific currencies and promises based on specific currencies, just as, in talking about 'men' we are talking about specific populations. Currencies common to more than one political unit involve political as well as economic association, with associated sharing of loss and gain far remote from the tendencies to fission examined in this book.

This section is not intended as an essay on inflation, even if I were competent for such a task. I seek only to explore to the minimum extent needed, a critical area of instability in relations within the human milieu. The points which I have sought to make may be summarized as follows:

1. There has always been an element of uncertainty in the relations of a society with its physical milieu and in the relations of its members with each other and with their society and in its relations with other societies. Cultural development has moved some of these uncertainties from the first field (society/environment) to the second (interpersonal) and third (inter-society) as men have increasingly come to provide each other's milieu. This has not reduced the total volume of uncertainty or increased the stability of the human systems which it has elaborated. But it has greatly increased the demands which its human elements make on each other.

2. To some extent a society can spread these risks, or concentrate them on the individuals best able to bear them or cushion them to a limited extent by keeping reserves of the few forms of wealth which admit of storage. But it cannot eliminate them, and to an even greater extent it cannot simply allow them to lie where they fall. This is partly because, as human systems develop, the results of the uncertainties fall ever more capriciously on an ever widening circle of people who are ever more able and willing to resist; and partly because of rigidities which have become built in to the political, economic and cultural expectations of the societies affected, especially those which I have identified as the heirs of the Enlightenment.

3. Money and credit, created in a large number of irregularly related currencies, have become a particularly important and recalcitrant element in the stability and instability of human systems. However well regulated, they would not wholly neutralize the instabilities inherent in the other three areas which I have distinguished – the physical, the technological, and the commercial. But at their present level of confusion they can make the instability of those other and closely related areas incomparably worse. Indeed I find it impossible even to guess which of today's nation states

would survive and in what form unless financial order is reimposed, both nationally and internationally to an extent not yet in sight.

4. This is impeded today partly by lack of information about what is going on and partly by disagreement even among experts about what ought to be going on, which I have already mentioned. It is also impeded by rigidities, some of which I have also described. I will add a brief note on three which seem to me specially important.

(a) The experience of past decades has built in to the minds of most people in most developed countries, at least among those of the 'West', that the economic system is set to produce more goods and services per capita indefinitely. And for several decades that has indeed occurred. The satisfaction which this might have been expected to produce has been muted by discontent with patterns of distribution. But the average increase has been there. The mere suggestion that it might stop or even be reversed still raises incredulity and suspicion among the great majority of the people concerned.

(b) This being so, the attention of the vast majority has shifted from goods and services to money. Given money, the accessibility of goods and services in ever greater volume and variety is taken for granted. The idea that goods and services might be lacking for any reason other than an individual's lack of buying power is almost wholly dead. (It is happening no further away than Poland but there it is assumed to be due to their different system of production and distribution.)

(c) Access to money is almost universally identified with having a job at a fixed wage. This has until recently been expected to rise in real terms year by year irrespective of the fortunes of the undertaking if it be in the private sector, or of the country if it be in the public sector. This assumption of increasing affluence is being strongly challenged in Britain as I write this and as strongly affirmed by those who think that the short fall, if real, is the avoidable result of financial policy. But the first part of the claim, the claim to a job, though less well supported by historical experience, is even more strongly affirmed; and naturally so, since it is of even more importance to most of the country's labour force, who are also a large part of its electorate. I examine it in the next chapter.

Before doing so, I wish to repeat a point which is relevant both to this section and to the next. If I am right in thinking that we are coming to the abrupt end of a cultural phase, it is essential not to view the future on the basis of assumptions formed in the past, at least until these have been reexamined in the light of today's situation. I recently reviewed a publication by a noted scholar in which he stated with total confidence that whatever be regarded as the purpose of education, it certainly does not exist to provide jobs for teachers. I expressed dissent. The transmission of the human heritage from one generation to another is a task so important and so many sided that it may be impossible to comprehend it within a list of purposes, however long. But in such a list, however short, I would certainly include the recruiting, training, and employment of teachers, not only to instruct the young, not only to keep the teachers out of the queues of unemployed, but to create and maintain a corps of people dedicated to this most important of functions and fit to develop and defend it as well as to perform it. They, as well as their charges, are members of their society and are changed by their own activity and in turn influence for good or ill the whole of that society, not only their young charges. Human systems are not mere goal-seeking assemblies of insentient parts not otherwise active and they cannot be described simply in terms of purpose.

Unemployment

Poverty has been recurrent, if not endemic, among human populations, as among other animal populations, since the dawn of history. In all of them, from time to time, some or many of their members have known scarcity of what they class as needs, and many of them have perished in consequence. By this biological definition of poverty many are perishing now.

Many human populations have developed a second, a more subjective, definition of poverty as a lack of resources and conditions which they have come to expect as minimal. The succession of social surveys which marked the development of social responsibility in Britain through the later nineteenth and twentieth centuries progressively abandoned a merely biological definition of the poverty level in favour of one which took increasing account of the subjective standards of expectation of its day.

Among those who thus awakened concern, one class has differed sharply from all the others and has aroused, as it still arouses, an extraordinary variety of strong and often contradictory emotions. This is the class of the unemployed. At least five conflicting myths about unemployment are potent in our society even today.

1. There need be no unemployed. An economy growing under the constant stimulus of new technology will create new jobs as well as new wealth. Those unemployed in such a society can only be so temporarily, during a state of transition from one job to another, unless they are incompetent or unwilling or worse.

2. Unemployment is avoidable but not by the automatic working of a free market alone. It is a feature of those booms and slumps which mark the self-regulation of any error-controlled system. These can be smoothed by using the public power to create or restrain demand. Any residual disturbance can be met by insurance. Subsidy should be a rare and residual remedy.

3. Unemployment is unavoidable. Even more than other forms of poverty there is nothing adequate to be done about it, because even money sufficient to alleviate its worst hardships does not serve to give the recipient that status in society which only a productive role (or property) can bestow, whilst money adequate to alleviate the resultant need would remove the incentive to work.

4. Unemployment is not only unavoidable but necessary. It is the variable resource needed, if industry is to be able to respond quickly both to stimulus and to restriction.

5. Unemployment in an affluent society is only an old-fashioned word for leisure, carrying pejorative assumptions which are now quite unwarranted. Self-generated activities will develop a nonmarket sector of mutual service and self-service which, with little assistance from private employment or public funds, will keep everyone busy, happy, and sufficiently rich. Why should everyone in an affluent society rely for income or status on employment by someone else?

Each of these attitudes has its own history. The first, that there need be no unemployed, found its earliest expression in England, so far as I am aware in the Poor Law of 1601. The law dealt with all forms of poverty and made each parish responsible for alleviating its own poverty. But it draws a significant distinction between unemployment and other forms of poverty. Other forms could be dealt with by money grants. The unemployed needed not money but paid work. Let the parishes 'set them to work'. The Act had no deep theoretical backing. It was perhaps little more than a reaction against the appearance in increasing numbers of able-bodied unemployed men. This in turn was partly due to the dissolution of the feudal structure and feudal expectations and partly to the dissolution of the only large-scale institution for the relief of poverty, the monasteries.

The parishes were given neither guidance nor money in their uncharted task. Predictably they failed. The doctrine was, none the less, repeated in more emphatic form in the Poor Law of 1834. It was a necessary article of faith in a society intoxicated with the earlier stages of an industrial revolution. It was also sharpened by fear of a class which was certain to contain, as well as many of the unfortunate, the ill-endowed and the ill-prepared, all the parasites and predators whom such a society was likely to breed. (The unemployed class would not, of course, include those parasites and predators whose existence was masked by property.)

The unemployed were thus a double reproach to society and incurred a double odium which was reflected in the administration of the Poor Law in so far as it affected the unemployed. This survived to embitter memories of the interwar depression and to give unemployment, alone among the sources of poverty, something of the stigma of an injury inflicted by the act or default of government, rather than a natural status such as marked the other classes – childhood, injury, sickness and old age.

The second attitude, that unemployment is avoidable but not by the automatic working of a free market alone, owes its popularity to J. M. Keynes. It came as a revelation at a time when rearmament and the war were applying a Keynesian solution to the horrors of the Great Depression; and it nourished the Western world for three decades thereafter. Many would say that it has never been fully tried, since it has been far more attractive as a stimulus than as a check. Today in a country which, at the time when I write this, combines some three million unemployed with deficit financing at the rate of some £10 billion yearly, it is less honoured than it used to be, though it is still powerful.

The third attitude, that unemployment is unavoidable, is the oldest. Its earliest expression known to me is a gospel parable in which labourers are described as waiting in the market place to be hired for money by the day and often waiting all day in vain. The situation is clearly expected to be regarded as familiar by those who first heard it thus described. It would not have seemed so familiar to Britons at that time but it was to become so. It was taken for granted by Malthus in the early nineteenth century.

But its starkness had been muted in 1880 by Bismarck when he persuaded Kaiser Wilhelm I that the cheapest, if not the only, way to reconcile an increasingly large and self-conscious labour force to cooperating in a free capitalist society which was bound to distribute property with gross inequality was by using the principle of insurance to offset all poverty risks, including the risk of unemployment. Insured benefits were the only form of property which could be universalized in such a society.

The decision to include unemployment among the insurable risks of an industrial society was important and had its own driving force. Large numbers of unemployed men, especially urban unemployed, were not only a reproach to the consciences of the well-to-do but also a threat to their safety. Gilbert,[3] an American historian of British social legislation, dates the emergence of this threat into common consciousness from a riot of unemployed men in London in 1883. Action in Britain was much slower than in the new German Empire but the German model was influential. It was studied on the ground by at least two of the Liberal British Cabinet which came to power in 1906 and it was followed in the social legislation of that Government in the eight years prior to the outbreak of the First World War.

The proposal to apply insurance to unemployment as well as to other forms of poverty awakened opposition more passionate than is easily understood today. This special hostility is due, I think, to the fact that it challenged at least two of the myths most dear to that generation. One was the myth of the self-regulating economy. The other was the myth that the motivation to seek work at any wage rather than none was essential to the working of the system and far too precious to weaken even in the slightest degree.

Both myths perished in the Depression. No one could suppose that two million workers had suddenly become disposed to a life of indolence even at the cost of penury. No one could suppose that a modest cushion against transient unemployment would fatally sap the will to work. At the same time Keynesian economics raised hopes that in a properly managed economy unemployment would generally be transient and the cost of the cushion correspondingly modest. Beveridge, calmly writing his plan for Britain's social future in the battered and burning London of 1941–1942, could assume that he was dealing with an insurable risk, except for the occasional unfortunate. It was, I think, the more important of his only two mistaken assumptions.

Another change, particularly interesting to students of systems, had occurred by 1918 to give to the depression which followed on the first war a different impact from all those which had preceded it. Unemployment had become unacceptable. A more self-conscious, more powerful and more fully enfranchised working force was no longer willing to be used as the primary regulating mechanism of a fluctuating economy. What economists described as self-regulation the human 'regulators' described as unacceptable instability of employment. Stability of employment, as well as a larger slice of profits, had emerged as a major political goal for a very large number of working men and women. A new stabilizing policy was demanded.

The hope that it can be found is more battered now than it was in the three decades before 1970 and the fourth myth, that unemployment is not only unavoidable but necessary, is again becoming more influential and more openly avowed but for different reasons.

In the nineteenth century, when industry was far more labour intensive, the engagement and the laying off of workers was by far the quickest and most effective response to increase or decrease in demand. Labour provided the governor of the system. It was largely casual, engaged or dismissed from day to day; and the lowness of its wages was offset by its numbers. Labour costs formed a higher proportion of most industrial costs than they do today. It made perfectly good economic sense to insist that a pool of unemployed labour was a necessary resource for industry, which could not expect the demand of a free market to remain constant or reliably linear. Labour was defined, at least in theory, as a resource to be hired as cheaply as possible and only to the extent that it could be profitably employed. Full employment, like subsidized unemployment, could only weaken the regulator on which the whole system depended.

Although industry today is less labour intensive, wages have risen and the financial and other costs of reducing labour have also risen. Hiring and firing is a less effective, as well as a less acceptable way to adjust the output of industry to fluctuating needs. A pool of unemployed labour is, none the less, regarded by many as useful to offset the new bargaining strength of labour. It is a reminder that though the organized employed are strong, the unemployed are as yet both unorganized and weak. The need to keep a job limits the measures which can be taken to raise its value. And it becomes ever more accepted that even an active economy abounding in new technology is likely to diminish the number of paid jobs, even if it multiplies both overall wealth and the rewards of such jobs as remain.

Hence the fifth view, unemployment should be redefined as leisure. Holders of this view are affronted by the inconsistency of demanding paid work for all as a means of distributing a product produced by ever fewer and assume that Western technological societies are still set upon a course of indefinitely expanding affluence and diminishing labour. In this view, what we need are radically new attitudes to unemployment and leisure.

These five attitudes cannot be dismissed merely because they are mutually inconsistent. They all exist and they can all point to some area in which they are valid. A technological economy does create some new jobs, though, as the Luddites correctly perceived, there is no reason to suppose that these will offset in numbers those which they eliminate or, still less, that they will benefit the workers whom they displace or even those workers' children. An economy can be so managed as to reduce, though not to eliminate, fluctuations in employment, though, of course, the pursuit of that objective will have costs in terms of other objectives. Unemployment, where it exists, cannot be wholly offset by subsidy, still less by anything which can validly be called insurance; but the loss of income which it represents does need to be replaced by some other form of income to whatever extent is acceptable to the community concerned. The threat of mass unemployment is a necessary restraint on monopoly pressure for high wages unless and until some better accord can be reached on the principles which should fix the levels of reward. Some people if long unemployed will find ways to meet their own needs, perhaps more effectively than others can do for them, but not to the extent of freeing them from all dependence on the basic economy.

None the less the five attitudes and the histories which have evolved them have currently produced nothing short of an intellectual Bedlam.

Despite deficit financing, unemployment grows. As labour grows more expensive, technology increases its efforts to displace men by machines and has ever more scope for doing so at a cost which, to it, is 'economic'. As work becomes more capital intensive, it costs more to create new jobs. As existing jobs become more protected both by workers' organizations and by statutory right, employers reducing their labour force rely increasingly on 'natural wastage', that is on not replacing those who leave or die, thus restricting the inflow of new workers and casting the burden of unemployment increasingly on the young. The new technology of information processing threatens with redundancy large sections of the labour force which before were its most active growing point. Few believe any longer in even the theoretic possibility of full employment.

But the death of the myth that full employment is possible has profoundly different impacts on the parties principally concerned. Employers as such are concerned only to have sufficient qualified applicants for such jobs as they cannot devolve on machines; preferably an excess rather than a deficiency of such applicants in order to strengthen their weakened hands in their effort to contain wage costs. The social and financial costs of unemployment do not appear directly in their accounts.

Governments are concerned with the individual prosperity of their entrepreneurs who are a major source of revenue – but also, and even more, with the prosperity of every individual in their country's labour force who changes from a financial asset to a financial liability whenever she or he loses his job and very likely changes his allegiance as an elector also. They are concerned with their country's competitive status in world markets; but they are also concerned for the financial status of every individual citizen, both as a taxpayer and as an elector. For the myth that full employment is attainable by the exercise of public control is not to be purged from the assumptions of those who most depend on it, merely because economists have changed their minds or because theories have been disappointed in practice.

Trade unions are not indifferent to unemployment. But their primary duty is to their members, who are people at work. They are interested in work sharing only in so far as it does not involve wage sharing. But it must involve wage sharing, for there is not enough for all, and this for two good, though different, reasons already mentioned. First, the concept of what is enough has become a relative concept, related not to the physical needs or even to the aspirations of 'average' men but to the 'average' amount of their incomes. And, secondly, the amount available in total for consumer incomes is falling, not rising, and is likely to continue to fall even if the gross national product were to rise. For, as already observed, the gross national product must provide for investment and collective services as well as for consumer incomes; and both investment and collective services are likely to rise at the expense of consumer incomes in a world which becomes ever more crowded and which must devote ever more effort to meeting its needs from ever more expensive resources. Moreover, gross national product itself is an unreal figure in so far as it includes an unsustainable rate of public borrowing.

Within the ranks of the employed there are presently insoluble disputes about the relativity of reward. I have elsewhere distinguished nine more or less ethical, but mutually inconsistent, criteria which are used regularly and accepted as relevant by both sides in wage negotiations. The way in which agreement is reached, if it is reached, is among the most complex and obscure psychological problems of our day. But differences between the rewards attached to different jobs, though weighty matters, are minor when compared with the difference between employment and unemployment.

The country is divided today into two nations as sharply distinguished as those described by Disraeli, but radically different. They are the employed and the unemployed. Two small classes escape the classification – those with property sufficient to assure them of an adequate, inflation-proof income, and those with skills sufficiently rare and highly valued to assure them individually of an ample income either in employment or in the state which we now significantly call self-employed. These classes are qualitatively significant but small in numbers compared with the two nations which either lack a job or depend on a job which it is their main object to defend. Unpaid work is increasingly suspect as diminishing the area in which paid jobs might be found. Even the job of the housewife is diminishing in prestige and importance as our society in the name of sexual equality encourages both parents even of the youngest children to work full time – if they can compete successfully for what jobs remain.

On the other hand the same society is ingenious in finding ways to support more people of potentially working age than it can find paid work for. In the period reviewed in this book, our own society has devised a host of acceptable ecological niches to accommodate these, notably a huge extension of education at one end of the scale and of early retirement at the other.

It has also made an enormous business of catering for leisure activities – indeed two businesses; one, the entertainment industry, revelling in new technological facilities for one-way communication and promising an even more bewildering variety of choice; the other, the 'do it yourself' industry, catering for the needs of those who can no longer afford to hire the skills they need for their technology-dependent lives. It is these, the 'amateur' builders and decorators, motor mechanics and electronic engineers who provide what evidence there is for the fifth of the conflicting myths which I described earlier, that unemployment should be redefined as leisure. It is welcome though scarcely new. The volume of such work in terms of individual man- (and woman-) hours can scarcely yet be comparable with what it was up to even a hundred years ago, when every house was literally a 'manufactory', a place where most of the requirements for its own living were made by hand.

This is the situation which I described earlier as an intellectual Bedlam. The description does not seem to me less justified after further analysis. It seems to me clearly to constitute a fearful and growing area of instability in the human milieu. I analyse it chiefly as an example of three aspects of human systems which I have already emphasized.

First, unemployment, like inflation, is the name we give to a relationship. Our verbal habit of giving names to relationships is liable to reify them and obscure their real nature.

Secondly, the relation which the term 'unemployment' describes, is a dual one. It exists in 'the real world out there'. It also exists in the variety of mental representations which we make of the real world out there, which is the nearest we can get to reality. The two are not the same but they are closely interrelated. We are constantly revising our understanding of our relationships and also working on the relationships themselves to make them more understandable. The regularities which we find in human life are in varying degrees imposed by ourselves. For example, full employment and stable money may or may not be combinable aspirations; but even if they are so in theory, they will not be so in practice unless all those whose cooperation is needed to make them so understand what the aspiration requires of them and agree to accept the cost of acting accordingly. And this understanding is not merely a grasp of general laws but a grasp of a specific ongoing situation, embedded in space and time and context.

It follows, thirdly, that the unemployment situation is not to be understood in abstraction from the way it is perceived by those who participate in it. For they as participants are part of it and their understandings are part of them. That is why human beings engaged in governance at any level spend so much time trying to persuade each other what the situation shall be deemed to be, even though no representation can do justice to the infinite particularity of human life.

It is worth asking whether any member of those earliest hunting tribes was ever unemployed. Indeed he was. A hunter with a broken bow cannot hunt, however abundant the game; nor can a hunter who finds no game, however well armed he is. The first lacks the technology to use what he regards as a resource. The second lacks the resource to which his technology is adapted. It is no help to either that centuries later the woodland may be arable land, needing tools other than the bow.

The unemployed man today lacks both technology and resource, but not necessarily because they do not exist. The technology is in the idle factory where he last worked. The resources probably wait only to be called for. But they can only be called for if users express through a market both their wish to possess the product and their ability to pay for it. Their ability to pay may be lacking simply because they are, as producers, unemployed; but this is by no means the only possible or necessarily the most probable reason. If the factory is idle because it can no longer meet a market need at a competitive price, it is no more use than a broken bow. If the resources it formerly used can no longer be made by its technology into a marketable product, they are no more use than absent game.

The market has its own rigidities. One is more rigid than it used to be. The idle, hungry hunter will work very hard and very long for very little. Not so his descendant. He works in a world of men and money which owes him a living. He even knows how much it owes him – even if it does not agree. But even if he worked excessively for whatever value his labour would produce, he would not necessarily survive thereby, any more than the famished hunter. A rigid wage structure exaggerates the inherent uncertainties of a market economy. But no structure, however flexible, will of itself support the producer of what it fails to make marketable.

It is not surprising that the only superabundant resource today is human labour. It is not surprising to a historian – though it would have been to most economists until very recently, perhaps to some even today – that human labour does not grow less expensive because it is superabundant. It is not surprising that the price of human labour speeds the technological urge to replace it by machines. It is not surprising that those who receive that price, that is, those in work, are collectively unwilling to support those who do not work.

The fact remains that no system can be expected to support such instability for long. So no one should be surprised when it ceases to do so – however unwelcome and bizarre the collapse may be.

Footnotes

1. T. H. Huxley. *Evolution and Ethics*, op. cit.
2. *North-South: A Programme for Survival*, op. cit.
3. B. B. Gilbert. *The Foundation of National Insurance in Great Britain*, London, Michael Joseph, 1966.

CHAPTER 18

THE CHANGING ROLE OF THE TECHNOLOGIST

During the past hundred years there have been radical changes in the perceptions of technology by those whom its activities affect for good and ill. These have been partly due to a reassessment of what can be expected of technology and, more recently, to a change in the role of technologists themselves.

Until a century ago the technologist, unlike all the other power elites which I have mentioned, had unquestionably the status of the Red Cross Knight. The Red Cross Knight is a symbol of immense power and resource, wholly to be trusted because wholly dedicated to doing good and unquestionably able to distinguish good from bad. He rides around slaying giants, who are wholly bad by definition, and leaving his fellow men happier and safer than before.

This reputation was not surprising. The technologist was specially associated with two major and welcome revolutions. One was a revolution in consumption. Shops became full of goods in a variety and at prices which had never before been within the reach of any but the rich – and often not even of them. The other, perhaps an even more potent symbol, was the revolution in transportation. Not yet in individual transportation. Apart from that most beneficent invention, the bicycle, individuals going their own way had still to rely on their own or their horses' legs. But extending transport by land and sea was more than a convenience for the traveller. It was symbolic of a major enlargement of one of the basic constraints of human life. And it seemed at first wholly to be welcomed.

A famous example was the opening of the bridge over the Menai Strait. The strait is full of ships of every size and kind. The Anglesey and Caernarvon shores are black with silent crowds, tense and waiting. High above their heads across the gorge springs the huge, airy structure of the bridge, the like of which no one has seen before. And high on the structure a small figure in frock coat and top hat, Brunel, watches the last piece symbolically bolted into place.

The job is done. Brunel raises his hat. And at the signal every ship's whistle squeals, every siren blares, every throat cheers and every heart lifts. The technologist has sewn together two more pieces of man's fragmented world.

Bridge building was a highly symbolic act and the technologist was its high priest.

By 1914 two more aspects of the technological revolution were on the horizon – mechanical power available anywhere for the turning of a switch; and mobility increased to a further still immeasurable degree by the infant motor car and the embryo aircraft. Individual men, each potentially powerful and mobile past telling! It seemed an unbelievable realization of two of mankind's oldest dreams.

There was a price; but it fell most heavily on those who participated least in what it bought.

The First World War crystallized two of technology's inherent threats. Although the previous two centuries had made a difference to the techniques of war, as well as peace, this had been little experienced from the receiving end by the technologically advanced countries. Nor had it been so dramatic as the changes in the arts of peace. The breech-loading rifle had replaced the musket; the shell-firing fieldpiece had replaced the cannon; the machine gun had made its fearful debut at Omdurman. But these were developments rather than innovations.

The First World War brought home two facts, neither of them new but neither of them previously realized. The first was the technical efficiency of war as a means of killing men. The machine guns at Omdurman are estimated to have killed 15,000 Sudanese at a cost of 26 British casualties. Even the Somme had no more dramatic a lesson. But the names of the Sudanese did not appear in casualty lists in *The Times*.

The second fact brought home by the First World War was the irrelevance of conventions. It had been genuinely believed that even war had been tempered by the growing 'civility' of Europe. The use of gas by Germany, immediately followed by the use of it by the Allies, almost wholly destroyed this belief.

It also startled the still civil-minded world by applying even in war the calculus of economics to affairs in the realm of the right and wrong. What is the most economic way to kill a mass of men? What disadvantages need be taken into account? Innovation is the breath of life to technology. Why should it not be equally so in war?

The interwar years of industrial depression and financial collapse also had their lessons. Idle technology coexisted with unused resources. A system supposed to be self-regulating had ceased to be so. The regulator itself had ceased to be acceptable to those who were supposed to be its prime mover. No one blamed the technologist. But the event made visible a huge defect in the system which technology as such could do nothing to fill; nothing, at least, which technology as then understood – and as still understood – could be expected to fill. The system needed some degree of conscious regulation; but the problem and the potential means of regulating it were far outside the training and experience of technologists – and even of politicians.

The Second World War underlined the two lessons of the first and added another which was to dominate the post-war world. The mushroom cloud over Hiroshima heralded more than the ultimate weapon. It cast new doubts on the ability of *any* economic calculus to guide technological development. This became even greater after the war, when atomic power was heralded as the ultimate source of unlimited energy for peaceful purposes. Nontechnologists did not forget that a major element in the economic equation favouring nuclear power was the production of plutonium for weapons. The argument began before the cost of other sources of energy had begun to rise; still more before the need to conserve resources of other kinds had made any serious impact on the public mind. It divided scientists of high repute as well as common men. It bred a new distrust both of government and of technological calculations, a distrust which has been slowly gathering momentum ever since, as instabilities with the physical milieu have been added to instabilities in the human milieu.

Since the Second World War a further doubt has affected the reputation of the technologist. Some of his most confident developments have gone astray. Some have even had to be discontinued or reversed. And of these disasters, some have been due either to side effects which were predictable but ignored, or to other and independent technological developments which destroyed the assumptions on which the first were built.

A classic example of the first is DDT, a product which triumphantly did all that it claimed to do but which was banned in little more than a decade after it was introduced, though not before some of its disastrous side effects had become irreversible.

This episode raised further doubts. Did the sponsors of DDT fail to anticipate its side effects? If so, did they not show incompetence in the field of their own professed expertise? Surely an organic chemist should be able to anticipate how the food chain would concentrate poison in the bodies of animals further up the chain, including man?

Alternatively, did they know very well what they were doing but keep quiet about it? If so, were they not untrustworthy in their own professional field in which it was most difficult to monitor them?

Or worst of all, had the technological imperative reached a point at which there was no means to arrest it, however clearly foreseen its effects, until they had actually been experienced and had generated enough resistance to reverse the process? If so, were we not all caught in a system in which our vaunted powers of prediction were useless, because we were unable to respond to them until prediction had become present experience – and perhaps not even then?

The second of the dangers to which I referred is said to be exemplified by the St. Lawrence Seaway, an enormous enterprise carefully planned by two governments which, at least in the early stages after completion, failed to justify the enormous investment involved. One of the factors which disappointed these hopes was an independent change in the technology and economies of rail transport which reduced the economies to be expected from enabling ocean going ships to reach the Great Lakes during the open season. These changes may well have become visible only after resources were irrevocably committed to the Seaway project.

The example illustrates a dilemma which is bound to grow worse unless it is controlled by what could only be a very difficult and uncertain process. Technological innovation takes time to plan, to implement, and to pay for itself. The larger and more complex the plan, the greater this time factor becomes. But technological innovation also changes the world, at least to some extent, and thus makes it more unpredictable for other technological innovators. What happens when technology itself becomes a factor so disturbing that no individual technological change can be planned with sufficient confidence in the situation in which it will operate? The ground-nuts scheme, even if it had been admirably planned, would have operated in a world in which its most basic assumption – an impending shortage of fats – would have been radically changed by the independent invention of chemical detergents.

These doubts have divided planners for some decades. In theory one school avoids the pitfalls of an uncertain future by moving only by short but hopefully incremental steps. The other accepts the need to act on a large scale if at all and pins its hopes on improved 'forecasting'. In practice, neither can wholly follow its principles. For the first, short term planning, involves sometimes 'choosing' no action when action is clearly needed and right action is not impossible, whilst the second, improved forecasting, seeks to predict without even trying to control sufficiently to make its predictions a little more probable. The alternative to independent initiative is a degree of control which, once established, is also likely to escalate.

Theoretically one alternative is to let the risks lie when they fall. The entrepreneur's business is by definition a risky one. But the risk-taking capacity of private capital has already been largely exhausted. No private capital would have built Concorde or bailed out British Steel or British Leyland, or even Rolls-Royce. The age of public salvage is already with us, even if the age of public enterprise is suspect and the age of public control still more so. Moreover, the technologist's mistakes do not fall only on the technologist or his entrepreneurial master. To suppose that they do is an outmoded economic convention. Often they cannot even be fully charted. DDT may have doomed to extinction all the mammals of the sea.

The decline of the technologist – from Red Cross Knight, through sorcerer to sorcerer's apprentice – is a symptom of the decline of the system which he served and characterized but did not invent. But it is not the last chapter in his history or the most recent one.

The common man begins to know at least as much as the technologist about unstable systems and he is often less inhibited in recognizing them by any personal stake in them. He does not generally feel safer for the arms race, but he knows that countless people and institutions make their livings from it. He begins to recognize the positive feedback built in to the self-exciting system of producers, advertisers and domestic consumers. And though he regards this as more benign in principle, it loses its charm when prices progressively outstrip real personal incomes. Stability becomes again a value as the expectation of endless more-for-less slips ever further astern. He has not yet accepted the idea of a permanently depreciating living standard, even as part of a more adequate distribution system. But the assurance of keeping what he has is no longer taken for granted.

There follows a radically new attitude towards change. Throughout nearly the whole of human history change has been the major threat to human life. Men are adaptable; they can learn to live even in harsh and hostile environments – so long as the environment remains constant enough to give them time to learn. A major change, climatic, demographic or cultural, sets them a new problem. If they form the habit (as we have done) of adapting by constantly changing that to which they are trying to adapt, they build uncertainty into the very structure of their lives. They institutionalize cluelessness. That no doubt is why an ever more scientific world is becoming ever less predictable and an ever more technological world ever less manageable.

Early technology was less open to this criticism. Roman aquaducts and roads, for example, freed men to some extent from the vagaries of the weather without introducing instabilities sufficient to counterbalance these stabilizing changes in the physical environment, at least in the short run. But technological man has long passed the stage when he can adapt to the changes which he himself has become organized to produce. He has become caught in a self-exciting system which is approaching its limitations. The fact is not yet clear to all nontechnologists but it is probably clearer to many of them than to the technologists who have become conditioned to live by change.

Moreover, the nontechnologist is conscious of other uncertainties, in addition to growing limitations on energy, resources and finance. He has withdrawn his confidence not only from the power élites but also from his fellow men on whom he so completely depends for the continuance of all his services. In a world increasingly interdependent but increasingly distrustful of all those on whom each depends, greater security seems to demand greater independence; and stability recovers its charm when change no longer necessarily means change for the better. Solar panels may not answer the world's energy demands but they will be sought and treasured by any household which they can make even partly independent of OPEC and even of the grid.

This new – or rather renewed – fear of change is chiefly focused by the two dangers which I have already discussed, unemployment and inflation. These, as I have sought to show, are today's form of mankind's oldest fear – the fear of diminishing returns and ultimately of no return from his search for subsistence. The primitive hunter knew it. The farmer knew it – and knows it now. Its familiar nature is masked for us today only because a net of human relations and institutions is interposed between each of us and the great collective enterprises which today sustain – or at least conduct – our kind's ancient search for survival.

And thus to the most basic fear of all, the fear of a self-defeating free-for-all battle to keep what one has and to get what one can even in a world where the total of what can be fought for is largely, though not wholly, dependent on some better form of distribution than a battle.

Technology does not increase equality of distribution either within one society or between one society and another. Nor does it make acceptable any other system of distribution, except by attributing a high and not unreasonable value to the services of its own practitioners. Yet it makes even more necessary and even more difficult the creation of some system of distribution which can be made sufficiently acceptable to survive. Here again, the contribution of technology has, through no fault of its own, been negative. For it has instilled deeply into the public mind, and into its own, the assumption that by its very existence it guarantees (or if fully used would guarantee) an increasing share for all. The trade unionist invited to accept no more of an increase in wage than will offset his increased cost of living is already being invited to qualify a basic assumption which technologists, as well as recent experience, have encouraged him to accept as inviolable. An invitation to accept less is so deeply contrary to these assumptions that no politician and few, if any, industrialists have yet ventured to present it except as a temporary measure, a brief interruption in the indefinite expansion of prosperity. Yet anyone familiar with the behaviour of systems should not need telling that they breed their own limitations and that in our day, or at most our children's day, the management of these limitations – not their evasion but their acceptance and management – is what politics will be all about.

The contrast between limitation and limitlessness is the contrast between ecology and classical economics. There was a time when it was possible (though even then perhaps undesirable) to assume that the earth was a limitless fund of resources for our needs, wants and whims, and a bottomless sink to receive our wastes, our failures, and our obsolescence. This is no longer a viable assumption; and the alternative is fighting its way into the common consciousness of both technologists and nontechnologists. It makes much faster progress with the second than the first. Technologists should know more about the behaviour of systems, but they are ill-placed, by interest and by tradition, to lead the culture in its belated recognition of the difference between cancerous and organic growth. Only a few mavericks, usually academic scientists[1] rather than technologists, contribute to the massive and unwelcome educational task of restoring some sense of reality and responsibility to a world which has for so long been technologically drunk.

A world technologically sober would not, of course, be a world less technologically active. At least three technological tasks are clamouring for more attention now. One is the basic inventive task which technology has always regarded as its own. The term 'appropriate technology', which is coming increasingly into use, reflects a new awareness that there are styles in technology as in all other cultural activities and that in many fields our current style is inappropriate, not only for the developing nations which wish to develop a more adequate technology but perhaps even more for the developed and overdeveloped countries themselves. The basic needs are now familiar.

They are all basically contained in the injunction to organize a sustainable human system – or at least some sustainable human systems in those places where degradation has not become irreversible. (They will not necessarily be in the Western world.) The basic task is, of course, not technological but political, financial, and educational – all aspects of human culture. But the technologist has an important though subordinate part to play. To stabilize the relations between human demands and available resources will require conservation, monitoring, and education; and all three will make demands on technology.

The conservation of resources has four aspects. None of them is purely global, though some of them have global implications. The first is the preservation of earth, air, and water (including the oceans) in a state fit for the indefinite support not only of men but of the vegetable and animal species on which he depends; and equally the adaptation of life in each habitat to the natural resources available. Water, for example, is not only indestructible but is naturally filtered by every circulation through the majestic water cycle which returns it periodically to the atmosphere and again precipitates it in its purified form. It remains true that the rain which falls in the world's few remaining rain forests is not presently expected to benefit the deserts of the Middle East. Even well-watered countries like Britain at present must sacrifice precious land on which to store the quantities of water on which they have learned to depend not only for agriculture and drinking but to wash away their sewage. Conservation is always a partly local activity.

Biological resources are described as renewable but they are not renewable to an unlimited extent. Any species of them may be permanently destroyed by human pressure. I have cited two cogent examples – the near exhaustion of wood used for fuel, and the depletion of the gene pool of cereals. The conservation of biological resources may therefore involve action no less drastic than the conservation of mineral resources which are not renewable even in theory – the third of the aspects of conservation to which I referred earlier.

Here again generalizations are to be avoided. Some mineral and even metal resources are not seriously eroded by human use and can be used again and again. The village of Avebury in Southern England is largely built of stone blocks cut from the megaliths which were erected more than forty centuries before to form the neolithic temple there. The pride of a technologist would not allow his most elegant fabrications in iron to dissolve in rust in a few years if his economic masters did not find that it paid them to let this happen.

The Age of Waste must obviously be succeeded by an Age of Conservation, an Age of Substitution and, in some fields, an Age of Abnegation; and these three will not come simultaneously everywhere or sequentially anywhere.

The scope for conservation is so vast in an Age of Waste as revolting as the present that it will offer the widest immediate scope for the technologist, at least in theory; but in practice it will no doubt depend on adapting more realistic systems of cost accounting than we use today.

The scope for substitution is more familiar. Consider the enormous substitutions of one material for another which have already marked this century, notably the development of aluminium, of asbestos, of synthetic fibres. These were powered solely by the imperatives of market economics. Fiscal and other government policies can alter the impact of market economics; and changes in the scope and time scale of the economic calculus are not beyond the power of governments even today.

Even abnegation is already in the forefront of contemporary politics. People the world over, especially nontechnologists, are aware that the most abundant, if not the only substance which technology has not merely produced but actually created is plutonium. It is not found in nature. It is more lethal to human life than any substance which is found in nature. It is not an achievement to be proud of. It is not an achievement to be ignored. Even the alchemist sought positive goals, such as the elixir of life and the transmutation of base metals into gold. Why do his descendants seek new elixirs of death?

Plutonium does not look like the key to a sustainable – and human – world.

So much for the first of the three tasks I mentioned. The second is the enormous monitoring task involved in charting and publicising even the most blatantly deviant trends in a world which today may be even more unstable than we realize. This field offers enormous scope for technological inventiveness. We have only just begun to measure a few of the most dangerous forms of pollution and the most urgent fields of depletion. There may well be some which have not been identified; and others will no doubt emerge. The new information technology makes possible the collection and presentation of data far more up to date than has ever been possible before.

It will generally be a thankless task. As usual the difficulties involved are far more political and cultural than technological. Things are moving. Most governments of industrially developed countries have some degree of environmental control. The Environmental Impact Agency of the American Government is a significant beginning. Coupled with the varieties of planning to control land use which have developed during this century and the more varied and controversial essays in economic planning, the total volume of effort to understand present trends and to guide them into the future would surprise any informed and concerned political mind of a century ago, even though we are more conscious of all that is left undone and all that we do not know how to do (let alone the side effects of even what little we do).

The third task, an essential condition of the success of the second (monitoring), is the educational task. The elementary facts about systems in general and human systems in particular, as spelled out in the earlier chapters of this book, are still not widely known, still less widely realized, though they can and should be taught in elementary schools.[2] Until they have entered deeply into the consciousness of a particular culture, they will have little, if any, effect either on the government of the country concerned or on its technologists.

Of course, individual instabilities will attract notice as they come seriously to affect the lives of ordinary men and women; but by then it may be too late for them or for their children. If our vaunted capacity for foresight is of any real use it must be able to affect action even a little before direct experience calls for action which will then already be too late.

The question most relevant to this book is – what role, if any, has the technologist in this educational task?

In principle there is nothing odd in expecting a professional to teach his clients what to expect of him. They usually expect too much. The architect works within a double framework of limiting laws – natural laws governing the stability of structures, and human regulations governing the size and nature of structures which may be erected on any particular site. He is also limited by his own conceptions of what is fit to be erected in any particular physical context and what will be most aesthetically satisfying in that context, as well as how best to reconcile his client's various functional and other requirements. The first two of all these limitations are matters beyond his control but not beyond his knowledge. It is his business to know and explain them. The remaining three are matters on which his client may differ but should at least consider with care his adviser's judgements. Deadlock may conceivably result; it is inherent in the professional's dual responsibility to his client and to his profession. All this is as true of the technologist as of any other professional. Why does he alone repudiate it? Why is he so arrogant? What other profession would be proud to claim, 'The difficult we do at once. The impossible takes a little longer'?

I will not offer even hypothetical answers to these questions. But I have no doubt that as a professional the technologist has an important educational function which he is best placed and best qualified to emphasize. He lives and works within a framework of natural laws which are not to be escaped, however complex their interaction. He should be better placed than others both to chart the most important areas of their interaction and to warn his fellows of the inherent dangers and implications.

And so to some extent he has begun to do – but only as the result of a most extraordinary development. This has left him deeply involved in an area for which his past history has radically unfitted him.

Footnotes

1. Professor Barry Commoner is an example – but they are still too rare.
2. I have suggested how this might be done in a paper published in the *Journal of Applied Systems Analysis*, vol. 7, April 1980, op. cit.

CHAPTER 19

ANALYSTS, MODELLERS, AND GOVERNORS[1]

Since the Second World War the most rapidly expanding field of professional study has been the field of human governance. I use the term 'governance' because policy making, government, management and administration are used in different senses by writers in the field and I need a term wide enough to include all aspects of the art of imposing on human affairs, whether in the public or the private sector, whatever kind and degree of order seems possible and desirable to those in seats of power.

I refer to this as a professional, rather than a scientific, field. The difference is, I think, important. All professional skills contain some quotient of academic knowledge; and universities from the earliest times have contained professional schools as well as academic disciplines. Medicine, law, architecture, and music have mediaeval academic roots. Engineering established its academic status in the nineteenth century and has since proliferated in its many branches. This century has seen further newcomers to the professional schools, including planning and social work. 'Governance' in various forms and degrees, is among the most recent.

But academic disciplines and professional schools have seldom got on well together. Professions other than the traditional ones have usually had a struggle to establish their academic status and sometimes an even harder one to maintain it, without losing their equally important link with the professions which they exist to serve. Some at the present time are making the worst of both worlds, regarded as second-class citizens by their academic colleagues because they are insufficiently 'pure', and by their professional colleagues because they are insufficiently practical.

The tension has been widened by the contemporary urge of all university studies to assimilate themselves to the model of the natural sciences. But an even more divisive factor, I think, is the criterion which determines the relevance of their curricula. Academic disciplines draw their boundaries in whatever way seems convenient to the pursuit of ever more specialized knowledge; and as they grow, they fragment. Professions, on the other hand, are defined by the kinds of service which their clients find useful enough to pay for. They have thus a different and inbuilt standard of relevance by which to define the academic knowledge which they need. They seek it wherever they can find it; and they generate it themselves if no academic discipline is interested or able to meet their need. Virology, for example, is today a well-established branch of biological science. But viruses were discovered by *medical* research, seeking pathogens which, before they were discovered, were known as 'filter-passing bacteria'. If no virus had been a human pathogen, how much would we know about viruses today?

Further, unlike the sciences, the professions tend not to fragment even while they diversify. Social work, for example, successfully insisted on a 'core training' for all social workers, from psychiatric social workers to probation officers. The Chartered Institute of Surveyors embraces a profession with many branches. Professionals have powerful practical, as well as ideological, interests in belonging to strong professional associations.

The profession of governance has long been studied in and out of universities but not until about a century ago in professional schools. As a professional study at least six contributory streams can be distinguished.

The earliest, so far as I can ascertain, were schools of public administration. These were concerned not with making policy but with the functions of implementing it and of providing the information which policy makers need. The actual making of policy was distinguished partly from a well-founded sense of its complexity and obscurity and partly in deference to the principle of representative government, which required the assumption that only elected representatives were 'policy makers'. The large administrative organizations which were coming into being in both public and private sectors were correctly seen as structures of roles, embodying complementary responsibilities, rights and powers which needed to be appropriately apportioned, understood and accepted, especially the scope of discretion allowed to each role in the structure.

A second contribution to the profession of governance early this century was the study of work organization. The scientific management of industry, or at least of industrial production, was pioneered by F. W. Taylor and dramatically illustrated by Henry Ford when he produced his 'people's car' the famous 'tin Lizzie'. The principle of division of labour was, of course, as old as Adam Smith. It was practised at least up to the Second World War by some of the finest Swiss watchmakers in conditions the reverse of those associated with mass production. Some of their jewel bearings passed through seven hands, each performing a highly skilled manual operation in a different cottage workshop. Yet when the Second World War cut down the supply of bearings reaching Allied hands, the whole resources of Western factory technology throughout the war proved unable to make good the shortfall without a rate of wastage several times as great as in all the cottage workshops.

Taylor's ideas produced Ford's people's car but in the long term the car's effect was more powerful in the social than in the technological field. The concentration of labour plus the debasement of skill had effects which Mary Parker Follet[2] was quick to point out. People organized for industry, as for anything else, became a human social system. This, the third contributory insight into the study of governing human systems, received a dramatic and unexpected confirmation from Elton Mayo's Hawthorne experiments. It was, and still is, pursued in England in the Tavistock Institute of Human Relations and it has become part of the general background of 'Personnel Management'.

During the 1930s two further streams, originally separate though destined to merge, perhaps too much, began to add their contributions, both practical and conceptual, to the study of governance. One was Operations Research. The OR man's original focus was on enquiring into the efficiency of given means to a given end, where the criteria of efficiency were also given. His remit extended to suggesting more efficient means to attain the same end when judged by the same criteria. This, however, was not the primary focus of his concern. He was essentially an efficiency auditor, though he was, of course, more likely to be called in when the client felt a need to better his efficiency if he could.

The OR man's impact was often wider than he or his client expected. The client often found it unexpectedly difficult to define all the 'ends' which some 'means' were intended to serve. He might even find 'operations' going on which served no identifiable end but which could not, he felt, be stopped without loss. Business was clearly not a simple application of means to ends, in which the means were indifferent except by some single quantifiable criterion such as economy of resources. Moreover, experiment soon showed that costs, and sometimes also benefits, were to be expected simply from change as such. The more the client tried to explain his business, the more complex and even obscure it tended to become. He was, none the less, the better for having to pause and explain to a critical outsider what he was doing and why – at least so long as he did not assume that whatever he could not explain to the satisfaction of the outsider must necessarily be wrong.

The OR man's horizons also widened. Any 'operation' which he examined could not be judged simply by its own efficiency as a means to its own end. It was part of a systemic whole, composed of related parts which sustained it through time only so long as it did not pass some critical limit of stability. These surely existed, though one could seldom predict with assurance when or how they would be breached. The analysis of systems emerged as an inseparable companion of operations research. Professor Rolfe Tomlinson[3] has coined the acronym ORASA for the combination of OR and Systems Analysis.

Operations Research was clearly a new profession and soon established its own professional organization. Its practitioners brought to the work a knowledge of such principles of management and government as they accepted as generally valid, and, perhaps more importantly, clear and logical minds accustomed to analysing situations from the point of view generated by accepted criteria of success. Virtually all professionals are systems analysts in this sense. The lawyer, questioning his client, needs to construct in his mind both a perception of the client's situation adequate at least for the purpose for which he is being consulted, and also a perception of the way that situation appears to his client. Both activities are forms of systems analysis.

The second of the two streams which I mentioned as destined to merge was the use of the computer as a tool for modelling situations. In so far as the effect of different variables on each other can be expressed in mathematical form and without excessive dependence on context, the computer can calculate them for a variety of values with incomparable speed and precision and can thus present a model of the situation on a wide variety of assumptions. Further, in so far as any planned or other intervention in such a process can be expressed in similar form, its effect can be predicted on any or all of the states modelled. The systems analyst becomes, to this extent, a systems modeller, and has at his disposal resources for predicting the result of such changes by a much more rigorous method than before. He has a new and powerful tool. How far its use can be extended depends partly on the development of computers and partly on the development of languages to which they can be designed to respond. It depends also and even more on the extent to which the interaction of persons, organizations and populations can be expressed in terms of laws sufficiently invariable and context free to be modelled in this way. The last question is the most important and has been the most fiercely debated. I return to it later.

At the time of the Second World War management and government were widely regarded, especially by their practitioners, as unteachable arts. Top executives of business had reached their positions usually by learning on the job and by promotion following what was regarded as successful performance and few saw any other way of developing their skills. The same was true of civil servants. Politicians were selected by electorates and judged by an even more obscure mixture of criteria; and they were even more convinced that their success could not be speeded or the road to it charted by academic study except in so far as this contributed to the background of an 'educated man', an expression which then had a meaning both wider and more precise than it has now. So the 'professional' and, still more, the academic study of government began slowly and was at first focused chiefly on the private sector, where the criteria of success seemed more explicit and more agreed.

The form of study which was evolving in America before the Second World War but which was first tried in England only in 1946 was a combination of two methods. One was the study of 'tool subjects' such as accounting and financial control, the use of statistics, the measurement of performance and productivity, organization theory and even personnel management. These, it was agreed, could be academically studied and were useful, even essential in some degree, to 'governors' at all levels. The more subtle and important part of the exercise, the development of 'judgement' was approached, still historically, through the study of case histories, a method which was also being widely adopted in training for social work. It was claimed that the student could widen and deepen his own experience on the job (and without the cost of errors) by sharing the experience of others who, in well-defined situations such as he might experience, had had to make critical decisions.

This method depends, of course, on the reliability of the historian who records the case history and it is a little simplistic in its assumption that the processes of making such decisions can be fully described in only one way. But it is useful and welcome in so far as it imparts some discipline and clarity, as well as richness, into our habitual process of learning from experience, including the experience of others. Indeed it is essential if these lessons are to be fully learned. For it involves detailed study after the event of all the processes which went to the making of particular decisions, including perhaps some which were hidden at the time by the actors from others and perhaps even from themselves. Rival interpretations may give rise to irresolvable controversy but they are no less useful on that account. A classical example is the study of the German decision in 1940 to attack through the Ardennes and of the Allies' exclusion of this even as a possibility. A more encouraging example is the handling of the Cuban missile crisis. Such historical examples have the advantage that they are usually documented more fully than others, though the historian may have to wait some decades before the most essential evidence is made public.

The study of recorded case histories can be extended by the practice of imaginary ones. This practice raises fascinating questions. How far can a role player really simulate in his own consciousness the responsibility and the stress of being the real man with whom the real buck really stops? Can we afford to become so conscious of our dramatic roles, as a preparation for playing them in real and different situations? I do not know the answers. There may be no general answers. I am not even sure that experience can teach us. But I have no doubt that these techniques, whatever their dangers, have a contribution to make both to education in governance and to education generally. I know a headmaster who, at a difficult interview with a deviant or recalcitrant student, secretly tapes the interview and plays it back to himself afterwards to see whether his performance stands up to his own criticism. He finds it an educative but sometimes a humbling experience.

Thus far training in governance has included acquiring ancillary skills and also learning to recognize errors and pathologies which may impede the exercise of judgement. Judgement itself remains an art, undefined except to some extent by its results; perhaps personal in that those who are recognized as excelling at it have markedly different styles not readily comparable; including diverse gifts; and incompletely describable because of perhaps irresolvable obscurities in our understanding of the human mind itself. This was sometimes expressed as the antithesis between 'art' and 'science'. But throughout this century this distinction has been growing more unacceptable as the empire of science extended its claims.

In mediaeval universities the term 'science' covered all forms of knowledge however acquired, as the term 'art' covered all skills (including of course the skilful use of knowledge). Rhetoric was no less a science than astronomy, but those who satisfied their examiners in these and the other required branches of knowledge acquired the title of Masters of Art.

Later, with the rise of the natural sciences, the word science became attached only to forms of knowledge which could be validated in a prescribed way and, as the prestige of science rose, the prestige of knowledge not so classified declined. Still later, as skills became increasingly embodied in technological processes which had to be fully specifiable and reproducible, any area of unspecified skill became suspect and the presumption grew that however obscure it might seem, it must really be precisely describable – and that meant describable in mathematical terms. So the latest developments in the art of judgement have been directed to converting judgement also into a fully specifiable skill. The development of computer hardware and, still more, computer software, have encouraged this drive.

One element in this development has been studies of game playing. These reflect and in turn encourage the belief that the object of all rational human endeavour is to achieve given 'ends' by the 'best' application of 'means', the criterion of 'best' being usually some measure of economy or effectiveness. This implies that all human endeavour can be broken down into a sequence of problems to be solved. This, I have argued, is a profoundly distorting and limiting concept to apply to a regulative process, but it is, none the less, widespread.

A personal experience illustrates both the limitations of the game-playing analogy and its power over excellent and influential minds. I once objected to one such excellent mind that playing chess could not be an adequate analogy to human governance, as he had suggested, because in chess the definition of success and the rules of the game are taken as given by the players, whilst in the governance of human life at all levels the criteria of success and the rules of the game are what the most important arguments are all about. He replied that, even if these changed over time and differed in different cultures, their differences caused him no concern. As a member of the U.S. President's Scientific Advisory Committee, when formulating with his colleagues the advice which they should give on whatever problem had been submitted to them (perhaps some aspect of environmental pollution) he 'felt as if he were playing chess'.

He is an eminent and very able man. And it is true that in the circumstances he described, the roles of the parties and their shared assumptions may well have created a base of unexamined assumption both about the nature of 'success' and about the 'rules of the game' which removed these from conscious debate, though not perhaps usefully so. It seems to me to remain significant that thoughtful and humane men can regard as an acceptable analogy to any form of human life a zero-sum game in which the players stand outside the board and its pieces and regard the pieces as purely instrumental, having no interests of their own in the use which is made of them. It was, of course, and too often still is, the attitude of the technologist using natural resources for human purposes. It is not acceptable as an analogy for the activity of a 'governor' at any level seeking to maintain acceptable order in a society of his fellow men, which includes himself.

Neither the dangers nor the uses of game playing are to be dismissed in a paragraph. Games (including some which are not 'zero-sum') have their uses as simulations of real situations and the study of them has contributed to our understandings of mental process. But it is to be remembered that of the last seventy years, ten have been spent by the leading Western nations in all-out war, which is our most extreme equivalent to the zero-sum game in the context of large-scale real life. Much of the remaining sixty years has been dominated, externally and internally, by mutual struggle or threat. The eclipse of the ethical dimension, as I have already noted, has depreciated the quality of human communication as much as technology has increased its volume and has left confrontation and trade-off as the only forms of human intercourse which can be fully accepted (though even this cannot be fully described). To this must be added the growing dominance of technology as successful manipulation of all forms of organic as well as inorganic matter, other than human beings, and the corresponding urge to assimilate governance to the otherwise universal pattern of manipulation. It is not surprising that the role of the governor should shrink, except in so far as it can be asssimilated to that of the analyst, and the modeller.

The trend is vividly illustrated by an activity which I have not yet mentioned, the forecasting of human futures. The term itself resonates with the assumption that in a scientific world the future must be predictable, at least in theory. And scientific optimism, encouraged by the promises of technological modelling, is prone to expect that what is possible in theory must some day be realized in practice.

The word 'forecasting' is, none the less, ambiguous; for in human affairs it has long been used in a conditional sense. 'If you go on spending at this rate you'll go bankrupt.' The prediction is conditional, intended as a warning to prevent its own fulfilment, a justification for the injunction – 'Cut down your spending!'

The scope for men to influence their own and each other's futures varies from nil to a high degree. Their scope for imposing a particular order on their future varies even more so. It is hard for the most rigid determinist to act on the belief that even the former scope is nil. The injunction – 'Think what you are doing!' implies a belief that such calling to consciousness will itself make a difference of some kind. And if it becomes apparent that the person advised is, at least for the time being, unable to face the realization of what he is doing, his advisers feel that to this extent he is lacking a normal faculty of the human mind. The example has its familiar parallels in the sphere of collective human life where a substantial majority of those concerned have not only to think what they are doing but to arrive at the same answer if their thinking is to be effective.

In consequence, attempts to forecast aspects of the future which are relevant to men today range from what purport to be predictions wholly beyond human control, to warnings which, at least in the view of those who utter them, will be spontaneously averted so soon as they are believed. It is a significant comment on our culture that forecasts of the future of technology are made more commonly than any others with the confidence of predictions. And the achievements of technology are most frequently expressed as the solving of a series of problems.

I have already expressed the view that the governance of human systems is not to be resolved into the solution of a series of problems. This view has recently been expressed by a very experienced practitioner of the art of ORASA, Professor Rolfe Tomlinson. In a recent paper[4] he refers to a review made by the British National Coal Board of the activities of its operational research unit (of which Professor Tomlinson was head) over a period of years. Only 15 percent of its activities over that period could be identified as 'problem solving'. The rest and the most prized result of its activities was to increase the understanding of some situation which was of concern to the board. The problem solving alone had more than paid for the unit over the period examined. But the deepened understanding was at least as greatly prized.

In the paper already cited Professor Tomlinson identifies what he calls seven dangerous half-truths about operations research and systems analysis. (He admits that the faint association, with the seven deadly sins is 'not coincidental'.) The first half-truth is 'ORASA is problem solving'. He does not underrate problem solving. At a low to middle level in the field of governance the technique of solving identified, fully describable problems is a useful 'tool subject' worth teaching in university courses. But the aim of education until now has been to deepen understanding, not merely to teach techniques.

Nor are new techniques merely an addition to a workman's bag of tools. They cannot help influencing his perceptions. They help to determine what he notices, as well as what he does about it. They limit as well as enable.

This is fearfully exemplified in Professor Tomlinson's sixth half-truth. 'All rigorous thought can be expressed in mathematical terms.' In fact the languages of words and of mathematics are complementary. The second developed much later and gave welcome rigour to some verbal statements, especially general statements of relationship for which it was more convenient than words. But it remained incapable of expressing at all many meanings which are essential to understanding any communication concerning human life. For these are derived from the direct experience of human life and they are embodied in the meanings and connotations of words which have been developed over millenia as a means of sharing direct experience and which have survived only because they have been found to serve this extraordinary purpose with astonishing success. A culture which contrives to overlook this basic instrument of its humanity must be very sick indeed.

Footnotes

1. This chapter is largely based on my paper entitled 'Systems Analysis – a Tool Subject or Judgement Demystified', published in *Policy Sciences*, vol. 14, 1981.
2. Mary Parker Follet, 1868–1933, from Massachusetts, a vocational guidance counsellor and author of *The New State* (1918) and *Creative Experience* (1924).
3. R. C. Tomlinson. 'Some Dangerous Misconceptions Concerning Operations Research and Applied Systems Analysis', *European Journal of Operational Research*, vol. 7, no. 2, June 1981.
4. Ibid.

CHAPTER 20

UNDERSTANDING, DECIDING, AND POLICY MAKING

The separation of analysis and modelling into distinctive techniques with their own specialists helps us to understand what the unaided mind does when seeking to understand a situation. This is even more apparent when the effort is a collective one; for then many operations which would otherwise be tacit appear explicitly in discussion and mutual persuasion. Consider what actually happens when a board of directors considers even something so simple as a wage claim. The claim's direct financial implications, if it were accepted, are the easiest to reckon and even to quantify. But these would not be the only effects even of acceptance. The probable outcome of refusal and of alternative offers can only be estimated, or even guessed. They involve 'modelling' mentally the attitude both of the representatives who are making the claim and of those whom they represent; the extent to which these attitudes may be changed for better or worse by attempts at persuasion of diverse kinds; the limitations under which both sides are acting and the possibilities of changing them; the part played by considerations of occupational status and of personal status; the existing level of trust; and so on. All these explorations are acts of analysis or of synthesis. Few, except the purely financial ones, can be expressed quantitatively. Few of the relations discerned can be expressed in terms of invariant or statistical relation. None the less the discussion, unless highly unsuccessful, will leave the members of the board with a more detailed and more agreed understanding of the situation and of the field of manoeuvre open to them.

This understanding will be changed by the board's next meeting with the union; and so will the situation itself. The understanding will be changed because each side will receive and interpret in its own way a flood of new information, verbal and nonverbal, received during the discussion. The situation will be changed in so far as the parties to it are changed by their own responses to the meeting.

These responses include a wide range of change both intellectual and emotional. I have chosen an example in which change in emotional responses may be sudden, extreme and critical; for the situation described as a wage negotiation is an ambivalent, and highly unstable one. It can pass in a few minutes from the joint search for a commonly acceptable answer to acceptance of the zero-sum conditions of a battlefield. This instability is due to the fact that the intermediate state of 'bargain' is virtually never present. For it is of the essence of a bargain that both parties, if they fail to agree, are free to go elsewhere. Failing this, the degeneration of negotiation into battle can be abrupt and unpredictable. The reverse process, from battle to negotiation, is more difficult and more rare and so even more dramatic when it occurs, as it sometimes does.

In brief, analysis and synthesis – for synthesis is the essence of modelling – are perfectly familiar exercises of the human mind. The factors which are distinguished in analysis, like the relations which are modelled in synthesis, can be expressed with widely varying degrees of precision. Even the distinction between those which can and those which cannot be mathematically represented, is liable to be greatly exaggerated by the promise of our new techniques of mathematical modelling. For on the one hand nearly all our mathematical techniques involve some degree of statistical or other simplification of the facts and relations modelled. Equally, on the other hand, even our vaguest sounding verbal expressions often have values of critical importance, even where we could not usefully expand them in words. Consider the crucial difference in understanding a situation represented by the alternatives: 'I trust A' and 'I don't trust A'. Neither can be expressed mathematically. Yet at an international negotiation I have see thirty delegates from fourteen countries change their collective mind in less than a minute simply from exposure to an individual whose good faith was important to their acceptance of his proposals and who, before they met him, they were sure could not possibly intend to do or even be able to do what he was proposing. Events showed that their change of mind was perfectly well founded. Their understanding of the situation wholly depended on their estimate of the character of a total stranger.

It is always difficult to stress one aspect of any matter without seeming to belittle the importance of others. We have every reason to be grateful for our new facilities for representing the interaction of variables of different hypothetical values, whenever the variables themselves and the laws of their interaction can be expressed in mathematical terms without unacceptable simplification. These facilities would have dazzled any technologist even thirty to forty years ago.

When, for example, the British coal industry was nationalized, the National Union of Mineworkers made a number of demands, all reasonable in themselves, none more so than the demand for a five-day week but none so full of implications, the effect of which needed analysis and modelling. Not merely the financial implications but the implications for energy supply (energy famines were a regular feature of the winters immediately following the war) for rail and other transport needed to be understood and the effects compared of alternative ways and timings for introducing a change of work patterns, the effect of which would spread far beyond the industry itself. Most of these comparisons could be judged by quantitative standards and most of them both admitted and depended on correct calculation based on reasonably firm data. The tireless statisticians who worked night after night to give multiple quantitative meanings to the alternative hypothetical proposals thrown up daily by the working party concerned would have been devoutly grateful for computer facilities which their children today may learn to take for granted at school.

None the less Tomlinson's warning is not to be ignored. Verbal symbols and mathematical symbols are almost wholly complementary instruments in the human mind's search for understanding. It is better not to argue about their relative importance, except perhaps to remind someone who is obsessed with the importance of one of them that the other also has its dominant field – and that not only because its field has not yet been absorbed by its alternative.

It is not to be expected that human beings should fully understand their own understanding. For that capacity, whatever it includes, is their only instrument for understanding anything. It seems to me improbable, if not illogical, to expect any system to contain a complete model of itself. We should rather, I think, be surprised that we understand as much of our own understandings as we do. I have already stressed the fact that in interpreting the human world we cannot help using our own experience, both conscious and unconscious, as an aid to the analysis and modelling of other people's experience and understanding. And since verbal language has developed largely through the efforts of individuals to exchange experience, it is not surprising that its most unchallenged and unchallengeable field should be the field of human relations. This is not to say that simple observation, such as supplies the data for the natural scientist's hypotheses, may not be fruitful in the field of human relations also. It does, however, stress the truth that the viewpoint of the agent experient cannot be contained by that of the observer, any more than the reverse.

So far I have sought to present the search for understanding as a combined process of analysis and synthesis in which both verbal and mathematical symbols have a part to play. It remains to explore the relation between understanding and deciding, and also between understanding and policy making, by which I mean changing (or confirming) the regulatory norms by which the mind concerned chooses to be guided in future action in so far as it has any scope for choice.

Understanding does not of itself tell us what to do, still less what policy to follow. It may indeed make these decisions more difficult, though one may reasonably hope that it will on the whole improve their outcome. This too is one of those facts which, once familiar, is in danger of being obscured by the obsessive passion to reduce all exercises of discretion to some form of calculation.

The fallacy is latent even at the stage before the search for understanding begins. Why seek to understand this situation rather than another? Why seek understanding at all? I have emphasized in an earlier chapter that some 'concern' has to be postulated to explain even the earliest steps in the search for understanding.

This concern may be awakened simply by some perceived promise or threat, though even so it remains to ask why the occasion is perceived as promising or threatening. It may equally be awakened by the felt need of the human mind to complete its own interpretation of the world in which it finds itself to whatever extent will satisfy its curiosity; a dimension in which human minds manifestly differ very widely.

The distinction drawn by Marx and already quoted between philosophers who are content to seek understanding for its own sake and activists who seek it only to guide action, distinguishes two extreme positions in a spectrum along which different minds can be arranged with some confidence. But whether the directive comes from the felt need to understand or the felt need to act or some combination of the two, some specific felt need there must be – not to explain mental activity as such, for human beings like other animals are active by definition, but to explain the direction which the activity takes. I have already expressed my dissatisfaction with efforts directed to resolve this complex hierarchy of concerns into basic biological urges unaffected either by a society's culture or by that 'culture of one' which comes to distinguish each individual as experience and reflection develops his or her own complex of responses and criteria.

In the context of governance, the roles of the 'governor' are usually sufficient to explain substantially why he seeks understanding in particular directions and with particular emphasis and urgency. His role determines his field of responsibility. His experience signals those areas in which he is being least successful or in which he has the most promising opportunities for intervention. Even for such a role player the signals which call for attention and the criteria which determine success are usually more subtle and more complex, though not necessarily more conflicting than appears superficially. The statesman serves a country, belongs to a party, and manages a personal career, and the three react on each other in ways which cannot wholly be attributed to a hierarchy of cogency irrespective of context. The conflicts which arise between them have been the stuff of ethical debate ever since men began to attribute moral responsibility to each other and to themselves. A major function of a culture has been to impose some degree of uniformity, at least among those who have most frequent dealings with each other. Naturally these imperatives have been most unconditional in those areas which have been deemed most socially important.

We need not go back for examples to the tribe which drove out its deviant member to die in the desert. For most ordinary Britons in 1914 British participation in the First World War was justified and required simply by the requirements of the treaty whereby the country had joined in guaranteeing the integrity of Belgium a century before. The obligation to keep a treaty was then almost universally regarded as a collective obligation involving the national honour. The circumstances which led to the creation of Belgium might have changed but the obligation to defend its frontiers remained.

Since 1914 there have been radical changes in the views commonly accepted in Western countries about the criteria for action, individual or collective. The point is well illustrated by a passage in a well-known book by Peter Berger and others[1] which purports to describe and explain the change of usage which in English-speaking countries has made the concept of honour almost unusable today, whilst the concept of dignity has attained a universally respected status. According to Berger and his coauthors honour is a word connoting privilege and so no longer acceptable in an egalitarian society, whilst the word dignity has come to summarize all those rights to which every human being is inalienably entitled.

In fact the word honour has always connoted a code of duties; and although these were once regarded as binding only on persons of a certain social degree (who alone were expected to defend their honour in a duel) this class distinction had died out, at least in England, long before this century began. The obligation of national honour which sent so many volunteers to the First World War was an obligation attaching to a share in a national inheritance.

Dignity, by contrast, was an ambivalent word, implying the respect due to certain offices and their holders as such but readily withdrawn from those who sought to bolster their personal worth by identifying with their office and 'standing on their dignity'. The change since 1914 is indeed as great as Berger describes but its historical course and origin seems to me to have been the precise reverse of what he suggests, at least in Britain.

It is, of course, common knowledge how much such cultural imperatives have lost their force in the West during the present century. It is much less common to hear it admitted that this change has made human choice more difficult and less explicable than before, rather than the reverse. Analysis and synthesis are indeed the basic tools of any cost-benefit analysis. But they do not of themselves determine the weight to be given to any cost or any benefit. They do not even distinguish between a benefit and a cost. Even if the rational anticipation of results and the estimation of risks and uncertainties were far more complete than they can possibly be even in theory, this would not of itself prescribe what value should be attached to any of them.

Yet this process is far from being without effect. It presents to the concerned mind a representation of the situation which has evoked it, greatly extended in both past and future time. This representation in turn evokes response. I have argued elsewhere that the process of decision making and, still more, of policy making is a process of intensive and accelerated learning and that this includes learning what to want as well as how to get. Both the tacit norms and the explicit values which the agent brings to the process are changed by the process itself. The men who leave the conference table or the negotiating table (whether they count their interaction as successful or not) are not the same men as those who first sat down together. In the language which I introduced in Chapter 6 they have changed the settings of their appreciative systems. Their deepened understanding has been one main agency in this change. The other has been their own response to the total experience, resulting from and expressed in their new appreciation of their situation. The combined result is less predictable in proportion to the degree of change involved.

These speculations take us to the edge of our understanding of ourselves, possibly to the edge of what we can hope to understand. I express them not because I think they can do more than reflect the outlines of a familiar and important picture but because even those outlines are in danger of being lost to view. They are attested chiefly by human history and human biography – apart from direct personal experience, a fact of life which should not be ignored merely because it is often misleading. They are in danger. For if we consistently ignore a human capacity, even one which we manifestly possess, we shall cease to practise it, cease to prize it, and conceivably forget it beyond hope of recall.

This we cannot afford to do, especially at the present time. For if the argument of this book has any validity at all, it is to suggest that all today's human populations, perhaps particularly those heirs of the Enlightenment who have so successfully pioneered the huge cultural changes of the last two hundred years, need now to achieve an even more radical reversal, a change not only in their understanding, as observers, of the developing situation in which they are trapped, but also a change in their appreciation, as agents and as experients, of what these changes require of them. The demand will, of course, exceed their capacities; it is doing so already. But at least they cannot afford to handicap themselves by assuming that mathematical calculation, however refined, will make unnecessary an effort at evaluation which at best may be far beyond their powers.

Footnote

1. P. Berger et. al. *The Homeless Mind*, New York, Random House, 1975.

CHAPTER 21

HOW DIFFERENT ARE HUMAN SYSTEMS?

There can be no doubt that the organizations in which human beings are always found have the characteristics of systems as I described them in Chapter 2. It remains to ask in what respects, if any, they differ from those other kinds of system with which we most readily compare them.

These standards of comparison are mainly of two kinds – the ecological model and the technological model. The ecological model has developed through the interaction of life forms in a specific habitat, which is to some extent their own creation. The rain forest grew in the Amazon basin which favoured its growth and created conditions which favoured some forms and discouraged others. Its relative stability as a mature form is a *resultant* of countless forces acting on each other, sometimes to encourage, sometimes to restrain. Many of these forces are inherent in the individual forms themselves but their effect on each other is infinitely variable. The same pursuit of light, for example, encourages vegetable forms to grow vertically and restricts their growth horizontally. The resultant order, though not wholly constant, is sufficiently so through time to be recognized as a continuing system both by its enduring characteristics and by its contrast with different ecological systems to which different conditions have given different but equally enduring characteristics.

Ecological order is not only a resultant; it also has results. Some of them are important to men. Rain forests produce oxygen. Swamps produce malarial mosquitoes. Both have countless other results, favourable and otherwise to human life. In so far as men have and use power to intervene either to change or merely to preserve ecological order, it becomes not merely a resultant but a potential field for human design. However much this power is exercised, the system will remain a system. However little it is exercised, a new determinant will have appeared on the scene, using new criteria. The system thus modified, however slightly, will invite judgement not merely as more or less stable but as more or less successful by these new standards, and perhaps later by others which are found to be involved.

The concept of success is a complex one. It implies criteria by which success is to be judged; criteria which are cultural, sometimes almost wholly individual, as well as biological. Even the biological criteria are more complex and conflicting than they look. Rain forests may be necessary to the biosphere as a home for man but a less than optimal environment for those men who live in them. Malaria is a burden but wetlands have their biological uses for men. Cultural and personal criteria are far more complex and conflicting.

The concept of purpose obscures the concept of success still farther. For first it assumes that the purpose is worth pursuing and thus commits the evaluating mind either to some ultimate objective which is worth pursuing for its own sake, or to an infinite regress in which every goal is sought as a means to some even more remote 'end'. It also commits the evaluating mind to the absurd assumption that 'means' are in themselves value-free, comparable only by their efficiency in attaining some desired end. This dominance of purpose as a human motivation is a relatively new deviation in our understanding of human motivation and one which technologists are particularly liable to accept without sufficient question, since they are so frequently called on to find means to ends chosen by others.

The concept of success is wider than the concept of purpose; but it too involves judgement by criteria which are essentially supplied by human minds. The Amazon jungle does not have a purpose or need a purpose to justify its existence; and even if it ceased to exist, it would be anthropomorphic to say that it had 'failed'. Equally the tribes which inhabit it do not have or need a purpose to justify their existence; and although they and their members no doubt have many 'purposes', their standards of success are both more and other than the fulfilment of their purposes. Our own Western societies have defined success in life in a great variety of ways, even within the last two centuries – from glorifying God to serving mankind to making a fortune. But in every case, even the last, the success lay in the activity itself, rather than in its results. A man ambitious to become Prime Minister looks forward primarily to exercising all the relationships which that office will open to him. He may also look forward to the euphoria of his election night but if he died in the course of it both he and his supporters would feel that fate had robbed him of the fruits of his success.

This obsession with goals or ends which are to be attained or not attained once for all, is fatal to any adequate conception of system, human or otherwise. It is not, of course, a total illusion. Animals seek to avoid death, although the survival of a species or even of a population is not necessarily served thereby. It may even be threatened, as many human populations are threatened in varying degrees by the increase in longevity. We find it hard to withhold the categories of success and failure from the rabbit eluding the hare or the fly eluding the fly catcher. It is, none the less, anthropomorphic to equate death with failure. Death and life are part of the same process, for mice or men. Our habits of thought about success have been greatly confused by the concept of biological evolution, or rather by its cultural effect, coming when it did, in identifying survival with success.

Success is a judgement made by human minds by reference to human criteria. Even so it appeals to three different sets of criteria, each of which ideally needs a separate pair of words to connote match or mismatch with the criteria involved.

One set reports the outcome of comparison of the specific result of an action with the agent's intention. A murder is successful if the murderer kills his victim; if not it is a failure. The demolition of a block of unwanted flats, if well done, is as successful as their equally efficient erection.

The second set of criteria reports the outcome of comparing all the discernible results of an action, whether intended or not, with all the criteria then entertained by anyone who is affected by those results and whose judgement cannot be – or at least is not – ignored. This is, of course, an open-ended definition. No one can trace through an indefinite span of future time all the results which may flow from even a trivial action; nor can anyone assess the criteria which future ages will apply. I have cited DDT as an example of an activity which succeeded by the first set of criteria but failed by the second. Among the criteria of the second class which condemned it is one, namely its ecological effect on the sea-living mammals, which would probably have had less effect a hundred years before and which may well have an even greater effect even a few decades hence. Criteria of success are structures of the human mind and change with time. They may emerge – or even disappear with time. And it is they alone which define what shall be regarded as success in the second of the senses which I have attributed to that word.

In doing so they are bound to raise basic difficulties of at last three kinds. One is the difficulty of comparing disparate variables. At what point does somewhat polluted air become preferable to the cost of keeping it even cleaner? Is a cheap sewer preferable to a river you can safely bathe in?

The second difficulty in defining success is uncertainty. Most future promises and threats are not predictable with absolute assurance; some are highly uncertain. But their importance in human calculations does not diminish in linear or other regular relation to their probability. An unacceptable threat does not necessarily become acceptable merely because it is improbable. Human decisions are often made by the fact that one risk is found too serious to accept or, if it exists, to increase, however unpalatable the alternatives may look. Nor do human minds usually agree on this crucial issue of acceptability. Some of the most bitter controversies of our time, notably the controversy around the future use of nuclear energy, depend precisely on different valuations of this kind – not on estimates of probability but on judgements of acceptability.

The third difficulty in defining success is time. How far ahead should the policy maker look? Beyond some horizon, which varies with the issue, all estimates of future results become lost in a fog of uncertainty. But should he not look at least as far as he can? At one extreme stands the mutualist, grumbling – 'Posterity has done nothing for me. Why should I bother about it?' At the other extreme stands the devotee of complementary obligations, overwhelmed by his indebtedness to the past and acutely conscious that he can pay that debt only to the future. I have already suggested that human beings may be able to extend their awareness of future as well as past time to an extent which we have not even guessed. Let us hope so.

Contemporary education does not seem to place this goal high on its agenda. I have heard an eminent systems scientist, when asked whether he thought history was bunk, reply that although he would not go so far as that, he would confidently assert that an adequate description of any system at a precise 'moment in time' would include all the information about the past which a man living at that moment of time could need to guide him into the future. I will leave it to the reader to work out how far this would meet the needs of a 'governor' at any level.

A publication of the Open University observes that human systems are the only kind of system which can be said to succeed or fail. It avoids attempting a definition of success but it defines failure as including both failure to accomplish the intended purpose and also its accomplishment offset by so many unwelcome accompaniments that the accomplishment is reckoned as not worth its price. (I have given examples of both these kinds of failure.) The definition seems admirable to me (with the qualifications I have mentioned) so long as we confine the expression 'human systems' to systems which are made for one or more specific purposes though without total disregard for their other effects. In other words to systems which are probably judged by the second of my sets of criteria already defined. It is worth noting that technologists designing a system are usually given one or, at most, two sets of criteria of success, the others being introduced in the form of constraints within which their solutions must be kept.

But can all human systems be defined in terms of purpose? This brings me to the third and widest context in which we use the criteria of success and failure. A village is a human system – but has it a purpose? It is a set of more or less self-sustaining relationships, a continuing way of life for people and also a set of conditions of life for people. It may deliberately set out to change one or more of these conditions. It may build a village hall for meetings. It may take an active part in developing or controlling the development of its physical growth. But none of those account for the village in the sense in which a railway service or a telephone exchange can be accounted for by the purpose which it is designed to serve.

It seems that we need to make a distinction between human systems and man-made systems. A man-made system might be wholly automatic. It would, none the less, be explicable as a means of serving a human purpose. A human system might consist wholly of human persons, all capable of purposeful action and usually active in ways explicable by some purpose. But it would not be explicable wholly in terms of human purpose, unless 'purpose' were given a meaning far wider than is either normal or convenient. People are not merely instruments either of other people's purposes or even of their own. We have criteria for judging excellence and default which are not to be expressed in terms of purposes achieved or not achieved but of standards realized, standards defaulted on and even standards reset.

The reality of this distinction is breaking through into contemporary consciousness despite the powerful imagery of means-ends technology. Consider the contemporary pursuit of 'social indices', the contemporary concern for 'quality of life'. These reflect the scientist's understandable passion for reducing things to measurable form and relations to regular laws. The pursuit is to be commended so long as it does not come to imply its converse – that only the measurable and the regular are properly knowable. Those who are dissatisfied with the quality of their lives or the conditions in which they live do not need objective yardsticks to stir their emotions or to provoke their actions; and their judgements of dissatisfaction will be no weaker for lack of such yardsticks. They are based not on calculation but on comparison with self-set standards.

It seems that I have now come as near to answering the question implicit in the title to this book as I at least am likely to get. It can be summarized as follows:

1. A human system must be distinguished from a man-made system no less than from an ecological system.

2. All human systems are also ecological systems in that such stability as they have is in part the undesigned *resultant* of their interaction with the world around them, including (increasingly) the other human systems on which they depend. But they differ from other ecological systems in that they include (and probably cannot help including) a not always beneficent element of design, which in turn implies partly tacit criteria of success.

3. All human systems are also to some extent man-made systems in that such stability (and success) as they have is in part the designed result of their interaction with the world around them including (increasingly) the other human systems on which they depend. But they differ from other man-made systems in that they include a greater element of judgement as well as calculation. In other words, the criteria which necessarily direct all exercises in calculation are themselves not necessarily taken for granted and may be the central issue in the design process.

4. Even man-made systems are not wholly technological. The constitution of the United States, for example, is a man-made system. Usually to a greater extent than purely technological systems, these systems of explicit rights and duties define, rather than taking for granted, the standards by which they are to be judged. Even the most technological of man-made systems are to some extent norm-setting as well as norm-holding systems. If we define this nontechnological element as in the widest sense political, we can compare one man-made system with another by reference to the extent of the political element explicitly or tacitly involved. I have already referred to the course of development by which Western societies, when unduly influenced by technological models, discovered that any group of people, even though gathered together for a purely technological purpose, could not be organized as if they were no more than constituents of a machine.

5. Yet even the most political of man-made systems remains something

less than a human system so long as it is only an object inviting study or even design by outsiders. The essence of a human system is that it is composed of human beings who bring it into being by their actions and their experiences. I have referred earlier to the gulf which separates the observer from the agent experient even where the two roles are combined in the same person and are being played in the same context and as nearly simultaneously as our nature permits – which means, as I believe, with a shifting from one stance to the other so frequent, rapid and appropriate as to be unnoticed, and so difficult as to be very rare.

The Constitution of the United States has survived the test of two centuries with remarkable success. Yet its actual meaning in the particular contexts in which alone it can be invoked have involved the best judicial minds of the country in constant debate and often in irresolvable disagreement since the Constitution came into force and will continue to do so however often it is amended. Every other country with a well-developed judiciary tells the same story. Must it not have something to tell us about the process by which decisions are reached by particular minds in particular cases of other kinds, however well equipped and similarly equipped they may be with general principles, whenever they engage in the regulation of human systems?

I think it must; and one of the things on which I think it must shed some light is why and how human systems are different.

Some light; not total clarity. For part of the difference is the tacit element in the criteria for success of human system as distinct from man-made systems in any form.

Perhaps this is as far as we can get. It seems to be as far as I can get. But one addendum is perhaps needed, since I have taken for granted a major point which others may not consciously assume. Who are these governors about whom I have been so provocatively speaking? Who exercises this activity to which I have given the probably offensive name of governance? And over whom?

I invite the reader to share what may be an unfamiliar view of political power – a concept almost wholly removed from physical force.[1]

Let us describe as political power all power which is exercised by anyone in so far as it affects anyone else, whether intentionally or not, whether knowingly or not. And let us describe as a responsible exercise of power any exercise which takes into account, however partially or mistakenly, the effect of that exercise of power on another, whether that other has any power to hold the other to account or not.

To avoid the connotations of governance, let us refer to everyone in his or her capacity as agent simply as 'doers' and to everyone in his or her capacity as affected by other people's doings as the 'done by'.

Clearly we are all in some contexts 'doers' and we are all in some other contexts 'done by'. Clearly also in an ever more interdependent world of ever more human environments, we are all more often done by than doers. And in an ever more responsible world we should all, as doers, be more constrained by awareness of the effect of our doings on the done by. I am not saying that our world is becoming more responsible. But the demand that it should do so is a virtually necessary result of its increased interdependence. We are back at that most elementary of systemic truths that all organization constrains, as well as enables.

We are back also at the theme which has dominated the second part of this book – the radical change which has overtaken the understanding of 'reasonable men' concerning the most basic conditions of their well-being and even their survival, and which has derived from the successes of the Enlightenment no less than from its failures.

In a world in which the doers were seen as the few – and the selfish few – it was reasonable to hope that a world controlled by the many would give the many a far greater share of its resources; and further, that in such a world liberty would be the only requirement needed by the many. They would cease for ever to be 'done by'. The movement to control by the many did indeed pay great rewards, unequally distributed but not negligible, even to most of the many. Neither the hidden hand of the market, nor the visible hand of the bureaucrat, nor the wisdom of the legislature, nor the liberation of the human spirit per se has realized Condorcet's dream. But surely they would have produced at least a higher subjective degree of satisfaction, if some other force had not been at work to neutralize it.

That other force, I have suggested in this book, is the increase of constraint on every done-by by every doer, due inescapably to his increasing involvement in the very system which has also set the standards of his enablements at a level never conceived by Condorcet. The counterpart of this, is of course, the corresponding increase in the constraint exercised on every doer by the reluctance of so many done-by to accept the increased constraints in even the most benign activities of the doers. The conventional picture of our time as a time of all-powerful doers and helpless done by, the very picture which the Enlightenment believed that it was abolishing for ever, is I believe as dead, at least in the West, as any revolutionary of two centuries ago could have hoped. But its replacement involves a concept of universal responsibility such as no Utopian since Plato ever hoped to get even from his 'Guardians'.

No wonder the political growing point of the world is the manufacture of consensus.

Human systems have become very difficult for human beings to maintain. They demand from whole populations levels of understanding and tolerance seldom before found even among the few. Time is short – but so is the whole human time span. Who knows what regulatory powers might not emerge at least among some of the different populations which face the future – even if it be a future measured only in decades?

We need not expect only one answer. Different treasures from the rich and diverse human heritage may survive and even flourish in different places. Precious innovations still undreamed may be spawned by necessity.

'Evolution', as T. H. Huxley wrote in the essay so often quoted, 'encourages no millenial expectations.' Man as designer would not achieve a millenial design and dwell in it in happiness ever after. None the less he is a designer and we should not assume that his creative powers have run into a total cul-de-sac.

We can take comfort from the fact, not always readily admitted but attested by every designer and not least by every creative technologist, that our creative powers are largely tacit.

Footnote

1. I have developed this more fully in a paper 'L'Art d'Être Gouverné' (The Art of Being Governed) published in *Analyse et Prevision Toure VIII*, no. 1–2, July–August, 1969.

BIBLIOGRAPHY

Annual Abstract of Statistics. London, HMSO, 1982.
Barnard, C. *The Functions of the Executive.* Cambridge, Mass., Harvard University Press, 1938.
Benedict, R. *The Chrysanthemum and the Sword.* London, Secker & Warburg, 1947.
Berger, P. et al. *The Homeless Mind.* New York, Random House, 1975.
Bhagavad Gita (English translation), London, Murray, 1931.
Bibby, C. *Four Thousand Years Ago.* London, William Collins, 1962.
Cross, J. A. *British Public Administration.* London. University Tutorial Press, 1970.
Dahrendorf, R. *After Social Democracy.* Unservile State Papers, no. 25, London, Liberal Publication Department, 1980.
Davis, W. J. *The Seventh Year.* New York, W. W. Norton, 1979.
Dicey, A. V. *Lectures on the Relation Between the Law and Public Opinion in England.* London, Macmillan, 1905.
Diderot, D. *Le Neveu de Rameau* (English translation). Harmondsworth, Penguin, 1974.
Driberg, J. H. *Initiation and Nine Other Poems; translations from poems of the Didinga and Lango Tribes.* Waltham St. Lawrence, Golden Cockerell Press, 1932.
Erickson, E. *Insight and Responsibility.* New York, W. W. Norton, 1964.
Fisher, H. A. L. *A History of Europe.* London, Arnold, 1936.
Florman, S. C. *The Existential Pleasures of Engineering.* New York, St. Martin's Press, 1976.
Follet, M. P. *Creative Experience.* 1924.
Follet, M. P. *The New State,* 1918.
Fussell, P. *The Great War and Modern Memory.* Oxford, Oxford University Press, 1975.
Gilbert, B. B. *The Foundation of National Insurance in Great Britain.* London, Michael Joseph, 1966.
Gluckman, H. M. *The Judicial Process Among the Barotse of Northern Rhodesia.* Manchester, Manchester University Press, 1955.
Harris, M. *Cannibals and Kings.* Glasgow, William Collins, 1977.
Harris, M. *The Rise of Anthropological Theory.* London, Routledge & Kegan Paul, 1969.

Hill, C. *The World Turned Upside Down*. London, M. T. Smith, 1972.
Huxley, T. H. *Evolution and Ethics and Other Essays*. London, Macmillan, 1894.
Löwe, A. *The Price of Liberty: a German on Contemporary Britain*. Day to Day Pamphlets no. 36. London, Hogarth Press, 1937.
MacIntyre, A. *A Short History of Ethics*. London, Routledge & Kegan Paul, 1967.
North-South: A Programme for Survival. Report of the Independent Commission on International Development Issues, under the chairmanship of Willy Brandt. London, Pan, 1980.
Polanyi, M. *Beyond Nihilism*. Eddington Lecture. Cambridge, Cambridge University Press, 1960.
Polanyi, M. 'History and Hope'. *Virginia Quarterly Review*, vol. 3, no. 2, 1962.
Polyani, M. In *Personal Knowledge: Towards a Post-critical Philosophy*. London, Routledge & Kegan Paul, 1973.
Rappaport, R. *Pigs for Ancestors*. New Haven, Yale University Press, 1968.
Rhinelander, P. H. 'Is Man Incomprehensible to Man?'. Stanford Alumni Association, 1973.
Robson, W. *Welfare State and Welfare Society*. London, Allen & Unwin, 1976.
Seeley, J. R. *Ecce Homo* (first published London 1866). London and New York, Everyman Library, vol. 305, 1908.
Snow, C. P. *The Two Cultures and a Second Look*. New York, Mentor, 1964.
Stout, S. *British Government*. Oxford, Oxford University Press, 1953.
Tanner, J. *Foetus into Man*. Cambridge, Mass., Harvard University Press, 1978.
Toffler, A. *The Third Wave*. London, William Collins, 1980.
Tomlinson, R. C. 'Some Dangerous Misconceptions Concerning Operations Research and Applied Systems Analysis', in *European Journal of Operational Research*, vol. 7, no. 2. June 1981.
Trilling, L. *Sincerity and Authenticity*. Oxford, Oxford University Press, 1972.
Vickers, G. 'Education in Systems Thinking', *Journal of Applied Systems Analysis*, vol. 7, April 1980.
Vickers, G. 'Equality of Opportunity', *Futures*, February 1979.
Vickers, G. 'L'Art d'Etre Gouverné' (The Art of Being Governed), in *Analyse et Prevision Toure VIII*, no. 1-2, July–August, 1969.
Vickers, G. 'Systems Analysis – a Tool Subject or Judgement Demystified', in *Policy Sciences*, vol. 14. 1981.
Vickers, G. 'The Weakness of Western Culture', *Futures*, December, 1977, p. 457.
Waddington, C. H. *The Ethical Animal*. London, W. H. Allen. 1960.
World Conservation Strategy. International Union for Conservation of Nature and Natural Resources, Glaind, Switzerland, 1980.
Woodward, L. *The Age of Reform*. London, Oxford University Press, 1964.

Index

academic disciplines and professional schools 152–4
acculturation
  limits 61–2
  process 59–60
action, appreciation and 54–8
adaptability
  of human beings 145–6
  of human societies 87
administration, public 153
affluence, increasing 130
After Social Democracy (R. Dahrendorf) 110, 111n
Age of Reform, The (L. Woodward) 75n3
aggression 93 *see also* war
alienation 84–5, 89, 91
analysis
  and modelling 8, 155, 162–4, 167
  and synthesis 163, 165, 167
Anti-Corn Law League 70, 115
appreciation 57, 59
  and action 54–8
  and language 43, 44
appreciative systems 43, 44, 55–6
Aquinas, Thomas 94, 100
armaments industry 5, 124
arms race 119, 145
art and science 157–8
Art of Being Governed, The (G. Vickers) 177n1
atomic power 118–19, 143
attitudes
  social 38, 96
  towards change 145
authenticity 89, 91–2
authorities 1, 84
authority 45, 104
autonomy 1, 81, 86, 87 *see also* constraints; interdependence
  and conscience 94
  of nations 76, 77, 81, 87
  personal 3, 81–8, 96
  within social groups 89–97
Avebury (Wiltshire) 58n1, 149

bargaining 44, 163
Barnard, Chester 45, 53n1
Barotse, British administration of 37, 41
Bateson, G. 82
belonging 62 *see also* social groups
  dimensions of 98–104
  foci of 101–4
  sense of 98, 102–4
Benedict, Ruth 95, 97n7
Bentham, Jeremy 64, 69, 72, 86
Berger, P. 166, 167, 168n
Bernard, Claude 20
Beveridge, sir W. 86, 134
Beyond Nihilism (M. Polanyi) 97n1
Bhagavad Gita 93, 97n6
Bibby, G. 115, 121n3
biological
  control 20–6, 27, 30
  evolution 18–19, 24–6, 27, 41
Brandt Commission (1980) 34, 124–5
Brandt Report 39n2, 124–5
British Government
  changes in 74
  expenditure 74–5
British Government (S. Stout) 75n4
British Public Administration (J. A. Cross) 75n5
Brunel, I. K. 141, 142
Buddhism 60

Camus, A. 92
Cannibals and Kings (M. Harris) 39n7
Cannon, W. B. 21
change, rate of 48–9
Christianity 61
Chrysanthemum and the Sword, The (R. Benedict) 97n7
class, social 102
Clausewitz, Karl von 52
COMECON (Council for Mutual Economic Aid) 107
commitments and constraints 98
Commoner, B. 151n1
communication
  human 41, 42–6, 59, 98

Index 181

levels of 43–5
non-verbal 43, 162
tendency to degenerate 52-3
verbal 162, 163, 164–5
community, sense of 63–4
computers 6–8, 164
 in systems analysis 155
concern 54–6, 165–6
concerns, human 17, 48
Condorcet, M. J. (Marquis de) 100, 176
conduct, codes of 56–7
conflict
 and negotiation 163
 between academic disciplines and professional schools 152–4
 in role 166
conscience, individual 94, 99–100
conservation of resources 148–50
 by abnegation 149–50
 by preservation 148
 by substitution 149
 education in 150
constant state 22
constraints 2, 47–8, 141, 176 *see also* autonomy
 and commitments 98
 environmental 109–10
 extension of 96
 freedom from 66
 of interdependence 14, 17, 62, 82
control 6, 8, 17 *see also* regulation
 automatic 10, 69, 71, 75, 143
 biological 20–6, 27, 30
 by price 70, 71
 computerised 6–7
 conscious 143
 cultural 37–9
 cybernetic 10, 22–3
 ecological 24, 29–30, 37–8
 of body temperature 20–1
 of environment 148–50
 of form 13
corporations, multi-national 124
Council for Mutual Economic Aid (COMECON) 107
Creative Experience (M. P. Follett) 161n2
credit 38, 124, 129
Crick, F. H. 24
 Cross, J. A. 75n5
cultural
 bonds 59–64
 change 48–9

community 109
control compared with ecological control 37–8
differences 66
culture 41, 46–9
 and law 90–1
 as consensus 38, 62, 88
 comparative 95
cultures 3, 4, 9, 41 *see also* sub-cultures
currency *see* money supply
cybernetics 10, 22, 23

Dahrendorf, R. 110, 111n
Darwin, Charles 6, 18, 27, 28, 116
 on *Beagle* 46
Davis, W. J. 121n4
DDT (dichloro-diphenyltrichloroethane) 143, 145, 171
de la Rivière, Mercier
 quoted 70
Declaration of Children's Rights 86
Declaration of Human Rights 86
democracies 45
democracy, representative 64, 76–7
democratic principles 45, 49
deoxyribonucleic acid (DNA) 24
Depression Great 133, 134
Descartes, René 12
determinism
 in doctrine 71, 73
 in history 5–6
 of Karl Marx 73
 of Adam Smith 61, 73
determinists 160
Dicey A. V. 64n1
Diderot, D. 92, 97n3
dignity, ambivalence of 166–7
diminishing returns 146
directors, boards of 162
disobedience, peaceful 91
Disraeli, B. (Lord Beaconsfield) 138
DNA (deoxyribonucleic acid) 24
dominance 83–4 *see also* pecking order
Driberg, J. H. 36, 39n5, 49, 64, 77
Driesch, H. A. E. 21, 22

Ecce Homo (J. R. Seeley) 51, 88n3
ecology 27, 147–8
ecological
 control 30, 37–8, 109
 ethic 61
 imperative 37–8

order 37–8, 169–70
relationships 122
systems 10, 24, 26, 27–31, 29, 122, 174
economic
  colonialism 124
  development 124–5
  expansion 103, 116, 130
  interdependence 123
  recession 110
economics, Keynesian 134
education 24
  aims of 161, 172
  importance of 131, 145–6, 150
  technologist's role in 151
Education in Systems Thinking (G. Vickers) 88n2
EEC (European Economic Community) 107
Einstein, Albert 12
Eisenhower, D. D. (President) 124
empathy 58
empires, collapse of 76
employment, full 135–7 *see also* unemployment
ends and means 10, 173
energy 21, 116 *see also* power
  and matter 12
  solar 119, 146
Engels, F. 5
Enlightenment, the 85, 88, 99–100, 176
  atmosphere of 73
  heirs of 129, 168
  ideology of 71
  individualism of 78
entelechy 21
entrepreneurs 145
  and wage claims 162
entropy 12
epistemology 38
equality 83
Equality of Opportunity (G. Vickers) 26n
Erikson, E. 47, 53n3
ethical
  dimension 95–6, 103
  process compared with cosmic 122
  standards 19, 25–6, 38, 62, 174
Ethical Animal, The (C. H. Waddington) 11n3
ethics 8, 38, 56–7
  and natural law 94–5
  and technology 25
ethology 3, 27, 31, 122
European Economic Community (EEC) 107

evolution
  and technology 25
  biological 18–19, 24–6, 27, 41
  cultural 19
  social 19, 25
  speed of 48–9, 103
  technological 6
Evolution and Ethics and Other Essays (T. H. Huxley) 32n2, 29n4, 64n2, 140n1
exchange 127
  international 107, 108–9, 114–5, 117, 122–3, 125, 128
Existential Pleasures of Engineering, The (S. C. Florman) 112, 121n1
existentialism 92
expectations
  and role 4, 59
  self 38, 56–7, 60, 62
  shared 38, 57, 59–60, 65–6, 82–3

feedback
  negative 10, 22–3, 69
  positive 51, 124, 128, 145–6
finance, international 38, 128
financial instability 127–30
Fisher H. A. L. 4, 11n1, 35, 39n3
Florman, S. C. 112, 121n1
Foetus into Man (J. Tanner) 32n3
Follet, Mary P. 154, 161n
food resources 113–14
Ford, Henry 153, 154
form
  and ecology 26
  and growth 13
  in relation to substance 12
  stability of 12–13, 15–17, 28, 29
Foundation of National Insurance in Great Britain, The (B. B. Gilbert) 140n3
Four Thousand years Ago (G. Bibby) 115, 121n3
Fragment on Government (J. Bentham) 72
freedom
  of association 78–9
  personal 89–90, 96, 100 *see also* autonomy
Freud, S. 92
Functions of the Executive, The (C. Barnard) 53n1
Fussell, P. 64n3

game playing 158–9
Gilbert, B. B. 134, 140n3
Ghandi, M. K. (Mahatma) 65, 91

Gluckman, Max 37, 39n6, 49
governance, human 6, 112, 152–4, 160, 166, 173–7
  and chess 158
  forms of 28
government 41, 49–50, 156
  British, changes in 74
  distrust of 143
  representative 153
  study of art of 156–7
governor, activity of 159, 166
Great Depression 133, 134
Great War and Modern Memory, The (P. Fussell) 64n3
gross national product 137
growth
  and interdependence 14
  and form 13

Halifax, Lord (Viceroy of India) 65
Harris, M. 4, 5, 6, 11n2, 37, 39n7
Hawthorne experiments 154
Hegel, G. W. F. 4
helmsman analogy with negative feedback 22–3, 69
hierarchies 2, 16–17, 54, 96–7
  in biology 30
Hill, Christopher 72, 75n1
history
  and scientific ideology 6–7
  human 7, 18, 33–9
  of systems 7, 35
  personal 18
History of Europe, A (H. A. L. Fisher) 11n7, 39n3
Hobbes, T. 85
Homeless Mind, The (P. Berger) 168n
honour, as an unusable word 166–7
Hudson's Bay Company 29
human,
  adaptability 87–8, 145–6
  labour 140
  rights 4, 86
Human Relations, Tavistock Institute of 154
human systems 2–4, 9, 28–9, 54, 88, 169–77
  see also political systems
  and purpose 170, 173
  and success 170–3
  and standards 25–6
  autonomy of 87
  bonding of 59–64
  coherence of 38, 101–3
  emergence of 18, 33–8
  governance of 29, 160 *see also* governance
  history of 7, 35
  instability 65–6, 107–11, 138–9, 145
  interdependence of 37
  peculiarities 41–53
  regulation 69–75
  stability 29, 31, 49, 65–6
  threats towards 107, 109–11
Hume, David 61
Huxley, T. H. 28, 29, 32n2, 35, 39n4, 61, 64n2, 122, 140n7
  quoted 61, 177

individual
  conscience 94, 99–100
  liberty 49, 78, 100
  persons 2, 18, 99
inflation 108, 109, 110, 123, 146
  and standard of living 125–31
  and trade 125–6
information 6
  computerised 6–7
  processing 2, 3–4, 136
  transmission 44
Initiation and Nine other Poems (J. H. Driberg) 39n5
innovation, technological 142, 144
Insight and Responsibility (E. Erikson) 53n3
instability *see also* stability
  financial 127–30
  in human systems 65–6, 107–11, 138–9, 145
  individual 150
  of economic development 124–5
  of relations 122–21, 122–40, 138–9
  of systems 145
institutions, growth of 74
  see also human systems
integrative forces 123
interdependence 2, 14–15, 17, 22, 25–6, 37, 176 *see also* autonomy
  economic 123, 145
  of groups 83, 88
  of individuals 81, 82–3, 86–7, 100
  of nations 81, 145, 49–50
International Union for the Conservation of Nature and National Resources, (IUCN) 27, 32n1, 42, 117, 118
international exchange 107, 108–9, 114–15, 117, 122–3, 125, 128

intuition 58
Is Man Comprehensible to Man? (P. H. Rhinelander) 97n5

Judaism 61
Judaeo-Christian tradition 61, 94, 95
Judicial Process among the Barotse, The (M. Gluckman) 37, 39n6

Keynes, J. M. 133
Keynesian economics 134

labour
  division of 153–4
  abundance of 140
language 41, 42–3, 164
law
  and culture 90–1
  natural 29, 94-5
League of Nations 93
Leavis, F. R. 46
lebensraum 119
Lectures on the Relation between the Law and Public Opinion in England (A. V. Dicey) 64n1
leisure 54, 138
  and unemployment 132, 135–6, 138
liberty, individual 49, 78, 100
life
  force (vitalism) 14
  quality of 173
living standards 145, 173
  and inflation 125–31
Löwe, Adolph 100, 104n1

MacIntyre, A. 78, 80n2
Malthus, T. R. 133
management 156, 209
  personnel 154
  professional 152
  scientific 153
  taught as case history 156–7
market economy 71, 75
markets 71, 139
  rigidities of 140
Marshall Plan 63
Marx, Karl 4, 5, 6, 64, 69, 85, 165
  determinism of 73
  doctrines of 6, 71, 101
  ideology of 61
Marxism 75
Marxist analysis 6

Maslow, A. H. 54
materialism 61, 71
matter and energy 12
Mayo, E. 154
means and ends 10, 173
membership *see* belonging
minorities
  power of 52
  sectional 2
modelling
  and analysis 8, 155, 162–4, 167
  models 163–4, 165, 169
money supply
  and inflation 125–30
  and trust 128
  and wages 130
  control 127–8, 129–30
  functions 128, 130
  measurement 127
moral
  imperatives 61
  standards 19, 25–6, 38, 62, 174
morality 60
More, Sir Thomas 94
mores, social 89–90
motivation 170

national product, gross 137
nationalism 77–8, 102–3
  foci for 101–4
nations, emergence of 76–9, 81
Nations, League of 93
Nations, United 86, 93
negative feedback 10, 22–3, 69
negotiation 44, 163
Neveu de Rameau, Le (D. Diderot) 97n3
New State, The (M. P. Follett) 161n2
Nietzsche, F. 93
nuclear power 118–19, 143

OPEC (Organisation of Petroleum Exporting Countries) 81, 117, 146
operations research (OR) 154
operations research and systems analysis (ORASA) 155–6, 160
order
  ecological 37–8, 169–70
  pecking 57 *see also* dominance
  political 85
  social 38–9, 72–3, 78, 85
organization 14–15, 17
  and systemic thinking 9

Index 185

as the enemy 100
theory 1
organizations, human 9 *see also* societies; human systems

pecking order 57 *see also* dominance
peace, universal 49
personal identity 2, 18, 99
Personal Knowledge: Towards a Postcritical Philosophy (M. Polanyi) 11n4
personnel management 154
photosynthesis 30, 118
Pigs for the Ancestors (R. Rappaport) 53n4
planning, fallibility of 25
Polanyi, M. 11n4, 89, 97n1
political
  betterment 103
  consensus 229
  organization 73–5
  power 175-6
  systems 69–75, 169–77 *see also* human systems
policy making 162
pollution
  monitoring 149
  problems of 149–50
Poor Law 132, 133
population
  controls 56, 113–16
  density 56
  growth 108
positive feedback 51, 124, 128, 145–6
power
  concentration of 108
  elites 112
  nuclear 118-19, 143
  social 112
  solar 119, 146
preformation, theory of 21
Price of Liberty, The (H. Löwe) 100, 104n1
process, cosmic compared with ethical 122
processing of information 23–4, 136
professional schools and academic disciplines 152–4
protests, 'principled' 90–6
purpose, concept of 170

Rappaport, R. 50, 53n4
rationality 57–8
reason 57–8
reductionism 14
Reform Act (1832) 73

regulation 8, 10–11 *see also* control
  and growth 17, 19
  automatic 10, 69, 71, 75, 143
  biological 20–6, 27, 30
  by price 70, 71
  conscious 143
  ecological 24, 29–30, 37–8
  governmental 64, 74–5
  in war 63
  of form 13
  of political systems 69–75
  of relationships 120, 152
  organic 20–22
  technological 23–5
Relations, Human, Tavistock Institute of 154
relationships 17, 65–6, 139
  between whole and parts 15–18
  complementary 81–5
  ecological 122
  ethological 122
  external 2, 17, 48–9
  group to group 65–6, 82–3, 129
  instability of 112–121, 122–40
  internal 2, 17
  international 81, 107
  person to group 65–6, 85–6, 129
  person to person 65–6, 81, 82–3, 129
  professional 45
  regulation of 120, 152
  social 17, 36–7
  stability of 66 *see also* stability of systems
  uncertainties in 129
religion, as focus for social cohesion 101–2
religions 60–1
resources
  abnegation of 149
  conservation of 148–50
  monitoring 149–50
  need for education about 150–1
  shortage of 110
  substitution of 149
responsibility, personal 5, 94, 99–100
returns, diminishing 146
revolution
  American 73
  cultural 120
  English 73
  French 73, 100
  green 117
  in consumption 141
  in information control and processing 118

186 Human Systems are Different

in transportation 114, 141
nuclear 118
political 120
technological 112–21
Rhinelander, P. H. 92, 97n5
rights, human 4, 86
Rise of Anthropological Theory, The (M. Harris) 4, 11n2
risks
  in technology 143–5
  spreading of 129
Robson, W. 86, 88n4
role 3, 4, 56–7, 59, 78, 102
  conflicts 166
  players 111, 157, 166
  playing 4, 82–4, 92, 102
Rosseau, J. J. 85, 86

St. Lawrence Seaway 144
Sade, D. A. F. (Marquis de) 91, 92
Sartre, J. P. 92
science and art 157–8
Seeley, J. R. 51, 85–6, 88n3
self-determination 77, 78–9, 96
service
  and servitude 100
  public 102
Seventh Year, The (W. J. Davis) 121n4
Short History of Ethics, A (A. MacIntyre) 78, 80n2
Simon, Herbert 100
Sincerity and Authenticity (L. Trilling) 97n2
Skinner, B. F. 87, 93
Smith, Adam 61, 64, 69, 71, 72
  and division of labour 153–4
  and markets 69, 85
  determinism of 61, 73
Snow, C. P. 46, 53n2
social
  class 102
  consensus 38, 96
  Darwinism 28
  engineering 72
  interdependence 37
  legislation 96
  mores 89–90
  order 38–9, 72–3, 78, 85
  power 112
  relationships 17, 36–7
  standards 25, 38–9, 91
social groups 11, 75
  foci for 101–4

growth of 3–4
membership of 98–101
interdependence of 37
societies *see also* human systems
  bonding of 59–64
  coherence of 38, 101–3
  political 75
  stability of 29, 31, 49, 65–6
space, access to 119
stability *see also* instability
  and stasis 21
  of form 12–13, 15–17, 28, 29
  of internal milieu 20
  of systems 10–11, 29, 31, 49, 65–6, 103, 107–11, 169
standards
  ethical 19, 25–6, 38, 62, 174
  of living *see* living standards
  regulative 8, 38, 56–73
  social 25, 38–9, 91
stasis 21
state, constant 22
states (nations)
  emergence of 76–9, 81
  totalitarian 45
Stout, S. 75n4
sub-cultures 62, 66, 102
sub-systems 78
substance, in relation to form 15
success 170–3
  and survival 171
  criteria for 171, 175
symbiosis 27, 50
symbols
  mathematical 163, 165
  verbal 164, 165
synthesis and analysis 163, 165, 167
systems
  appreciative 43, 44, 55–6
  financial 38
systemic
  analysis 104
  instability 103
  interdependence 86–7
  relationships 28, 107
  thinking 1, 9, 82, 125
  truths 176
  whole 155
systems 1, 17
  analysis 154–6, 160
  analysts 8, 155
  and politics 147

appreciative 43, 44
  as tools of understanding 17, 22
  behaviour of 147
  ecological 10, 24, 26, 27–31, 122, 174
  general interest 79
  human *see* human systems
  inorganic 14–15
  instability of 145
  limitations of 147
  man-made 174
  open 12–19
  political 69–75, 169–77 *see also* human systems
  relevance of 17
  single interest 79
  stability of 10–11, 29, 31, 49, 65–6, 103, 107–11, 169
  sub-systems 78
  taxonomy of 7
  theory 96, 132
  thinking 3, 82

Tanner, J. 32n3
Tavistock Institute of Human Relations 154
Taylor, F. W. 78, 153, 154
technological
  evolution 6
  innovation 142, 144
  regulation 23–5
  revolution 112–21, 141
  systems 6
technologists 8, 10–11, 116–17, 122, 123–4, 177
  arrogance of 151
  as forecasters 159
  attitudes of 159
  educational function of 151
  role of 112, 141–51
technology 8, 10–11, 35, 112, 115–21, 123, 124, 126
  achievements of 160
  and ethics 25
  and innovation 142, 144
  appropriate 148
  dominance of 159
  failures of 143–5
  future of 143
  means-ends 10, 173
  self-regulating 142
teleology 22
thermostats 22 *see also* feedback, negative
Third Wave, The (A. Toffler) 87

threats
  as communication 44, 51
  avoidance of 23
  ecological 61
  of minorities 52
  of war 51, 52
  to society 64
Toffler, A. 87
Tomlinson, R. 155, 160, 161, 161n3, 164
Toynbee, A. 4
trade 125 *see also* international exchange
trade unions 78–9, 109, 137
transport and exchange 114–5
Trilling, L. 92, 97n2,4
Two Cultures and a Second Look, The (C. P. Snow) 53n2
understanding 57, 162, 164–6, 167–8
  and systemic thinking 9
  and systems 17
unemployment 108, 109, 111, 123, 131–40, 146
  and deficit financing 133
  and labour 140
  and leisure 132, 135–6, 138
  and poverty 131
  and the elector 137
  as relationship 139
  attitudes towards 131–7
  in primitive societies 139
  insurance 96, 133–4
  self-regulation of 132, 135
  trade unions and 137
Union of Socialist Soviet Republics (USSR) 4, 77, 123, 124
United Nations 86, 93
United States of America (USA) 73, 77, 90, 124
  constitution of 174, 175
utilitarianism 72, 75

Vickers, G. 26n, 88n, 177n
violence as non-verbal communication 43–4
vitalism (life force) 14
vitalist 22

Waddington, C. H. 11n3
wages 130, 147
  negotiations about 137
  rigidity in 140
Walden II (B. F. Skinner) 87
Wallace, A. R. 18, 27

war 41, 50–3, 63, 77, 107, 108, 109 *see also* World War I & II
  as a bond in society 63–4
  as level of communication 52
  as source of instability 108, 123–4
  atomic 143
  increased threat of 123
  technical changes in 142
water cycle 117
water conservation 148
Watson, J. D. 24
Watt, James 22
wealth, inequality of 108, 109
Wealth of Nations, The (Adam Smith) 72
welfare, mutual 70
Welfare State and Welfare Society (W. Robson) 86, 88n4
wholeness 1, 14
  and relationship with parts 15–17
Wiener, Norbert 22
Wilberforce, W. 90
Woodward, L. 75n3
World Conservation Strategy (IUCN) 32n1
World Food Congress (1974) 35
World Turned Upside Down, The (C. Hill) 72, 75n1
World War I 86, 95, 101, 142, 166, 167
World War II 62, 73, 86, 108, 143, 152, 154, 156